A RACE TO REMEMBER

A RACE TO REMEMBER

THE PETER NORMAN STORY

JoJo PUBLISHING

DAMIAN JOHNSTONE & MATT NORMAN

A Race to Remember – The Peter Norman Story

By Damian Johnstone and Matt Norman

Published by JoJo Publishing

'Yarra's Edge'
2203/80 Lorimer Street
Docklands VIC 3008
Australia

Email: jo-media@bigpond.net.au or visit www.jojopublishing.com

National Library of Australia
Cataloguing-in-Publication data

Johnstone, Damian
A Race to Remember : the Peter Norman story

ISBN 9780980495027 (pbk.)

Norman, Peter, 1942-2006.
Olympic Games (19th : 1968 : Mexico City, Mexico)
Track and field athletes--Australia--Biography.
Physical education teachers--Victoria--Biography.
Teachers and community--Victoria.
Olympics--Participation, Australian.

796.422092

Editor: Gill Smith
Designer / typesetter: Rob Ryan @ Z Design Media
Printed in Australia by McPherson's Printing Group

CONTENTS

I still wasn't sure if they would go through with it. A guy up in the stand used to sing the American national anthem every time it came up. When we turned to face the flags, both Tommie and John were behind me, so I couldn't see what was happening. But I knew they'd actually gone through with it when the voice from up in the stands got about four bars into the national anthem and then faded out to nothing. The stadium just went quiet. I immediately thought, 'They've done it. Good on 'em!'

Peter Norman

PREFACE

In August 1960, I was living with my family in Heathcote, a small town 112 kilometres from Melbourne in north-central Victoria. I had just celebrated my ninth birthday when I discovered the Olympic Games. From late August to mid September 1960, I scoured the daily pages of the *Sun News-Pictorial* for news on the exploits of new heroes in my life, particularly swimmers Dawn Fraser and Murray Rose, and athletes Herb Elliott, Peter Snell, Dixie Willis, Abebe Bikila and Rafer Johnson. By the end of the Olympics my favourite athlete was the USA's Wilma Rudolph. I was amazed to read that Wilma, the twentieth in a family of 22 children, had been crippled by polio at the age of four, then had to struggle to walk even a few metres without a cumbersome leg brace until she was twelve. Her family had struggled against poverty and racism, yet here she was, at the age of 20, winning gold medals in the 100 and 200 metres sprints and the relay.

Wilma had retired by the time of the 1964 Tokyo Olympics, but she would always remain a special favourite. I was now hooked on the Olympics and followed the Tokyo Games with great interest. By 1968 I was closely following the career of a young Melbourne runner, Peter Norman, who appeared to be a medal chance in the forthcoming Mexico Olympics. I had also been impressed to read over the previous two years that Peter was prepared to stand up for what he believed in, namely his Salvation Army faith.

I was thrilled with Peter's success at the Games and that he had supported the two Americans, Tommie Smith and John Carlos, during the medal ceremony for the 200 metres sprint. But I admit that I didn't fully comprehend what that support meant at the time. Peter's actions mean so much more these days. I wrote to Peter after the Olympics congratulating him on his incredible performance in winning a silver medal in the 200 metres. On Sunday 15 December 1968, I got the shock of my life when a car pulled up in our driveway in Heathcote and out came Peter Norman and his then wife Ruth. Peter was on his way to Bendigo to speak at the Golden Square Methodist Church evening service. Instead of travelling to Bendigo by the most direct route, Peter drove via Heathcote, thereby adding some extra 30 minutes or so to his journey.

Much of that visit is a blur 40 years later, but I remember not having film in my little instamatic camera. So while Peter and Ruth had a cuppa and talked to my parents and four sisters – Maree, Geraldine, Loreto and Kathryn – and younger brother Brendan (my older brother Michael wasn't home), I felt like I broke Tommie Smith's world record sprinting up to the local service station to buy a black-and-white film. Much to our delight, Peter graciously allowed us all to try on his silver medal. My father Harold was not normally a person to get starstruck, whereas my mother Carmel was, but both were very taken with Peter and Ruth, and their visit was a talking point at home for weeks. I exchanged a couple of letters with Peter soon after that visit, but apart from a very brief meeting at Olympic Park in 1972, sadly we never conversed again. I continued, however, over ensuing years, to add any newspaper articles about Peter to scrapbooks I was keeping.

The photos taken in Heathcote on that day remain among my most prized possessions. While I have met other Olympians since, that day remains the one and only time I have ever had an Olympic medal around my neck. No other athlete has ever impressed me quite like Peter, not only because of the kindness he showed to a young kid from the bush, but also because of the strength of character that he showed over his life as he battled and overcame a number of obstacles.

Peter's sudden death on 3 October 2006 came as a huge shock. My wife Therese and I attended Peter's funeral service at the Williamstown Town Hall. It was very important that we paid our respects to the person who had been so kind to me all those years ago. While listening to Ray Weinberg's outstanding eulogy I realised there were so many aspects of Peter's life about which I was not aware. I felt the need to learn more. So grew the seeds for this biography.

While conducting early interviews, I learnt that Peter's nephew Matt Norman was making a documentary chronicling Peter's silver medal win and his involvement in the so-called 'Black Power' salute at the 1968 Olympics. I was ecstatic to learn that Matt was going to explore on film that moment when three courageous athletes took a stand and delivered a powerful and provocative human rights message to the world – a message that is still remembered 40 years later.

During subsequent discussions with Matt, I learnt that he had interviewed Peter about his life and his involvement in the medal ceremony both on film and audiotape during the three years before his death. These, along with interviews with Tommie Smith, John Carlos and other key figures, became the cornerstones of Matt's film *Salute*.

To do justice to Peter's life story, it was crucial that I gained access to Matt's interview material. Our discussions eventually led to him being named co-author of Peter's biography in exchange for access to, and the rights to use, material from *Salute*. Matt was keen to see Peter's story told in print. He provided great assistance and has been a wonderful source of encouragement during the writing of this book. It's been a great journey Matt! Many thanks to you and Rebecca for your support. I value our friendship.

My wife Therese has shown me incredible love and support during the past 35 years, but she has excelled in so many ways over the past two years during the researching and writing of this book; in fact, it was her idea that I write it. Thank you, Therese, for your belief, constant encouragement and sacrifice, and for 'pumping up my tyres' when I was down, but above all for your undying love. I dedicate this book to you with all my love.

Our children – Glenn, Clare (who provided invaluable input for several chapters) and Karen (and their respective partners Louise, Dave and Rick) – have been gigantic supporters of this project from day one. You'll never know how much your support, given in countless ways, has meant. I loved you all from the moment I set eyes on you and always will.

Peter's story could never have been written without the unconditional and total support and cooperation that I have received from Peter's mother Thelma (regretfully, I was not fortunate enough to meet Peter's father George) and the extended Norman family (including Peter's siblings – Laurie, Heather and Elaine – and their families; his first wife, Ruth, and their children Janita, Sandy and Gary and their families; and Peter's second wife, Jan, and their two daughters Belinda and Emma). I'm sure it was a joy for all to discuss their many happy memories of Peter. But I also know other discussions undoubtedly evoked feelings of great hurt and sorrow, and resurrected memories previously locked away. My sincere thanks to you all for welcoming this stranger into your homes and for being so hospitable and so open and frank with me.

Many of Peter's friends, teammates, competitors and work colleagues also gave their time freely for interviews – some on many occasions – for which I am grateful. Gary and Glenda Holdsworth, Bob Lay, Greg Lewis, John McAdam and Phil May deserve particular mention and thanks. They have been constant sources of information and encouragement. I am also grateful to John Francisco and Ray Harbert for providing extensive details on Peter's career with the Collingwood Harriers athletic club.

This book would not have been possible without the following people: Elaine Ambler, Trevor Beecham, Kevin Berry, Ray and Denise Boyd, Raelene Boyle AO OBE, Di Burge AO, Margaret (Shewan) Callender, Ron Clarke MBE, Bev (Mathwin) Claughton, Danny Corcoran, Perry Crosswhite AO, Peter Dixon, Maurie and Daisy Drew, Gary Eddy, Iris Elmi, Tom Elmi, Arch Galloway, Alec Gardiner, Bob Gardiner, Tom Huntley, Paul Jenes, Graham Johnston, Sandy and Chris Kadri, Robin and Rhonda Kidney, Jenny Lamy, Susan McAdam, Ken McBride, Geoff Mathwin, Ruth Membrey, Sandy Miller, Brian Mott, Belinda Norman, Emma Norman, Gary and Lara Norman, Heather Norman, Herb Norman, Jan Norman, Janita Norman, Laurie and Jill Norman, Thelma Norman, Judy Patching AO MBE, Lawrie Peckham, Pam (Kilborn) Ryan, David Shewan, Neville Sillitoe, Ron Simmons, Helen (Shewan) Snashell, John Steffensen, Bob Stuart, Ray Weinberg AO, Max Wells, Ron Wells, Jeff Westlake, Helen (Pletzer) Whelan, Vern and Ruby Williamson, and Graham Young.

My thanks also to the following people, who all helped in various ways: Graham (Gus) Bailey, Cliff Bastow, Michael Bodey, Irene Bradley, Irene Bright, Mike Brudenell, Dr David Burgin, John Challis, Reg Chiller, David Culbert, Eira Cozens, Bob Dees, Jeff Dodds, Ian Dunstan, Judith (Treadwell) Evans, Ken Greatorex, Bill and Teresa Hicks, Kevin Hillier, Colin Hirst, Bruce Ivey, Reg Jones, David Kusznir, Jeff Lang, Norma Lawson, Howard Leigh, Norma and Frank Leonard, Justin Lewis, Greg Marcon, Trevor Marsh, Alec Martin, Terry Miller, Catherine Mills, Joe Minogue, Gary Moorcroft, Bill Muir, Graeme Olden, Peter Rechter, Len Reddoch, Lachlan Schonfelder, Larry Simmons, John Smith (for his two bob's worth), Nigel and Jill Smith, Robert Smith, Vince Spiteri, Martin Stewart, Steve Thom, Raymond Threlfall, Pat Toohey, Steve Tupper, Scotty Turner, John Whittington, and Arthur Winchall.

I also wish to acknowledge that all quotes from Peter Norman, Tommie Smith, John Carlos and Payton Jordan in this biography have been taken from *Salute*, unless otherwise indicated. In addition I acknowledge and extend my thanks to Paul Jenes, Peter Hamilton and David Tarbotton for the use of their Australian Athletics statistical data (<www.athletics.com.au/history>).

My sincere thanks to the wonderful team at JoJo Publishing. Managing editor Charlotte Strong showed faith in the project and in me from the outset. This meant a great deal to me, as did her sound advice, encouragement and tireless efforts (in so many aspects) to produce the best book possible. It's been a pleasure working with you, Charlotte. I am most grateful. I also appreciate the great support provided by Barry Dorr and Jo Costello. I look forward to hearing more about your athletic career (in Melbourne) when the dust settles Barry. Special thanks are extended to my super-duper editor Gill Smith. Gill has been a delight to work with. She has worked tirelessly to ensure the best possible manuscript and has been a great source of advice and guidance. Her banter also helped to make the editing phase a most enjoyable experience. Special thanks also to designer and typesetter Rob Ryan for his amazing cover and marvellous text design. Great work Rob!

Finally, without Peter George Norman himself, this book would never have been written. Peter, you have left us with some incredible memories.

Damian Johnstone
May 2008

1

THE IMPOSSIBLE DREAM

On 16 October 1968 the image of two black American athletes, heads bowed, black-gloved fists raised into the night sky in the so-called Black Power salute, shook not only the many thousands watching the event unfold live in Mexico City's Estadío Olimpico but also sent shockwaves throughout the world. In the intervening 40 years, the event has become an iconic image, not just of the Olympic Games but also of the twentieth century. While most focus their attention on the two Americans, Tommie Smith and John Carlos, there was a third individual on the 200 metres victory dais that night. A white Australian athlete stood tall, proudly wearing alongside his silver medal a civil rights badge in support of the silent protest made by Smith and Carlos against racial discrimination.

The Australian could quite easily have disassociated himself from the protest and refused to participate in the medal presentation ceremony. He knew in advance what the Americans intended to do when he accompanied them onto the dais. He knew that he would almost certainly face repercussions for his support. He also knew only too well that his actions were likely to be seen by many as hypocritical. After all, his own country had an appalling record for having treated its Indigenous people as less than second-class citizens, refusing to formally acknowledge them in national census counts until the year before the Olympics. But Peter Norman was a man of conviction and great moral fibre. Racial discrimination was abhorrent to him – he firmly believed that all people were created equal and had a natural-born right to be treated that way.

Peter said of the ceremony:

> It's been said that sharing my silver medal with that incident on the victory dais detracted from my performance. On the contrary! Getting across the line between the two of them in the actual race itself was my moment of glory. The victory ceremony in no way detracted from that. I was very proud to run second and I was very proud to be on the victory dais with them when they made their statement. I'm a firm believer that in a victory ceremony for the Olympics, there's three guys standing up there. Each one's been given about a square metre of God's earth to stand on and what any one of the three choose to do with his square metre of earth at that stage is entirely up to them. If I hadn't been happy with what they did, I wouldn't have asked for the badge.

Peter believed that if it hadn't been for the 'demonstration', his would have been just another silver medal picked up by Australia: 'No-one would have ever heard of Peter Norman!'[1]

Peter's place as a key player in one of the Olympics' most memorable moments was set in motion with his selection into the Australian Olympic team following his victory in the 1968 Australian 200 metres championship.

Right up to the time the Australian national championships and selection trials for Mexico were held in late March 1968 in Sydney, New South Wales sprinter Bob Lay was the holder of the national 200 metre record of 20.8 seconds. 'Bob had the fastest start of just about anyone in the world,' said Peter.

> He was fairly lightly built by comparison to Gary, Greg and I, but damn hard to beat. That day in Sydney, it was Gary Holdsworth, Greg Lewis, myself, Bob Lay, Phil King and American Jim Kemp. Bob once again equalled his Australian record of 20.8 but that was only good enough for second last. The only man he beat home was Jim Kemp. Greg and I both clocked the same time of 20.5. That was the new Australian record and both Greg and I went to Mexico on that run.

The whole field ran under 21 seconds, which was incredible given the state of the ES Marks Field cinder track. It was an old track bound together by used sump oil, so it wasn't really conducive to fast times. 'That was when Peter moved from being a bloody good 200 metres runner to an exceptionally good 200 metres runner,' said Lay. 'Peter would be the fastest last 50 metre runner I've seen in this country. He suddenly found something that none of us could find, and he kept repeating it. This was Peter's time. He'd threatened so much. He hit a purple patch and he went over to Mexico with so much confidence.'

Greg Lewis had already won the 100 metres and was in good shape going into the 200 metres event at the championships. He recalled saying to Peter, 'This is it mate, you'll win the 200 tomorrow. I've got the 100 in the bag. We're right for Mexico.' Lewis recalled Peter turned and tousled his hair and said, 'There be one little fat piglet that won't let me have it all my own way. Greg's response was, 'You've gotta expect some competition. On Sunday, I'm looking pretty good till the last ten metres and he steams past.' Later that same day, Lewis and Peter joined teammates Gary Holdsworth and Phil King to win the 1968 Australian 4 × 100 metres relay championship.

There wasn't a great deal of knowledge in Australia about tartan tracks at this time. Peter's coach, Neville Sillitoe, had found some material in American magazines and from what he had read, he expected Peter to run better on the tartan tracks in Mexico. In the lead-up to the Olympics, Peter ran inside the Olympic 100 and 200 metres qualifying standard some thirteen times – all on cinder tracks. Most of the faster times than his in the world at that stage had been run on synthetic tracks in major competitions, for which there had been strong lead-up events.

Sillitoe described Peter's string of under 21-second runs leading up to Olympics as being 'one of the most remarkable achievements in Australian athletic history'. He rated Peter's climaxing effort in winning the Australian championship on Sunday 24 March 1968 on an average track as being 'excellent'.[2] Sillitoe put Peter's improvement down to maturity as an athlete: 'Peter developed late, but he worked and worked and improved. His character was there. He had experience behind him. His training techniques were right and he just went bang.'

In winning the Australian championship in 20.5 seconds, Peter wiped the oldest Australian running record from the book. He took 0.1 seconds from the time set by American Bob Morrow when he won the 200 metres gold medal at the 1956 Melbourne Olympics. On hearing the official time, Peter immediately apologised to Sillitoe for letting him down.

> Norman apologised because he began slowly from the blocks and was giving his five rivals a big start after the first 50 metres. 'Neville has spent hours improving my start. That was where we were to win today, but I was last away,' Norman said. Norman 'flew' in the straight and was locked in a neck and neck tussle with Greg Lewis over the final twenty-five metres. Norman's final throw to the tape clinched victory.[3]

Sportswriter Steve Hayward wrote at the time that he believed Peter could cut his 200 metres time by 0.2 seconds if he could sharpen his start: 'His getaway in yesterday's final was bad. He was last in the six man field at the straight entrance with 100 yards to go, but he finished like a runaway train … His win yesterday stamped him as a probable finalist in the Olympic 200 metres final. And he has strong prospects of winning a medal.'[4]

Sillitoe thought Peter would make the final: 'I would have been disappointed had he not.' Sillitoe described how Peter's preparation didn't change because of Mexico's altitude, but training became more intensive: 'We resorted to having handicapped races against the likes of Ricky Dunbar. He wasn't there every session but he did some work with us. I'd have Peter start behind so as to get more out of him. Plus we ran in every meet possible, no matter where it was.'

Peter recalled that he and Lewis were having real trouble. There was nothing new they could do against each other that the other didn't know about.

> We had to get some racing under our belts, but as it was out of season, there was just Gary, Greg and myself. Ricky Dunbar was a professional runner and we weren't allowed to run against professionals, but Rick, known as 'The Flying Scot', offered to train with us. The first Sunday morning he was there we were running time trials over 100 metres. Rick said, 'If I'm to be any value, I'll take four metres.' So Rick set himself up as the hare for us. Rick was also out of season, and wasn't in top gear, but was willing to race against us to make us run faster. That proved very beneficial for what happened in Mexico. He did a magic thing for us.

Hayward noted in mid September that Dunbar was 'well short of form, but he punished himself in trial after trial'. He described Dunbar's support as an act of courage as well as graciousness.[5] Peter showed his appreciation for Dunbar's help by sending him a postcard from Mexico City, which read in part: 'Let me say once again thanks a million for your help at the time that we needed it most.'

Before leaving for Mexico, Peter was given a farewell party at the home of Florrie Carruthers, his mother Thelma's eldest sister. Peter's sister Heather made a cake and decorated it with the map of Mexico, the Australian and Mexican flags, and a runner on a track. Some friends of Florrie's eldest son from a light operatic company sang 'The Impossible Dream' for Peter at the party, which he thought very special.[6]

The upcoming Olympics was not the only world event on the minds of Australians in 1968. The country's participation in the war in Vietnam was a highly controversial issue. In 1962, in what was then seen as an insignificant event, a team of 30 Australian army officers had joined American advisory forces training Vietnamese military personnel in South Vietnam. Over the next three years, additional resources were added to the team and inevitably the advisers were drawn into counter-terrorism activities. Selective national service was introduced in 1964. But as there was no war, the great political conscription battle that took place in Australia in 1916 and 1917 was not repeated. However, in late April 1965, Prime Minister Menzies announced that Australia would send a full battalion of troops to support the USA in Vietnam. 'Australia was at war once again. Nevertheless the general attitude of the Australian public to events in Southeast Asia would not turn until later in the decade.'[7]

By 1968 the Australian government, now led by Prime Minister John Gorton (who had assumed office following Harold Holt's drowning), was facing a huge groundswell of opposition to the continued deployment of national servicemen in Vietnam and the country's participation in the Vietnam War. Anti-war demonstrations were heating up all over the nation. By now more than 8000 combat soldiers, 40 per cent of them conscripts, had been committed to the war. At the time, it was arguably the most controversial war in Australia's history, fought for three major reasons: anti-communism, Australia's geographical position and its traditional reliance on powerful allies.[8]

In 1968, Vietnam was just one of the world's trouble spots. In China, the Cultural Revolution was at its peak. In May 1966, Chairman Mao Zedong called on China's youth to overthrow the country's Communist Party leadership. Millions of radical youths, who came to be known around the world as the Red Guard, answered his call. China was plunged into complete turmoil. 'Hundreds of thousands died, millions more were brutalised and tortured, and much of China's cultural heritage was left in ruins.'[9] By the end of 1968, China was on the brink of civil war.

The USA was wracked by conflict and struggle. Activists were demanding an end to the intervention in Vietnam and black Americans were campaigning for civil rights and an end to racial inequalities and poverty. The assassination of Martin Luther King on 4 April 1968 led to an outpouring of rage and grief across America that resulted in over 40 deaths and many thousands of arrests. King, whose campaign for civil rights extended beyond the black community to all the poor of America, was in Memphis to support the strike of the city's garbage collectors. He walked onto the balcony of his motel room for some air when he was shot from a neighbouring boarding house. Senator Robert Kennedy's assassination on 6 June further provoked an already volatile situation. Kennedy was gunned down after celebrating his success in the California primary election for the Democratic presidential nomination.

Student demonstrations paralysed France, Germany and Brazil. In Czechoslovakia the liberal Dubcek regime was crushed by the Soviet Union and its Warsaw Pact allies. This ended the so-called Prague Spring, a period of liberalisation and reform in Czechoslovakia in which censorship was relaxed and popular freedoms were constitutionally guaranteed.

On the Olympic front, the International Olympic Committee (IOC) was facing the growth of a collective politicised movement of black American athletes who had formed the Olympic Project for Human Rights (OPHR), spearheaded by sociologist Harry Edwards. The OPHR understood the elemental stakes involved in sport, demanded racial equality within it and were threatening to boycott the Games in Mexico City if their demands for equality were not met.[10] IOC president Avery Brundage fuelled an already volatile situation when discussing the fundamental basis of the Olympic movement: 'There is no discrimination whatsoever because of race, religion, colour or political affiliations … A boycott would only disadvantage the athletes themselves. I don't think any of these boys would be foolish enough to demonstrate at the Olympic Games. If they do, they'll be promptly sent home.'[11] The athletes ultimately decided before the Olympics that they would not boycott the Games; rather they would carry out their protests in their own way during the Games. One thing was certain, however. No black American athlete would accept a medal from Brundage, even if he were foolish enough to attempt to give out medals at a presentation ceremony. They considered him to be the supreme racist.

Many black African nations, unhappy with the IOC's initial decision to allow South Africa to compete in the Games, also threatened boycotts. These threats forced the IOC to reverse its decision. Several European countries also threatened to withdraw from any competition against the Soviets because of their actions in Czechoslovakia. Olympic great Emil Zátopek called for the suspension from the Olympics of Warsaw Pact countries.

There was also major concern over the rarefied atmosphere of Mexico City. Doctors, officials, coaches and athletes alike from lowland countries feared the effects competition in the thin air of Mexico City would have on competitors. Australian team doctor Brian Corrigan described the IOC's decision to hold the Olympics in Mexico City as the blunder to trump all blunders. He says the decision, under the autocratic leadership of Brundage, to ignore the medical warnings about the 'dire consequences' of staging the Games at an altitude of 2240 metres above sea level 'will remain forever a blight on the record of the old buffers in the IOC'. He added that, while no competitor died during competition, as had been predicted by some sports medicine specialists, it was 'more good luck than planning'.[12]

In the weeks leading up to the Games, the host city was under siege. There was a history of confrontation during student demonstrations in Mexico City and elsewhere in the country. 'Student demonstrators contended that the government had no place spending $150 million on a sports spectacle while millions of Mexican citizens still lived in poverty. Indeed, students had been insisting for months that they would deliberately disrupt the Games. They were also demanding the firing of top police officials, dissolution of the city's notorious riot squad, and abolition of various national anti-subversion laws.'[13]

Ten days before the opening ceremony, on 2 October 1968, government troops opened fire on a crowd of unarmed students in the La Plaza de las Tres Culturas in Tlatelolco, Mexico City. The site, about 24 kilometres from the Olympic Village, was a common meeting point for students. Over 250 people were killed and many hundreds more were injured. Kate Doyle, director of the Mexico Documentation Project for the US National Security Archive, wrote that the extent of the violence stunned the country.

> When the shooting stopped, hundreds of people lay dead or wounded, as army and police forces seized surviving protesters and dragged them away. Although months of nationwide student strikes had prompted an increasingly hard-line response from the Diaz Ordaz regime, no one was prepared for the bloodbath that Tlatelolco became. More shocking still was the cover-up that kicked in as soon as the smoke cleared. Eyewitnesses to the killings pointed to the President's 'security forces', who entered the Plaza bristling with weapons, backed by armoured vehicles. But the government claimed that extremists and Communist agitators had initiated the violence.[14]

The IOC would not be drawn into the tragedy, referring to it as an 'internal affair'. Brundage refused to concede that there was any connection between the massacre and the Olympics and was adamant that the Games would proceed on schedule.

Julius (known as Judy) Lockington Patching had been selected by the Australian Olympic Federation in January 1968 to be the general manager of the Australian Olympic team. Patching was an outstanding selection as he understood what it was to be an athlete, having competed at club and interstate level.

Following his retirement from competition in 1947, Patching gained vast experience as an official. He was a member of the Victorian Amateur Athletic Association council, and had been on the technical committee for the organisation of the 1956 Melbourne Olympics. Patching became a starter in 1947 and was chief starter at the 1956 Olympics. He subsequently became a Victorian delegate on the Australian Athletic Union. He had been the section manager of the athletics team at the 1960 Rome Olympics and the assistant general manager at the 1964 Tokyo Olympics before becoming the general manager in Mexico.[15] Patching strongly believed that athletes performed at their best when their state of mind was settled, rather than being worried about some 'stupid official'.

Patching was very concerned about how Australian athletes would cope with Mexico City's altitude. Harry Hopman, who had been the general manager of many successful Australian Davis Cup tennis teams, told Patching that his teams always went to Mexico City at least a month before to acclimatise before one game of tennis was played. 'The Australian Olympic Committee executive went along with this,' says Patching. 'We were in Mexico City five weeks before the Games started.' Altitude was only one of the issues faced by the team. 'We had to be very careful with food, particularly because of "Montezuma's revenge" as they called it, or a superior guts ache of shocking proportions, that devastated you. We had very wise doctors and strict rules regarding team hygiene.' Patching also purchased water purifiers from New Zealand: 'We took the water purifiers and hooked them up to our system. We ended up providing water to New Zealand and the British from our system.'[16]

NOTES

1 'Where are they now?', Channel 7, 1988.

2 *Australian Amateur Athletics* magazine, December 1968 – January 1969.

3 'Record, then an apology', *The Sun*, 23 March 1968.

4 'Record but now he is running late', *The Herald*, 25 March 1968.

5 'Ricky to the rescue', *The Herald*, 12 September 1968.

6 Peter sent his Aunty Florrie a postcard from Mexico: 'Dear Aunty Flo and Uncle Dave, I am just writing to say thank you again for the send-off party. It really made me feel good. I have often thought of that night since I have been over here. Would you please pass on my regards and thanks to Bob and Cliff for the way they sang "The Impossible Dream" that night. As things worked out, my dream nearly came off. Still a silver medal is okay with me.'

7 Peter Luck, *This Fabulous Century*, Circus Books, Melbourne, 1979, pp. 98–9.

8 Australian troops were finally withdrawn from Vietnam in 1971. Australia's participation in the war cost 415 Australian lives with 2344 wounded. See Luck, *This Fabulous Century*, pp. 105–7.

9 'China marks Cultural Revolution', BBC News, Beijing, 16 May 2006.

10 Amy Bass, *Not the Triumph but the Struggle*, University of Minnesota Press, Minneapolis, 2002, pp. 3–4.

11 Avery Brundage, interview footage, *Salute*, 2008.

12 Brian Corrigan, *The Life of Brian – Confessions of an Olympic Doctor*, ABC Books, Sydney, 2001, p. 6.

13 Douglas Hartmann, *Race, Culture, and the Revolt of the Black Athlete*, University of Chicago Press, Chicago, 2003, pp. 150–1.

14 Kate Doyle, 'Tlatelolco massacre: declassified U.S. documents on Mexico and the events of 1968', <www.mexconnect.com/mex_/history/tlatelolco/nsaintro.html>.

15 Patching had been a member of the Geelong Guild athletics team before joining the navy in 1934 at seventeen. He was the navy's all-round athletics champion on three occasions. After thirteen years in the navy, Judy rejoined his former club and competed in open track-and-field athletics. He ultimately captained a Geelong Guild premiership team. Judy was a good all-round competitor, having originally been a sprinter before moving to the 440 yard hurdles. He described himself as a 'good, but never brilliant athlete – good enough to be selected for Victoria, but not good enough to get in an Australian team'.

16 Peter told a friend in a postcard from Mexico that he missed some of the niceties of home. 'Mexico is a great place but I won't be sorry to get back home. The first thing that I want to do is to have a pie and a glass of water. That's two things you just can't get over here. After the first two or three days, the doctor told us that it was safer to drink beer than the water, so that was enough of a hint for us. You can guess what happened after that.'

2

HE BLOSSOMED LIKE A CACTUS FLOWER

Ray Weinberg was the coach of the 1968 Australian Olympic athletics team. Before leaving Australia, Weinberg obtained information from each athlete's personal coach as to what they wanted the athletes to do on the trip. 'Ray's interest in our training program and in wanting to get to know each of us gave him an insight into how the team was going to perform in Mexico,' said Peter.

> Ray supervised Neville's program for Greg and I. Ray had been through it. He knew what it was like to compete at the highest level. He was an Olympic hurdler, an Olympic finalist, so he knew what it was like to be in the Village, to travel in the team, to be away from home at the age we were at and he was smart enough to make the team feel part of a family.[1]

Weinberg admitted:

> I don't think we realised how difficult it was going to be till the first day we got there. We were on the fourth floor of our apartment block and I said to the team, 'Don't use the lift, walk up the stairs and give yourself every chance to get acclimatised.' So they loaded their luggage into the lifts and sent it up. But no athlete reached the fourth floor, so I thought we've got a problem.

The death by heart attack of athletics section manager Jim Howlin, at aged 52, on 23 October 1968, shocked the Australian athletics team. *The Sun* newspaper reported that Howlin had become ill some two weeks before: 'He spent several days in bed at the Australian headquarters in the Olympic Village, before being transferred to hospital.'[2]

Howlin's death meant that Weinberg had to also assume the role of team manager. 'Ray then became manager, coach and mentor, father figure, father confessor and all-round good guy,' declared Peter. 'Ray got the team together. We reassessed what we were going to do. We were a real team. Everyone in the team cared for everyone else and everyone else's performances.'[3] Peter added that Weinberg knew what the team wanted, when they wanted it and how they wanted it. 'He knew how to say no without saying no. He always finished up managing to convince us that it was our idea. Ray's psychology went a long way to getting some tremendous performances out of all the athletes.'[4]

Peter described Weinberg as

> a kind, understanding, loving sort of guy who loved a bit of fun, who knew when to put his foot down and when to let the reins out. He had the confidence of all 24 athletes in the team. The relationship right across the team was one of brothers and sisters. The younger females were little sisters and we were all big brothers to them. We looked after them, made sure they had someone with them whenever they went out, or when they went to the dining hall or to the recreation room. They were always involved in social activities. If we went into town, we'd round up a few of the guys, and you'd make sure the girls were involved because they had it pretty rough. They had Shirley Strickland who was a very hard taskmaster looking after them, so you'd make sure that they were okay. If they wanted to go shopping, you ensured they had some company. We were all different but it was such a great family.
>
> Ray was the main instigator of most social events, like a night out at a bar for instance, just for everyone to let their hair down, because we had a couple of weeks of pretty hard training and we'd been away for two weeks. Plus we'd lost our manager. Ray decided the whole team needed a good night out, so we had a

> good night out. The next day not too many of us trained, but from then on it was back to work, business as usual. Little incidents like that went a long way to making everyone feel comfortable within the team.

The athletics team was full of personalities and characters. One of the most popular team members was Phil May, the 1.95 metre Western Australian triple jumper, who ultimately finished sixth in the triple jump. According to Peter, May was very outspoken, had an opinion on everything, was always right and was the supreme bullshit artist.

> Phil was always jumping out of his skin. Ask Phil how he was going. 'Jumping out of my skin.' Phil and I were room-mates on a number of trips away and behaved ourselves impeccably! Phil was a great team man because he could always lift people's spirits. It would be nothing for him to have finished training and come over and pull the gun for the sprinters to do starts and walk down the track saying, 'That looked great, that looked fantastic.' Then someone else would watch Phil doing the triple jump and say, 'Phil you're jumping out of your skin. You look great.' We all were bullshitters to a certain degree. You raised each other's spirits and personal value by noticing what someone else had done. Phil was always there with that word of praise for the way you were training, the way you were moving, the way you looked. That type of person in the team is invaluable.

Peter roomed with high jumper and team captain Lawrie Peckham and fellow East Melbourne Harriers sprinter Greg Lewis in Mexico. They called their room the 'room of 1000 feet' because it was always littered with smelly shoes and socks. 'Peter and I did a lot together,' said Peckham, 'and that's where we became good friends. Because you room together, you go for meals together and you do everything together. I really enjoyed Peter's company in 1968. He was a good bloke, liked mucking around, enjoyed a beer, was very easy to get on with, and had a lot of common sense.' Peckham recalled Peter being sharp with one-liners: 'So was Greg Lewis. Peter's one-liners were more humorous than cutting though. Greg was a more abrasive character than Peter.'

Australian walker Bob Gardiner recalled visiting the 'room of 1000 feet' on a number of occasions: 'The floor was always littered with clothes. I remember Peter and Lawrie giving us a rendition of "Light My Fire". Lawrie played guitar and the two of them did this duet.' Peter recalled such music sessions with his 'very dear friend' Peckham. 'Like Phil, Lawrie was a room-mate of mine on a number of occasions including Mexico. I've got vivid memories of Lawrie sitting up in bed with a straw sombrero on, with something tucked under his arm, for a guitar, singing "Hey Jude" and all of us joining in the chorus.'

Legendary Australian Rules Collingwood footballer and media personality Lou Richards was instrumental in getting a dozen footballs for the track-and-field team to take to Mexico. Some were ultimately taken to Mexico, but others were used for fundraising activities as Peter related:

> We were going to get two competition uniforms to take to Mexico, plus a training tracksuit and a competition tracksuit, a couple of pairs of spikes and a pair of flats and our dress uniforms for marching in the parade and some casual clothes. We knew that some teams would be there in T-shirts etc. so we all signed half a dozen footballs and a few of us sold raffle tickets in pubs to raise money so that we could have T-shirts printed with the Australian insignia and the Australian track and field team name so we'd have some sort of identity while we were there. We used the other footballs for training purposes.

At the end of every meal, Peter, Peckham, Lewis and other athletes would play a game called 'salt and pepper chucking', which they had devised to take their minds off the pressure of competing. Peter explained:

> We'd set up a serviette canister at one end of the table, polish the table until you could see your face in the laminate and then slide the salt or the pepper shakers, whichever team you happened to be in, to get them as close as you could to the serviette container without touching it. It was like bowls or bocce.
>
> One night Greg Lewis and I were the salt, Lawrie Peckham, because he was a Collingwood supporter, and Lou Richards were the pepper. We played for an hour or so because there was a large storm outside and we didn't want to get wet. We made Lou an honorary salt-and-pepper chucker and he was actually a member

> of the world championship team that night. Several days later when I was going out onto the track for the competition, I heard this commotion and I looked up into the stand and saw this little grey-haired guy with a powder-blue suit on, pushing his way down through the people, past the guards. He got right down near the fence and leant over to wish me all the best. This was a real buzz to have the great Lou Richards do this. He was an absolute legend of the football world. And this was the final!

Peckham mainly hung out with Peter, Lewis, Weinberg and May. He described the salt-and-pepper chucking competition as being 'a stupid bloody game' but added that the crowds kept getting bigger and bigger every night. 'It did a lot to keep motivation and team spirit high.' So much so that he – who competed in three Olympics and four Commonwealth Games – described the 1968 team as being by far the best national athletics team he was ever in.[5]

Throughout his career, Peter had to be mindful of the effects of asthma. He knew he couldn't undertake a rigorous warm-up program before an event.

> If I went through the normal warm-up, there'd be nothing left to run the race. So I used to be less than diligent warming up, you might say. At the same time I got through all those years with minimum injuries through lack of stretching and warming up.
>
> It was pretty difficult to cope with asthma and not being able to breathe simply because Ventolin and sprays such as that just weren't available in those days. It was just at the start of drug testing and you had to be very careful what you ingested. Luckily in Mexico, we had a couple of very good doctors in Howard Toyne and Brian Corrigan who were very sympathetic to you being able to breathe as much as you could at that altitude, and at the same time not put yourself in jeopardy through taking a drug that was going to show up as a positive. So I was well doctored in Mexico.
>
> But asthma's not a thing that you want to muck around with. Being an asthmatic, it's very hard to get a lot of air down into your lungs and all the training sessions had to be spread out over a two-hour session in the morning and two hours in the afternoon.

Once I was doing a particularly vigorous type of training (with Greg Lewis) with very short recovery time between efforts and I completely lost my breath. I went over to the medical team to see if they could help. The students running the medical tent saw this as a big opportunity to save a life. They put me down on a little couch and held the oxygen mask over my face. I was trying to fight the mask off and they were holding me down and pushing it on even harder. It would have helped if they had turned it on because what they were doing was suffocating me at the time. There was nothing coming through the mask – so that was a close call through asthma.

Peter had to be given oxygen on another occasion after one of the fastest training sessions of his career. He was resting after two successive 150 metre dashes when he began gasping for breath. He recovered quickly after medical attendants at the training track behind the main Olympic stadium gave him oxygen. Peter later admitted that he didn't take enough time between the two sprints, running the second only about five minutes after the first. Peter's solid workout that day included four short sprints off the blocks at the start of the bend with Australia's women's sprint hope Dianne Burge.[6] She recalled the session with Peter:

Ray [Weinberg] organised the one-off training with Peter. It did as much for me as it did for Peter. It instantly bought out your competitive spirit. I was trying as hard as I damn well could for him not to catch me and he was working hard to catch me. I think that was probably one of the fastest times I ever ran. It really inspired me. I treasure that time. It was something I enjoyed. And it was really an honour to have been asked to do that with Peter. Peter was someone you respected. He didn't strut around. You knew what his thoughts and his beliefs were. He'd act accordingly. It wasn't just for show.

The powerful US track-and-field team flew into Mexico City on 7 October 1968. Coaching staff stressed to reporters that the threat of a black boycott was dead.

'We have been assured there will be no trouble whatsoever,' said Payton Jordan, head coach. 'The boys are here to win medals and

> that is all they are concerned with.' 'The black boycott issue is dead,' added Stan Wright, assistant coach. 'I have been very close to the black athletes. You can bet there will be no demonstrations.' John Carlos, one of the militants in the Black Protest Movement, corroborated his coach's statements with some mild reservations. 'We have no intention of disrupting the Games. But that does not mean we will not do something to accentuate the injustices that have been done to the black man in America.'[7]

Many black American athletes wore large Olympic Project for Human Rights (OPHR) badges on their tracksuits during training. Among them was John Carlos, who continued to talk up the idea of demonstrating at the Games. Carlos told Australian journalist Jim Webster that athletes would demonstrate in their own particular way. Asked what his form of protest would be, Carlos replied that if he won a gold medal, he'd accept it.

> I may throw it into a fire afterwards, but nothing is going to keep me from getting it. I would want everybody to see who won that medal. If you want to see how we are going to demonstrate, just stick around, fella. You'll see all in good time. We are determined to draw attention to the unfair treatment given to black Americans.

Carlos said that all black athletes in the team felt the same as him, but were not as outspoken as he. 'All you press, radio and television people chase after me when I'm on the track, but not off it. I'm just a nigger then and you wouldn't want to know me.'[8]

Smith, holder of eleven world records for indoor and outdoor sprints, was by now the world's standout sprinter, with Carlos being his main threat at the Games. Peter recalled catching up with Smith in the Olympic Village about 10 o'clock one night, soon after the US team had arrived.

> Tommie and I were having a chat. As we talked, I heard Carlos say, 'Hey who's the white boy?', as if Tommie had no right to be speaking to me. So Tommie introduced me to John, who then made some derogatory remark about where he was going to kick me. John was mean and nasty and more of a junkyard dog. At that stage I'd already run 20.3 and 20.2 in Mexico. There was no doubt John had got to hear about that and didn't want anything

> to do with this white sprinter who'd come on the scene and may have been a threat. Mind you I didn't see myself as any sort of threat at that stage.

Carlos kept up the psychological warfare and whenever he saw an Australian athlete he gave them a message to pass back to Peter: 'You tell that white boy I'm going to lick his ass.'[9] Peter was always pleased to receive Carlos's messages as he now knew that Smith was not the only runner on Carlos's mind. Peter knew, however, that Carlos would be mighty tough to beat in Mexico. He was well aware that Carlos had beaten Smith pretty convincingly in the American Olympic trials and that he'd actually run a world record of 19.7 seconds in doing so. But Peter was also aware that Carlos's record had not been ratified because he ran it in shoes with what were called 'brush spikes' (rows of tiny spikes across the sole of the shoe), which were deemed to be illegal. 'But you still had to think cometh the time, cometh the man,' said Peter. 'Tommie Smith was going to be that man. Carlos had run 19.7 and if he was capable of doing that in the Olympics, then Tommie was going to run 19.6. Larry Questad, the third American, had done very well in the trials, so he was obviously a threat too. There was always Mike Fray, Eddie Roberts, Harry Jerome from Canada and a couple of Nigerians, in fact any one of twenty guys could have been in that final.'

Mexico City provided a synthetic track for the first time in Olympic history. Peter had not run on a synthetic track until Mexico and he believed that it made a big difference to his performance.

> In Australia I was running on grass and cinder tracks. The synthetic track was just made for me because I was very much a power runner and I needed something with a bit of lift. The first time I ran there I found my knees up around my ears. Every time I put my foot down on the tartan it reacted exactly the same as last time. Every stride I took was lengthened by about four inches, which makes you run a lot faster. I couldn't believe what was happening.
>
> We had a couple of pre-Games trials beforehand and there were meets on weekends preceding the Olympics. In my first competitive run I went from 20.5 at home to 20.3. That was unheard of, and that was only a week or so out from the Games. Then I ran a personal best for the 100 and anchored the relay team

> home from a three yard deficit. I said, 'Hello there's something going on here.' The following meet I ran 20.2 and another 10.2 for the 100 and brought the relay team home again.

An informal international athletics meeting was held at the Olympic Village training track on 28 September 1968. Peter finished strongly in third place (in 10.3 seconds) in the 100 metres division. In the 4 × 100 metres relay, he ran a strong last leg to make up several metres and bring the Australians home in third place in 39.2 seconds. This was only 0.2 seconds behind the winning Cuban team. Australia had fared much better than expected in the relay. The following day, Australia again clocked 39.2 seconds, finishing second behind the strong Soviet team with Cuba third. They were beaten by only a third of a metre after an outstanding finishing burst by Peter. Starting the last 100 metres about three metres behind the Russians and level with the Cuban team, Peter threw himself desperately at the tape but just failed to catch the last Soviet runner.

Inexplicably Australian officials had not entered a men's relay team in Mexico, as Peter related.

> To get some extra exposure in the track meets before the Games, we entered a team consisting of Greg Lewis, the lead-off man, 6' 5" of Phil May down the back straight so he didn't have to go round any corners, Allan Crawley, the long jumper around the top turn, and me to bring them home. Phil in full flight down the back straight was something to see, arms and legs going everywhere, head held perfectly still looking every inch a sprinter. We managed to knock over both the Australian and British Commonwealth records with that scratch team after three quarters of an hour of bungled relay practice the night before. Just to prove it wasn't a fluke, the next day at a similar meet, the same team again broke both records. In those two runs we beat the French, Italians, Cubans and just missed the Russians by a matter of inches. The French and Cuban teams won medals so we may have made the Olympic final if we'd entered this ragged ol' team.

Weinberg said Peter always exuded an air of confidence, but when he got to Mexico he 'blossomed like a cactus flower. That relay team was winning essentially because Peter was developing phenomenal speed. He was just running athletes down. So we had high hopes for Peter's chances in the sprints.'

Peter would only run in the 200 metres in the Games, but had he run 10.3 seconds for the 100 metres in the 1968 Australian championships, as he was doing in the pre-Games events, he would have qualified to compete in the 100 metres in Mexico. However, this would have presented him with a dilemma as it would have meant competing on a Sunday. He told sportswriter Alan Trengove that he didn't know what he would have done had he qualified as it would have conflicted with his Salvation Army principles. 'In Melbourne I have run on Sundays, but at the same time I get in a bit of a commercial by wearing a tracksuit marked "Jesus Saves". I don't think I could have done that out on the main arena at the Olympics. I would certainly have had qualms about running here on Sunday.'[10]

Neville Sillitoe's confidence began to build as Peter hit form in Mexico, although he was concerned after learning Peter had strained a hamstring during the pre-Games meets and would be forced to restrict his training the following week. Sillitoe remembered telling Peter on the phone that he had to work through it; he couldn't afford to rest for a week. 'I encouraged him to keep training but to closely monitor it. If there was the slightest twinge, he had to stop.' Sillitoe had 'complete and utter confidence' that Weinberg would look after Peter's interests.

On 4 October 1968, Peter ran a fast solo 100 metres to test his injured hamstring and clocked 10.5 seconds. Weinberg told Australian journalists that Peter's leg had been given a thorough test and he had come through it very well. Ray said that Peter would definitely participate in the next day's international meeting on the University of Mexico track. Peter was in top form on 5 October 1968, winning the 200 metres in 20.2, which was only two-tenths outside the world record. Peter was second last, almost five metres behind the leaders at the halfway mark, before he unleashed a powerful finish. With 20 metres to go he was still three metres behind the two leading runners: 'But Norman gobbled up the two in front of him to win by a foot.'[11] Peter also won a 100 metres sprint in 10.3, his best time for the distance. After the race Peter told journalists that he had started slowly, and was not going to push himself because of his sore hamstring. 'But at the halfway mark, I found I was still with them and decided to have a go.' He added that he was running so easily that he just decided to relax and run through the tape.[12]

Australian journalist Robert Gray was suitably impressed with Peter's runs, describing Peter as being in the finest form of his career. He now saw Peter as the danger man to the much-talked-about expected US domination in the 200 metres. 'Norman now looms as a potential bronze medallist and almost certain finalist.' Gray believed, however, that Peter would have to change tactics to ensure a place in the Olympic final.

> At present he is starting slowly and letting his opposition get a yard or so up before he winds up for the race to the tape. Steaming around the bend like a tank, Norman has proved his strength over the second half of the journey. In the next week he must concentrate on lifting his early speed and keep close enough in touch with the tearaways to make the most of his finishing burst.[13]

NOTES

1 Born in October 1926, Ray Weinberg won seven Australian hurdles championships and finished second on four other occasions. He competed in the 110 metres hurdles at the 1948 London Olympics, making the semi-finals. He finished sixth in the final of the same event at the 1952 Olympics. He won a silver medal at the 1950 Commonwealth Games in the 120 yards hurdles.

2 'Death of athletics manager', *The Sun*, 25 October 1968.

3 Peter Norman, ABC radio talkback, 2000.

4 Peter Norman, 'Grandstand', ABC radio, July 1992.

5 Lawrie Peckham, who finished eighth in the high jump in Mexico, won ten Australian high jump titles and was twice runner-up and twice placed third. He won two successive Commonwealth Games high jump gold medals and narrowly missed winning a third consecutive gold medal, finishing a close second despite tearing a rib cartilage in the warm-up before the final. He was also a fine sprinter, triple jumper, discus thrower and shot-putter for the strong Melbourne interclub team Glenhuntly.

6 Dianne Burge won five Australian sprint titles. She competed at the 1964 Olympics, making the quarter-finals in the 100 metres. In 1967 she beat the best American sprinters, including Wyomia Tyus, on their home turf in the USA versus Commonwealth meet, taking out both the 100 and 200 metres in fast times. These performances made her an early sprint favourite for Mexico. But a severe bout of 'Montezuma's revenge' and hamstring problems affected her performances. She

ran sixth in the 100 metres final and was run out in the semi-finals of the 200 metres. Di retired after the Games. For many years, she was critical of her performance in Mexico, but gained a different perspective after watching all the sprints live at the 2000 Olympics. 'It wasn't until Sydney that I saw how hard it was to get through each round and make the finals. That was when it hit me. I had a new respect for myself and what I had done in Mexico.'

7 'Black boycott threat ended', *Sydney Morning Herald*, 8 October 1968.

8 'Anger the spur for a sprinter', *Sydney Morning Herald*, 9 October 1968.

9 Peter Fitzsimons, *Great Australian Sports Champions*, HarperSports, Sydney, 2006, p. 325.

10 'One man happy to miss a games run', *The Sun*, 7 October 1968.

11 'Sprint medal hopes soar', *The Sun*, 6 October 1968.

12 'Australians in brilliant games trials', *The Age*, 7 October 1968.

13 'Norman could surprise US sprint stars', *The Australian*, 7 October 1968.

3

HELL, I'VE RUN SECOND!

The XIX Olympic Games opened on Saturday 12 October 1968. Troops with rifles and submachine guns stood guard outside the main stadium in what newspapers described as the most tension-charged Olympics since the 1936 Games in Nazi Germany. Inside the stadium more than 6000 security men mingled with the crowd. But ultimately the troops need not have been there. A few hours before the Games opened, student leaders promised that they would not demonstrate during the Games and they kept their promise. Mexico, the land of the fiesta, stunned the world by turning on what was described then as

> the greatest and most colourful opening in the history of the Games. 90 000 people in short sleeves and gay summer dresses packed the Estadio Olimpico. The cavernous stadium was a riot of colour with the flags of 113 competing nations fluttering behind the grandstand.[1]

Australia was the tenth nation to march into the stadium. The 24 Australian female team members were a hit in their gold-coloured dresses touching some ten centimetres above the knee. The 119 male athletes by contrast were described in the press as looking 'like a sober and sombre squad of Australian bowlers. In their outdated straw hats, green blazers, white shirts, ties, cream slacks and brown shoes, they were as outdated as

Sherlock Holmes in the world of James Bond'. They 'marched well, but stodgily, almost as if they were going off to Vietnam and not to a festival of sport and culture'.[2]

A number of black American athletes gave a raised clenched-fist salute as they marched around the stadium during the opening ceremony. US 400 metre runner Ronald Freeman was quoted in the press as saying that the salute by black athletes was not a protest but rather a gesture of black solidarity. The press also noted that John Carlos declined to march in the opening ceremony, partly because of a cold, but also as his own means of protest. Carlos reportedly watched the ceremony on television in the Olympic Village. Asked if his absence from the stadium could be interpreted as being part of a long-discussed demonstration by the black Americans, Carlos said, 'You can call it that too.'[3]

History was made when the Olympic torch was carried into the stadium and the cauldron lit for the first time by a female, Mexico's 20-year-old 400 metres champion Enriqueta Basilio de Sotel.

The first round of the men's 200 metres was run on 15 October (the third day of competition). Carlos easily won the opening heat in 20.5 seconds. Tommie Smith equalled Henry Carr's Olympic record of 20.3 in winning heat two. The USA's Larry Questad won heat three in 20.7 and Jamaica's Mike Fray won heat four in 20.6. But Peter made all runners sit up and take notice when, running in lane seven, he won heat six in 20.2, thereby setting a new Olympic record. Greg Lewis followed up by winning heat seven in 20.7 seconds.

Before the start of Peter's first heat, the Italian runner Ito Giani, who was to run in the outside lane next to Peter, approached him, as Peter related.

> He said, 'Don't judge your race on me. I've got a bad hamstring and I'll be stopping just after the start. I've just gotta be able to tell my grandchildren that I ran in the Olympic Games.' I thought that was the greatest con I'd ever heard in my life because now I'm going to be watching him. But that's exactly what happened. He stepped two steps and then pulled up. Had he not mentioned that, and I'd seen him pull up, I might have thought it was a false start and I may have eased back. I took off like a scalded cat because I was determined that I wasn't going to run last. I was fourth or fifth coming into the straight, just behind David

> Steane and Roger Bambuck, and then nailed them about two-thirds down the straight and won in Olympic record time. It was probably the easiest of the runs I had there.

Peter hadn't forgotten Carlos's cutting remarks the night they were introduced by Smith. On his way to his heat, after Carlos had won his, Peter decided that he'd give Carlos a taste of his own medicine. He called loudly to teammate Lewis, 'That guy must be the third string American, he only ran a 20.5.' He made sure Carlos was in earshot when he made this remark, calculated to offend, and it stung Carlos enough for him to threaten about what he was going to do to 'that white boy'.[4]

In an effort to psyche out Peter and all other competitors, Carlos then promised a phenomenal time of 19.5 seconds in his second-round heat.[5] He had no chance of doing that because torrential rain after lunch flooded and deadened the track. Carlos had to settle for a second-round time of 20.6 seconds. Peter appeared to miss the start in his second-round heat by a few metres, but still won comfortably by 2.7 metres in 20.4. Smith equalled Peter's Olympic record in winning heat three. Another of the fancied runners, Mike Fray, won his heat in 20.3. Lewis moved through to join Peter in the semis by finishing second to Carlos in his heat. The stage was set for the running of the two semi-finals and final on Wednesday 16 October 1968.

The night before the finals, Ray Weinberg introduced Peter to Jesse Owens. 'He shook my hand and said, "You're going to do really well tomorrow." You can imagine the thrill that gave me.'[6] Peter described his meeting of the legendary Owens, who had won four gold medals at the 1936 Berlin Olympic Games, as being out of this world. Peter was well-versed on Owens's life and, in particular, his feats in Berlin and the times he'd run. 'I knew how when he'd been starting out in college athletics, the whole college team would go to some faraway meet, and all the white athletes would go through the front door of the hotel, while all the black athletes would go through the tradesman's entrance at the back, and then sleep six to a room.'[7]

On Wednesday afternoon on 16 October, two-and-a-half hours before the final, the eight 200 metres finalists virtually selected themselves. Carlos led all the way to take the first semi-final in a new Olympic record time of 20.1 seconds. Peter, starting badly as usual, was fifth into the straight, but finished a close second to Carlos with yet another 20.2. Fray and Roger Bambuck, both at 20.4, qualified third and fourth. Smith caught Lewis with 80 metres to go in the second semi-final and won drawing away, matching Carlos's 20.1 in the process. Edwin Roberts, Larry Questad and Joachim Eigenherr battled closely for second, finishing in that order, all running 20.4.

Discussing the semi-final, Peter said he didn't know enough about Carlos at that time:

> The first time I ran against him was in the semi-final and oh boy I certainly found out about him then because he was big, strong, and extremely fast. I set out like a scalded cat which wasn't very fast for me. Carlos ripped through on the inside and literally pulled me off my feet. The power that he was putting into the track just tore me apart. I was all over the place, totally off balance, until I got into the straight. Then I thought to myself, 'You've got to get something going here.' I closed on him very quickly, but just before the line, I knew I couldn't catch him. But I had to let him know I was there, so I called out across the track, 'You have this one John. I'll have the next.' It shows up beautifully in the slow-motion footage of the film where he turns and gives me a rather nasty wave before walking off the track.

Australia's second sprinter Lewis had run very well throughout the series. He was considered unlucky to miss the final, being just edged out by the German runner Eigenherr. 'Greg ran very well,' says Weinberg, 'and was run out in what proved to be the fastest of the two semi-finals.' The final would be contested by (starting from the inside lane of the track) Fray (no. 533 – Jamaica), Bambuck (no. 344 – France), Smith (no. 307 – USA), Carlos (no. 259 – USA), Questad (no. 297 – USA), Norman (no. 111 – Australia), Eigenherr (no. 9 – Germany) and Roberts (no. 776 – Trinidad Tobago) at 5.50 pm, Wednesday 16 October 1968.

Peter was aware that he was up against a formidable group of runners in the final.

> Eddie Roberts had medalled in the previous Games. Tommie Smith was the world record holder. John Carlos had beaten Tommie at the American trials. Larry Questad had beaten everyone except those two at the American trials. Roger

> Bambuck was the European record holder. Mike Fray was the Commonwealth record holder, and Joachim Eigenherr was a European champion.

Peter knew that Smith had limped badly as he slowed down and left the track after his semi-final, but at that point he had no idea how much trouble Smith was in. It was initially thought that Smith had suffered a cramp, but it was later revealed that he had strained his left adductor muscle, high up on his thigh near his groin. Smith later admitted his chances in the final, only about two hours away, looked dismal right then: 'I didn't think I was going to make it,' he said.[8] Ice was immediately applied to the area, which Smith says stopped the swelling and any bleeding there might have been. 'They left me in the training room, ice on and ice off, for about 45 minutes, until about 40 minutes before the final.'[9] Smith admitted years later that he was really afraid his leg would lock up, so he didn't practice any starts before the race: 'When the gun went, I prayed "God, it's on you man!"'[10]

After the semi-finals, Weinberg suggested to Peter that they find a quiet place in the dressing room to sit down and relax, which Peter thought was a great idea.

> Ray asked if there was anything I wanted. I said, 'I'd love to know the lane draw and I'd love a Coke.' Now under normal circumstances a coach would have probably said, 'A Coke! You can't have a Coke before you run in an Olympic final.' Not Ray. He wasn't going to argue with me. He said he'd see what he could do.
>
> He was gone for some time and then he burst into the dressing room. He handed me the Coke, which I found out later he'd shaken up and let all the gas out of it. He said, 'You won't believe it. You've got the perfect draw! All the Americans are inside of you, so you won't have to worry about them running away from you too early.' I said, 'I won't beat Tommie Smith so we'll discount him.' Ray said, 'Okay but you must have a show against the others. You've got Eigenherr and Roberts on the outside. Latch on to them around the bend. They'll get you going at your pace. By the time you really fire up, all the fast guys, Smith, Carlos and Questad, will be there with you and you

can just hang on to them around the bend.' Within probably two minutes he'd convinced me that if I had made the draw, that's the way I would have made it. It just sounded so logical.

Peter knew that he had a little bit of petrol left in his tank for the final, but he didn't know how much the other runners had left.

> I was very prepared up until we went out on the track, then the realisation of having one race to go hit me. I tried to do a start but it was painful. Everything felt uncomfortable. Think, think, think! Then they called the victory ceremony for the women's 400 metres won by Colette Besson from France (who caught Britain's pre-race favourite Lillian Board on the finishing line). We had to go off to the side of the track and wait for this victory ceremony. While the ceremony was going on, I had a sudden cool come over me. I thought this isn't real bad actually.[11]

Peter wanted to show the other competitors just how cool he was, so he made a point of speaking to each runner. He wished Smith all the best, observing that he couldn't see anyone beating him. Smith gave a laid-back reply saying, 'Thanks dude.'[12] He then went to Bambuck and suggested that he might like to make it two in a row for France, with Colette Besson having won the previous race. Bambuck waved him away. Fray from Jamaica and Roberts from Trinidad were standing talking. Peter walked up to them and put a hand on each of their shoulders and said, 'Come on guys, let's make this one, two, three for the Commonwealth! We'll knock the Yanks off.' Both looked at him strangely. Peter could think of something to say to everyone except Carlos.

> There's not much you can say to someone you haven't got a lot time for, as I didn't with Carlos at that stage. I was just about to walk past him to my lane when the phone rang on the side of the track. That was for the starter to get his instructions. At that stage John was in his lane behind his blocks. He was focused. He was locked in. We'd already had words in the semi-final and I was desperate to get an edge. When the phone rang, I casually said, 'Answer that John, it's probably for you.' Twelve months later, we're having a drink together in a restaurant and the phone rang and I said, 'Answer that John, it's probably for you.' He had

> forgotten all about this other business until then. John said, 'Hey man you don't catch me twice.' It was only then that I realised that just those couple of words before the event probably saved me 4/100ths of a second.

Darkness settled around the brightly lit Estadío Olimpico. The eight finalists were called to take their positions on the starting blocks. All was ready for one of the most highly anticipated finals at the Games. Tension was high, both on and off the track. An eerie silence fell over the stadium. Many wondered how badly hurt Smith was. Would his leg injury stand up to one more race? Even Smith did not know the answer to that. Or could Carlos reclaim the world record, which many considered had been wrongly denied him at the US Olympic selection trials? Would the USA take out all three medals? Or would 'the white boy', the previously unknown runner from 'Downunder', figure among the place-getters?

The answers to these questions would soon be known. The large crowd sat tensely on the edges of their seats. The runners were given the 'get set' signal by the starter. The eight best 200 metres runners in the world were about to face the ultimate test. Who would come out on top? But wait, more drama. There was movement on the blocks, so the runners were stood up. The tension continued to build. The starter signalled the runners to again take their blocks. A second attempt was about to be made to get the runners away. It was now crunch time. Bang! They were racing.

Track and Field News takes up the story:

> Carlos, in black socks and wearing his 'Olympic Project for Human Rights' button, blasted away with the gun, attacked the turn and led by a yard and a half going into the straight. He passed the 120 metre mark in 12.2. Smith, showing no sign of his injury, was also off quickly and entered the straight in second. Tommie then shifted into his unmatchable straightaway speed, caught Carlos at 140 metres, and the race for first was as well as over. Five metres from the finish, the elated Tommie threw both his long, thin arms in the air and broke into a wide smile. He finished still smiling and still waving, a move which may have cost him a tenth of a second or so, but one he couldn't keep himself from making. Norman entered the last 80 metres in about sixth position. But he came on like a bomb down the

> straightaway, closing in on the fading Carlos. US coach Stan Wright said later, 'Carlos lost his cool and looked to his left at Tommie. This probably lost him second to Norman, who was on his right.' Carlos's glance to the left in the final metres gave him a nice view of Tommie. But John missed seeing the Aussie pull ahead and take the silver medal. No one else was in the race for metal. Roberts, Bambuck and Questad came into the straightaway third, fourth and fifth. Norman pushed each of them back a place in the final standings. Fray and Eigenherr never got out of the last two spots.[13]

Cordner Nelson, then editor of *Track and Field News*, thought there was no way somebody he'd never heard of from Australia was going to split Smith and Carlos: 'So I was quite surprised when he did. I can still see that home stretch. Tommie Smith going full blast, Carlos fading away, and Norman coming on strong, passing him. It wasn't close. Norman really beat him!'[14]

In winning the event in 19.8 seconds, Smith had set new world, Olympic and American records. In finishing second and third respectively, Peter and Carlos had equalled the previous world record by running 20 seconds flat. Then followed Roberts (20.3), Bambuck (20.5), Questad (20.6), Fray (20.6) and Eigenherr (20.6).[15]

Peter wasn't blessed with the grace and natural ability of Smith or the blinding speed and strength of Carlos.

> I was once described as lacking the cat-like ability of Carlos and Smith and resembling more a rugby full-back as I bulldozed my way down the track. I think I was more that type of runner. I was strong. I was determined and what I lacked in natural ability I probably made up for in determination.
>
> Great sprinters can finish and start. I would have found it very hard to beat my grandmother out of the starting blocks. Sure the finish was there and I was always confident that it would come. I knew Carlos in particular would be away very fast. If I let him pull me off my feet like he did in the semi-final, then I'd be in trouble. So I had to imagine that those two white lines on each side of me were like thick walls and concentrate on what was happening between my two white lines.

I got a reasonable start. I ran at Eddie Roberts. Carlos went. I felt him go but it didn't have the same impact as it did in the semi-final. This time it didn't matter because I was gonna keep going as fast as I could and try not to make any mistakes. Coming into the straight I was about sixth. I gradually started to overhaul the rest of the field and with about 30 metres to go John started to look around. When he turned into the straight he was a gold medallist, but Tommie went past him as if he was standing still at the top of the straight.

John started to think about Mike Fray and looked to his left. John says he looked to see how Tommie was going, but Tommie was already out in front. The 'Tommie jet gear' had come into play about 75 metres from the blocks and no-one could stop him. He ran the last 10 metres of the race with both hands above his head and leaning back on an angle that's not really conducive to good sprinting. To have someone go past you so fast when you're going fairly well must have put doubt in John's mind. It must have torn John's heart out the same way that he tore my heart out in the semi-final. John lost concentration. He was looking for someone else to come past him. You can't do that in a sprint race. You can't make mistakes.

I never panicked because I was four or five metres down. I still thought I'd get a lot closer. I had no idea that the others would stop as they did, and make it look as if I was finishing like an absolute train. Tommie was still going away as we came into the tape, even though he had both his hands in the air. John's race had finished and a few others had nothing left. But I was running flat out. It's not as if I was saving myself. I was flat out at the start, but just couldn't keep up. Then I managed to maintain my top speed for perhaps a little longer than they did. As you can see in the film footage of the race, John sort of said to himself, 'Oh shit, the white boy!' He then looked across to his right and found that I was alongside him. Then I went on to cream him by four one-hundredths of a second.

The photo finish showed that Peter had finished just over a metre behind Smith and centimetres ahead of Carlos. Peter had become only the third Australian male sprinter to win an Olympic medal. Previously Hec Hogan had won bronze in the 100 metres in the 1956 Olympics and Stan Rowley also had won bronze in the 100 metres in the 1900 Olympics.

Carlos tried to explain away his poor finish to reporters after the race by claiming that he turned his head because he 'wanted to see where Tommie was, and if he could win it. If I thought he couldn't have won it, I would have tried harder to take it'.[16] Given Carlos's propensity to go on the attack when challenged, no reporter dared challenge his statement at the time.

Carlos claimed to have wanted Smith to win the gold medal.[17] He said that, although he was in control of the race, he deliberately slowed down to let Smith pass him. He also claimed to have looked back during the race and yelled out to Smith, 'Quit bullshitting if you want to win this race.' Carlos stated that had he not been so focused on getting Smith through the race, he would have watched Peter and 'beat him decisively'.

Carlos was deluding himself in 1968, if he honestly believed he could have turned his race around at will in those last few metres, let alone beaten Norman's withering finish. Carlos was absolutely spent just before the finish line. And it wasn't as if he hadn't been warned about Peter's thundering finish. Australian sportswriter Jim Webster observed that Peter had

> a peculiarity in his running that I don't think I've ever seen before. For about 120 metres, he ran without any great speed at all; inevitably he was still somewhere in the middle of the field. Then … whoosh, away he'd go. Suddenly he developed a turn of speed for those last 80 metres, the likes of which I've never seen before. I clearly remember warning John Carlos … about the way Norman unwound at the end of the race. The advice fell on deaf ears.[18]

US track coach Payton Jordan was not surprised at Peter's performance in the race.

> It played out pretty well like I figured. There was no doubt in my mind it was going to be a real race. The crowd realised it because they really got quiet before that race. I don't think in any other race there had that much silence and anticipation. This

> 200 metres was one of the epic races of my life. I told Larry [Questad] Peter was the guy to be aware of because he had a heck of a drive.[19]

Questad didn't see it that way. He remembered, 'We just kept talking sweep, sweep, sweep. We were very confident that we would win all three medals. Peter Norman is an enigma to me. He came from nowhere. I'd never come across his name. Who the hell's he? But he ran a hell of a race and I didn't!'[20]

Ousting Carlos for the silver medal gave Peter great personal delight at the time: 'Smith and I got on well, but Carlos called me "white boy" with animosity.'[21]

What was Peter thinking as he crossed the finishing line? 'Hell, I've run second,' he recalled.

> I knew Ray and Greg were in seats looking directly down the straight, so as I came across the line, they could see that I was in the position where I would have won a medal. I looked up and saw Ray. He had on this ridiculous white floppy hat so it was very easy to pick him out in the stand. He was holding up three fingers. It was pretty hard for him to tell from where he was front on, but I was able to very carefully hold up two fingers and indicate that I had run second, not third. So, yes, I was pretty happy.

Weinberg recalled Peter coming up to him after the race and saying, 'That was a lot of crap you were talking about before the race.' Weinberg was very happy to confess: 'Yes it was actually!'

Peter believed that he'd run the race of his life in the final.

> Looking back over it now I can't see too many places where I could have improved, which gives you a lot of satisfaction to know that win, lose or draw, you did as well as you could. I kept my concentration all the way, which is most important in a sprint race because from gun to tape the guy that makes the least amount of mistakes wins. In an Olympic final you've perhaps got three-tenths of a second between the fastest guy and the slowest guy on paper, so that concentration factor is absolutely vital.

Neville Sillitoe heard Peter's feats on the radio while teaching in

Melbourne. 'The final was broadcast direct to Australia. Peter's silver medal was just a great thrill. I was delighted for him because of the work that he'd put in and the hiccups he'd had along the way. I was delighted for myself as well.' Sillitoe wasn't one to throw compliments around freely, but Peter recalled Sillitoe had what he called his 'jelly bean system'.

> If you were bold enough to say to him, 'What you think of that, coach?', he would say, 'Oh, that was about a green jelly bean or a red jelly bean or a brown jelly bean.' The better the run, the darker the jelly bean he would offer. Not that there were ever any jelly beans. A couple of days after the 200 metres in Mexico, I got a little parcel. It was a little matchbox-sized box. Inside were two black jelly beans. No message. No name. Nothing! Just two black jelly beans. I knew where they'd come from. Neville was obviously pleased with what I'd done.

Peter's East Melbourne Harriers teammate Gary Holdsworth expected that Peter would run well in Mexico but nowhere near as well as he did. Holdsworth and Neville were both working together at Maribyrnong High School in Melbourne's west. Holdsworth recalled the day of the 200 metre finals.

> We were both at work. I was teaching. Neville had a period off. He came in and said, 'He's come second in his semi.' A little bit later he came back and said, 'He's come second in the final.' We were jumping up and down. People probably thought we were crazy. Peter would get to his peak quickly, but to keep him there was something else again. That's why his running in Mexico, being coached by a bloke who's in Melbourne, was so unbelievable.

Peter appreciated the sacrifices that Holdsworth had made to help prepare him for Mexico. He told the Australian press after the final that he attributed his success to the hard work that he, Holdsworth and Lewis had put in during the Australian winter. He also said he had no plans to retire immediately and his main aim during the coming Australian season was to lower the national 220 yards record of 20.9 seconds.[22]

Peter also told the press that Smith was 'the greatest. There's just no one else like him'. He described his own race as 'really great, but these blokes are just so good'. Told that he had not appeared to finish as brilliantly over the last 20 metres as he usually did, Peter said, 'I was finishing as well as I've ever done, but it doesn't make any impression when you're up against a man like Smith. You can finish all over other runners when they're donkeys, but not when they're fellows like this.'[23]

Peter's Australian teammates were thrilled with his silver medal win. Sprinter Di Burge said, 'It was such a shock to see an Australian male in the final of the 200 metres. We just couldn't believe it. We were all so excited and I was so thrilled for him.' Hurdler Pam (Kilborn) Ryan thought Peter would make the final, but she didn't think he had a hope of winning a medal. 'He didn't look great until 80 metres from home, then he just took off like a rabbit. If it had been another 10 metres further or if he'd gone earlier he would have won the jolly thing.' Lewis said Peter did 'that most magnificent, heroic thing, splitting those two unsplittable Americans. The sort of kudos he's got for doing that is a thimble full of praise, but no real appreciation of the fact that it was just a magnificent achievement'.

Bob Gardiner had known Peter longer than most of his Australian teammates, having first met him back in 1957 when Peter joined the Collingwood Harriers athletics club. Seeing Peter come through in the 200 metres final was, according to Gardiner, 'pretty stirring and emotional'. Gardiner was pleased with Peter's success because he thought highly of him: 'He was always ready for a laugh. He cared about people and when he talked to you, you felt he really was interested.'

Distance runner Ron Clarke had known Peter since they were teammates at the 1962 British Empire and Commonwealth Games. Clarke thought Peter was running well enough to make the final but said

> We were all astonished that he won silver. Coming second was out of the blue. But it's the best sprint performance we've had, even with Hec Hogan's third in Melbourne. Gee whiz, Smith and Carlos were top athletes. When you judge people, to me the judgement is on who they competed against.

The extended Norman family was ecstatic about Peter's success. His parents, youngest sister, wife and daughter were holidaying on the Atherton Tablelands in Queensland with family who were living in Queensland. They were having a picnic on top of a mountain when they heard the news of Peter's second place over the radio. 'We were sure on top of the mountain that day,' said Peter's mother, Thelma. 'We all did a dance, then had a big celebration.'[24]

Peter's oldest sister, Heather, had driven her future sister-in-law, Jill, to the Coburg Teachers College to sit an exam. The final was to be run at the same time as Jill's exam. 'You could see from the exam room out into the quadrangle,' recalled Heather. 'I told Jill that I would pin pieces of paper up on the window to indicate which place Peter had finished in. When it actually happened, I stuck two pieces of newspaper on the window, then sat back with my arms folded and just beamed. I was thrilled.' In the exam room somebody looked out and told Jill that Peter had run second. The whole exam room buzzed with excitement. Heather could have been suspended for communicating with a student during an exam, but fortunately her lecturer went into battle for her.

In the meantime, while the race was on, Peter's brother, Laurie, was a few hours' drive away from Melbourne. He heard the news on the radio at the end of a lecture at the Dookie Agricultural College, where he was studying agricultural science. While not the type to run around and shout to the heavens, Laurie was nevertheless still thrilled at his brother's success. He knew how hard Peter had worked to get to Mexico and saw the silver medal as just reward for his efforts.

NOTES

1 *Brisbane Courier Mail*, 14 October 1968.

2 *Brisbane Courier Mail*, 14 October 1968.

3 *Brisbane Courier Mail*, 14 October 1968.

4 'Silver lining', *The Australian*, *c*. 1999.

5 'Norman flies', *The Herald*, 16 October 1968.

6 'Follow the flame' interview, Channel 7, Melbourne, *c*. 2000.

7 Peter FitzSimons, *Great Australian Sports Champions*, HarperSports, Sydney, 2006, p. 325.

8 *Track and Field News*, Mountain View, CA, USA, October–November 1968.

9 Tommie Smith with David Steele, *Silent Gesture – The Autobiography of Tommie Smith*, Temple University Press, Philadelphia, 2007, p. 27.

10 Tommie Smith, interview footage, *Salute*, 2008.

11 Sadly, Lillian Board, one of the finest athletes of her generation, died of cancer in December 1970 at the young age of twenty-two.

12 'Silver lining', *The Australian*, *c*. 1999.

13 'Smith zips 19.8 hands high', *Track and Field News*, October–November 1968.

14 Cordner Nelson, interview footage, *Salute*, 2008.

15 Paul Jenes is Australia's leading research and statistical expert in athletics. He has also been president of the Association of Track and Field Statisticians. He described Peter's performance in splitting Smith and Carlos, which he witnessed live, as being 'quite extraordinary'. Jenes says there were two systems of timing in 1968: 'Mexico was electronically timed as well as manually timed. Peter's time was a straight 20.0 seconds on the watches, and that's what he was given. The electronic time was 20.01. In those days, they added .05 seconds to account for apparent differences between the manual and electronic system, so that's why the electronic time was given as 20.06 seconds. They found out later that this was nonsense, so they've removed that system since. Basically Peter ran 20.0 flat manually and the proper electronic time was 20.06.' The official converted times for all runners in the 200 metres were as follows: Smith (19.83), Norman (20.06), Carlos (20.10), Roberts (20.34), Bambuck (20.51), Questad (20.62), Fray (20.63) and Eigenherr (20.66).

16 '2 accept medals wearing black gloves', *The New York Times*, 17 October 1968.

17 CD Jackson, *Why? The Biography of John Carlos*, Milligan Books, Los Angeles, 2000, pp. 200–1.

18 *The Best of the Last 10 Years of Australian Sport*, HK Frost, Adelaide, 1978, pp. 104–5.

19 Payton Jordan, interview footage, *Salute*, 2008.

20 Larry Questad, interview footage, *Salute*, 2008.

21 'Power and glory at Mexico City', *The Sun*, 18 July 1984.

22 *The Age*, 18 October 1968.

23 'Peter claims first silver', *The Sun*, 18 October 1968.

24 Peter was happy that Ruth, his wife, and Janita, his daughter, were holidaying with family while he was in Mexico. He sent a number of postcards and letters to Ruth in which he told her how much he missed her and Janita: 'Dearest Ruth, Just a short note tonight to tell you that I love you with all my heart and I am missing you very much … the Village is getting pretty full now, but it still doesn't make up for my two special people. I love you both very much. See you soon my love. Your Peter.'

4

I DIDN'T RAISE A FIST, BUT I LENT A HAND

Once the race was over, the animosity between Peter and John Carlos dissipated. All the pre-race trash talk was forgotten. Peter related how 'down in the dressing rooms, Carlos and I made our peace by shaking hands and embracing and we've been very firm friends ever since'.

> The most important thing I did that day was shake John's hand after the race. That made me part of what he and Tommie were going to do. They knew they could trust me. We were on our own during preparations for the medal ceremony. There were a couple of officials floating around but they weren't taking much notice of us and we weren't taking much notice of them.
>
> The ceremony was well-rehearsed before we went out. We discussed it and went through the actions that were going to take place and the possible ramifications. We didn't go through physical rehearsal. It was rehearsed in our minds. I wasn't nervous about the demonstration that was about to take place. I was probably more nervous about being out there as an Olympic medallist.
>
> Tommie and John planned on wearing gloves on to the victory dais and going through certain motions. Then John discovered

> he had left his gloves back in the village. Tommie was still going to wear his. I suggested they wear one each as they were only going to hold up one hand. So that's what they did. John's got the glove on the left hand and Tommie the right hand. I suggested that if they had an Olympic Project for Human Rights badge[1] I'd wear it in support. As we were going out on to the track, Paul Hoffman, the cox of the US rowing eight, came over to congratulate the guys. The rowing team was supporting the African-American guys. Paul, who is white, had his badge on. As Paul reached over to shake hands with John, while John had his right hand clenched, he reached across with his left hand and undid Paul's badge. He then pinned it on my tracksuit. I proudly wore it on to the stand.

Paul Hoffman recalled thinking at the time, 'If this Australian wants my badge, then by God he's gonna have it! I'm glad I was able to give it to him. I know the guys on the stand were tremendously pleased to have his support.'[2]

When the time came for the victory ceremony, the three athletes paraded out to the dais to a fanfare of trumpets. Smith and Carlos had stockinged feet. Their socks were black. Both carried an easily identifiable Puma running shoe. Smith wore a black scarf around his neck. Carlos wore a black T-shirt and a string of African-style beads around his neck. The president of the International Amateur Athletic Federation, Lord David Burghley (the Marquess of Exeter),[3] presented each place-getter with their medals. Smith also received an olive sapling, an ancient emblem of peace. Having received their medals, the athletes turned to face the American and Australian flags raised over the north end of the stadium. As the band started to play 'The Star-Spangled Banner', Smith and Carlos bowed their heads. They each simultaneously raised a clenched fist, Smith his right and Carlos his left, encased in a black glove. Booing and jeering began to rain out across the stadium. Peter said:

> I still wasn't sure if they would go through with it. A guy up in the stand used to sing the American national anthem every time it came up. When we turned to face the flags both Tommie and John were behind me, so I couldn't see what was happening. But I knew they'd actually gone through with it when the voice from up in the stands got about four bars into the national anthem

> and then faded out to nothing. The stadium just went quiet. I immediately thought 'They've done it. Good on 'em!'

In accordance with Olympic protocol, Lord Burghley and other Olympic officials stood to attention for the duration of the American national anthem. The ceremony over, the three athletes left the presentation area to even louder booing and jeering. Smith and Carlos reacted by once again raising their black-gloved fists.

One time Melbourne interclub athlete Paul Jenes was very much aware of 'the black situation' in America because he was living there at the time of the Olympics. He attended all athletics sessions at the 1968 Games and was present during the victory ceremony. 'As they came out to get the medals, everybody applauded, then when the anthem stopped, the booing started. While I'm still cheering Peter as they came off, every possible derogatory comment towards a black man was hurled by a segment of white Americans. They were disgusting. It was pretty ugly.'

Ray Weinberg recalled that it had been mooted that something might happen on the dais. He cautioned Peter not to get caught up in anything.

> It would be easy as a young, pretty naive bloke to think 'I'll support these blokes. They've got a reasonable cause.' Peter very sensibly kept a low profile. They gave him a badge to wear. Peter stood there quietly, accepted his medal, turned and faced the American and Australian flags and that was his involvement. They respected Peter for what he had done and for the fact that he sympathetically understood their position. He handled it very well.

Fear was not a factor for Peter in the controversial medal ceremony. 'I didn't feel there was that sort of urgency to it. I hadn't encountered racial hatred of that sort of intensity before. The guys did a good job of covering up their fear or perhaps it was just that they were so committed to it, that it didn't matter.'[4]

Peter was aware of the racial turmoil in the USA, as he discussed:

> It was in all the papers. You couldn't watch television news broadcasts without seeing what was going on. The footage wasn't pretty. It was damn ugly. From an outsider's point of view, it didn't show black America in a very good light because that was the way they wanted to show it. They wanted to show it as

> blaming African-Americans for what was going on. The reports weren't saying they were standing up for what they believed in, for the rights of Americans, and for their right to be humans. They said they were fighting the system and not doing the right thing by the country. White was right. That was the way they put it on the television and in the papers.
>
> I always had my views on racial tolerance. I couldn't see why anyone would dislike or hate someone simply because they were a different colour. Colour doesn't matter. Nationality doesn't matter. I'd been involved with African-American athletes for a long time before Mexico and they were just buddies. They were competitors who you'd go out to dinner with, go to a jazz club with or go out to breakfast with on the way home. You liked someone because you liked them, not because of their colour. I was interested in civil rights but not from a political association. I was probably more interested in people. I think it's the Aussie tradition of giving everyone a fair go.

Peter knew, however, that Australia was not without fault when it came to its treatment of Indigenous Australians. He, like many Australians, was embarrassed about the country's treatment of Aboriginal people and the 'White Australia Policy'. At the end of the nineteenth century, colonisation had virtually destroyed, through slaughter, disease and dislocation, the Aboriginal community in Australia's southernmost state, Tasmania. This continued into the twentieth century and Aboriginal people were shot, exploited and humiliated across the country.

> Official government policy towards the Aboriginal race in Australia has ranged from Christian ministry to [so-called] savages around the turn of the century; to a policy of separate development or apartheid in the 1920s and 1930s; to a half-hearted attempt at assimilation in the 1940s and 1950s; to a situation in the 1960s where Aboriginals were eventually given some rights to determine their own future.[5]

Indigenous Australians were finally considered worthy of having the right to vote in Commonwealth government elections in 1962, but it wasn't until 1967 that a referendum allowed Aboriginal people to be counted in

Commonwealth, state and territory censuses.

That Peter also was no supporter of Australia's immigration policies of the time became apparent when he was questioned by reporters after the medal ceremony.

The White Australia Policy described Australia's approach to immigration from Federation in 1901 until the latter part of the twentieth century. The *Immigration Restriction Act 1901* placed restrictions on immigration of non-white people and provided for the removal from the Commonwealth of prohibited immigrants. The origins of the policy can partly be traced back to the 1850s when resentment expressed by white miners towards industrious Chinese diggers culminated in violence on goldfields in Victoria and New South Wales.

During World War II, many non-white refugees entered Australia. Most left voluntarily at the end of the war, but many had married Australians and wanted to stay. Following the war, many Australians, like the Norman family, began to argue against this racist policy. It was not only discriminatory, but it caused tremendous strain on affected families. It was also fast becoming a national embarrassment, given the severe criticism from other countries of Australia.

The late 1950s saw the introduction of a simpler system of entry permits that avoided references to questions of race. In March 1966 Immigration Minister Hubert Opperman[6] announced that applications for migration would be accepted from well-qualified people on the basis of their suitability as settlers, their ability to readily integrate and their possession of qualifications positively useful to Australia. At the same time, the government decided a number of 'temporary resident' non-Europeans, who were not required to leave Australia, could become permanent residents and citizens after five years. The government also eased restrictions on immigration of non-Europeans. These decisions were seen as a watershed in abolishing the White Australia Policy, and non-European migration began to increase. The final vestiges of the policy were removed in 1973.[7]

Peter strongly believed that had Smith and Carlos made their 'statement' anywhere other than on the Olympic dais, no-one would have given a damn. No-one would have taken notice and the statement would have been lost forever. He, Smith and Carlos all knew that at that particular time they had people in the stadium and the eyes and ears of the world's media focused on them. The three medal winners were very much aware that, for the first time in Olympic history, the American Broadcasting Company (ABC) was beaming the 1968 Olympics through affiliated networks to an estimated 400 million people worldwide. So the statement was either seen live or replayed in news broadcasts worldwide. In addition, for the next few days, they had press from all over the world writing about it, commenting about it in favour of or against – caring about it. It continued to be talked about and built up for quite some time.

Tony Charlton, a doyen of Australian sport broadcasting, was in Mexico to broadcast the athletics to Australian television stations. He conducted a brief interview with Smith immediately after the final. Charlton asked Smith about his injury, his thoughts on Peter's performance and the significance of events on the dais. Smith told Charlton that initially he didn't think he was going to be able to run in the final. Charlton, obviously somewhat sceptical about the extent of Smith's injury, immediately fired back the comment 'You're dismissing any prospect that this was a foxing performance to con the others into thinking you weren't fit!' Smith, with a huge grin on his face, admitted 'You're right, to a certain extent!'

Charlton then asked Smith how he felt about 'our own boy's achievement'. Smith responded, 'Man, this cat Norman! I was in Melbourne last year and he was running 21.1s. He told me, "I'll see you in Mexico." I said, "Okay," you know very nonchalantly, and there he is sitting right over there in fact.' Charlton, who to this day believes Olympic protocols should always be followed, made his own feelings known about what took place on the dais when he commented to Smith that 'there was quite a hiatus caused at the medal presentation by this black-gloved business!' He asked Smith to explain the significance of the event. Detecting that Charlton's views on the subject differed to his, Smith's demeanour immediately changed. A stern look had replaced a very broad smile as he responded.

> It represents black America. As a black man I am proud to be black. And to represent this, I wore black gloves and I ran in black socks and wore a black scarf around my neck to show the people that I'm proud to be black and racism in the United States is hopingly coming to some kind of improvements.[8]

Smith took the opportunity the following day to expand on his explanation of the symbolism to legendary American sports journalist and broadcaster Howard Cosell.

> The right glove that I wore on my right hand signified the power within black America. The left glove my teammate John Carlos wore on his left hand made an arc with my right hand and his left hand also to signify black unity. The scarf that was worn around my neck signified blackness. John Carlos and me wore black socks, without shoes, to also signify our poverty.[9]

Years later, Smith described his and Carlos's actions as being 'a silent gesture shown around the world. We didn't say a word. A picture is worth a thousand words'.[10]

The Australian press contingent was ecstatic about Peter's silver medal success. They also supported Peter's actions on the victory dais. Alan Trengove wrote that Peter won friends for Australia 'throughout the coloured world' by actively supporting the American civil rights movement by wearing an OPHR badge. 'Norman also agreed that it would be more effective if the negroes did not shake his hand on the dais. Negroes in Mexico City were delighted by Norman's gesture and at a mass press conference after the medal presentations, one negro hoisted Norman's arm aloft triumphantly.'[11]

Trengove reported that Peter told the press that he got 'pretty pally' with Smith when he was in Australia the previous summer, and when he was in Los Angeles in 1966. 'Being a believer in civil rights and in the principle that all men are created equal and are entitled to be treated as human beings, I thought this was a good opportunity to have a white man show himself on the Negro side.' Peter added that Smith knew of his sympathies long ago.

> The fourth formers at his school Williamstown Tech had expressed interest in the civil rights program and he had encouraged them to write to Smith. 'Whether I agree totally with what Smith and Carlos did on the stand is irrelevant,' Norman said. 'It takes a fair bit of guts when you back up your opinions with actions like that.' An American reporter reminded Norman that under Australia's immigration policy, Negroes were barred from settling in the country. Wasn't he afraid of criticism back home? Norman replied, 'I think you'll find the majority of Australians would favour what I did. And I'd also like to say that I don't necessarily agree with black power methods.'[12]

Trengove wrote that Peter had made his position clear after Smith and Carlos had delivered a long tirade against white people at the joint press conference.

> Smith said, 'We are black and we are proud to be black. White America will only give us credit for being Olympic champions, but black America will understand why we did this. And we're proud to say that black America is with us all the way.' Carlos said, 'There were people in the stadium who made it clear they regard Smith and myself as animals who have to do a job. After we've done the job we're not expected to think. We heard those boos and saw the thumbs down, and I want those people to know we are not low animals or rats or leeches.'[13]

Sports reporter Robert Gray related how, at the press conference, Smith and Carlos launched an attack on white people who 'treat Negroes as show horses and call them boy when they do well and throw a few peanuts'. Gray quoted Peter as saying, 'I am on their side. It took a lot of guts to do what they did. I don't think I'd be that brave. I've met Smith before in Australia and I know he doesn't hold my Government's principles on colored people against me personally.'[14]

Gray described Peter's silver medal win as the most freakish performance ever produced by an Australian athlete at the Olympic level.

> Never before has an Australian sprinter challenged the world's best and done so well, especially when it takes a man clipping two-tenths of a second off a world record to beat him … He did a nation proud by thundering home down the final stretch and splitting Tommie Smith and John Carlos, the two fastest men over the distance in the world … Carlos out sped him in a semi-final and it took a lot of competitive courage for Norman to bounce back with the last word in the final.[15]

Gray noted that Peter was the first Australian to ever last through to the final of an Olympic 200 metres, and that his time of 20 seconds won him the tag of the fastest white man the world had ever known over the distance. Over the years, Peter objected very strongly to this tag, saying on more than one occasion, 'Forget about the fastest white man in the world. They don't have age divisions or colour divisions in the top echelons of sport. You either are, or you are not, the fastest.'

After the race, Peter told Gray that 20 seconds flat had always been a target for him to aim at: 'I've got there now and I'll have to start thinking of getting down to Smith's new world record.'[16]

Gray felt that the most amazing thing about Peter's performance was that he, along with other track athletes in Australia, had to endure such poor facilities in comparison to American athletes: 'Tartan tracks are now laid down at every American university athletics field. In Norman's own words, "We haven't one tartan track in the whole of Australia, let alone a decent cinder track in any of the six states."' Gray added that Peter had a trace of bitterness in his voice when he told the world's press that training at Olympic Park, which was the best cinder track in Melbourne, was 'about as good as running on St Kilda beach. We just haven't got good facilities and our athletes suffer tremendously because of it'.[17]

Reaction in the American press varied from focusing primarily on Smith's outstanding run, with only brief reference made to his and Carlos's actions on the dais, through to scathing attacks on both athletes. Chicago sports columnist Brent Musburger described Smith and Carlos as 'black-skinned stormtroopers'.[18] The *Chicago Tribune* accused them of carrying out an act contemptuous of the USA, which had placed them on the team and paid their freight to Mexico City so that they could then insult their countrymen. The newspaper also blasted both athletes for creating an unwarranted intrusion of domestic politics into international competition.[19] The *New York Times* was critical of Smith's determination to win gold, so as to afford him the opportunity to protest on the victory dais, rather than winning for the honour and glory of his country.[20]

The *Charleston Gazette* focused on giving its readers a detailed account of the post-race press conference at which Carlos did most of the talking. The newspaper noted that Smith essentially nodded repeatedly in agreement with Carlos's statements throughout the conference. Carlos was quoted as saying that when he and Smith mounted the victory stand, he heard applause from the crowd of about 60 000, but he also heard a lot of boos and saw people gesturing with thumbs down, like a crowd at a bullfight.

> 'They look upon us as nothing but animals, low animals, roaches and ants,' Carlos said. 'We are sort of show horses out there for the white people. They give us peanuts, pat us on the back and say, "Well done, you did fine."' Then Carlos, his eyes glistening,

> added, 'I want you to print this and print it right. If white people don't care to see black men perform, they should not come out to the stadium.'[21]

Part way through the press conference Carlos took his bronze medal from around his neck and 'tossed it to his wife, standing in a yellow dress at the fringe of the crowd of reporters. "Here honey, this is yours," he said. "I don't want it." Then he added, "The next time I go to an Olympics, I'll pay my way and go as a spectator."'[22]

Peter said of the press coverage of the ceremony:

> The whole thing was blown up by the US press. They weren't denigrating the flag. They weren't denigrating the anthem being played. They weren't there to proclaim black supremacy. They were there to proclaim black equality. Equality was all they wanted. The American people took it as an absolute slight against 'Old Glory' and the national anthem and America as a whole. The symbolism went something like this. The heads were bowed in memory and respect of brothers and sisters that had made the supreme sacrifice in the cause of African-American unity. The raised arm and the clenched hand was a symbol of unity with the fingers coming together in a symbol of strength. It was never meant as a threatening gesture. The black socks, worn throughout the competition, and no shoes, was a sign of African-American poverty. The fact that they couldn't get jobs, weren't respected in jobs, couldn't get decent jobs or decent education. This symbolism went by the board because they didn't get a chance to explain it. All the press wanted to talk about were these militant young black athletes that had despoiled the Olympic dais.

Peter added that Smith and Carlos and other black athletes were also 'griping about' the fact that very highly qualified people in the inner administrative positions, and coaches and managers, were all chosen first because they were white, then because of their academic qualities and their use to the team. 'Then they'd put in a black assistant who would then act as a buffer between white administration and black athletes in boxing, track and field, and basketball.'[23]

Peter was very proud to wear the OPHR badge on to the dais: 'To wear the badge as a white individual made the statement even more powerful. And as Smith said, "I didn't raise a fist but I lent a hand", which I thought was pretty good.' Smith said that 'Peter's offer to wear the badge was significant to me. I heard John mention it to him and I thought, that's not really Peter. It's an American situation. Don't get Peter mixed up in this. He was that committed but I didn't know that.'[24]

Carlos insisted that Peter didn't have to wear the OPHR badge.

> Peter wasn't from the United States. Peter was not a black man. Peter didn't have to feel what I felt. When Peter put that button [badge] on his chest that was as powerful as us putting our fists in the sky. Peter was saying, 'Man I respect you. I respect human rights and I can do something with you.' Here was a guy from the other side of the world showing he believed in humanity, in love, and in God, and that showed his character.[25]

Carlos added that for Peter 'to wear the badge as a white individual, it made the statement even more powerful. During a crucial time in our lives, he was compassionate, understanding and he showed his manhood. I'll always respect and love him for that. Pete became my brother at that moment'.[26]

The morning after the victory ceremony, Peter went to the Australian administration area in the village to see if there were any telegrams for him.

> Being a bit of a big head I expected to get a few. Among the many telegrams I got was one from Dick Leffler, who was twelve times national hammer throwing champion, so I never argued with him when he had the odd shot at me for what I wore on my tracksuit. Dick's telegram simply said, 'After that Norman you can wear any bloody tracksuit you want.' I thought that was as good as a big pat on the back from Dick. It made me feel very proud. Dick died a few years ago. I went to his funeral and I wore a Papuan New Guinea tracksuit which has a big bird of paradise on the back, all different colours, and red and gold down the sleeves. People said to me, 'What's this at a funeral?' I said, 'That man said I could wear any tracksuit I wanted, so I did.' He would have loved that.

While Peter was collecting his telegrams and mail, Judy Patching called him into his office.

> 'Patch' has the ability to receive five pieces of conflicting information from five different people, agree with every one of them and then make up his own mind. He is very fair.[27] He asked me what in the hell had happened. When I told him I won a silver medal, Patch said, 'I know you won a silver medal but what happened after that?' He stood there knowingly, nodding his head, with a smile all over his face, as I went through it all with him. 'What about the badge?' 'Yeah I wore a badge on my tracksuit.' I explained how I got the badge. He said the badge hadn't gone unnoticed by the press. 'The Australian press and some of the other press are after your blood. They want you disciplined, sent home or some action taken against you for wearing the badge, so consider yourself severely reprimanded. Now have you got tickets to the hockey today?' I said, 'No I haven't.' He said, 'I can let you have four tickets.' So four of us went to the hockey that night. That was the degree of understanding that I got. Our manager understood what I had done was my choice and he didn't disagree with it violently enough to take any strict disciplinary action.

Trengove reported that Patching had cautioned Peter over his civil rights action and statements.

> Mr Patching said he wouldn't ask Norman not to wear his Negro civil rights badge when in an Australian uniform, but he would prefer that he didn't. Norman said he wouldn't wear the badge … Mr Patching also questioned Norman on statements he had made to journalists in support of the civil rights movement. The statements went all over the world. Mr Patching said he agreed with Norman that everyone had a right to hold and express an opinion. But he said Australian athletes should be careful what they said of a political nature when in a foreign country … 'As a general principle, I do not think politics should intrude into sport,' Patching said. 'At home the team members can say anything they want to, of course. But they shouldn't while they are representing their country overseas.' Mr Patching said he would instruct the Australian team section managers to tell competitors about this.[28]

Trengove went on to state that Sydney-based secretary of the Amateur Athletic Union of Australia Arthur Hodsdon fully supported Patching's comments. He quoted Hodsdon as saying, 'I strongly support Judy Patching. I have great respect for Patching. The way he has been so outspoken on this issue shows clearly he is the right man in the right position.' Trengove noted that Peter 'stressed today that he gave his approval only to the civil rights campaign and not to black power extremism. He said he thought Smith made a good point when he said that negroes were called Americans when they brought credit to their nation but were described as negroes when they did something bad. Smith, he said, had expressed appreciation for his support'.[29]

Trengove continued that several Australians had been 'chipped by American negroes and Africans about Australia's White Australia policy. Hurdler Gary Knoke said, "I told them they should put their own house in order before trying to tell us how to run our house."' Trengove had heard that many white athletes had criticised Smith and Carlos for politically exploiting the Games, but that others had said they acted perfectly within their rights. 'Norman was almost certainly the only Australian athlete who would have taken the action that he did. Triple jumper Phil May said, "You know Peter. He doesn't ram his views down your throat, but he thinks deeply about things. If he decides something is right, he will follow his conscience and no one will stop him."'[30]

The secretary of the Australian Olympic Federation, Sir Edgar Tanner, told Australian reporters that he 'did not think Norman realised quite what he was doing' when he wore a black power badge on the dais.[31]

Patching attended many of the track-and-field events in Mexico City. He was an athletics official at heart. He had a very close relationship and affinity with track and field and knew Peter and most of the team well from having been a race starter.

> I witnessed Peter running second. It was wonderful. And I witnessed him up on the dais. The hierarchy, Edgar Tanner and co, who were in Mexico, asked why had Peter worn the badge. That was very serious from their viewpoint. The Americans were forcing the issue. So I had the Australian brass [officials], Edgar Tanner included, contacting me individually, saying, 'This is serious. It is very reflective on Australia. You've really got to get

> stuck into him.' All they could expect me to do was admonish him. Well I didn't!
>
> I viewed it differently. He certainly wore a civil rights badge, but he didn't do anything wrong. He did everything right. What should I do? I needed to say, 'Congratulations, you did bloody well', and to say to him that the hierarchy had a point of view on what happened. But I also needed to say that from my point of view he'd done a great job for his country, we were all very proud of him, and here's a couple of tickets to tonight's hockey. So above all I congratulated him. That was the big thing. The other bit was positively secondary. [Edgar] Tanner let it drop at that. I think they had perhaps reflected on it all, because he hadn't done anything wrong.

Contrary to Peter's memory of his conversation with Patching the morning after the ceremony, Patching – while acknowledging that some sections of the American press were calling for action to be taken against the athletes – said that no Australian journalists were calling for Peter's blood.[32]

> I knew all the Australian journalists there and they were straight shooters. They were all of the opinion that Peter was a champion athlete. He was, in the eyes of everybody, except American officialdom, because it was a highly political thing. Obviously the American IOC people had been having a go at our IOC people and so they reacted. I don't know, but I presume that. But after that nothing happened from the brass point of view. It just disappeared obviously because Peter Norman had excelled. He'd done the impossible and you can't ask for more than that. And he'd done it in wonderful style. Bloody brilliant!

Patching added, 'Our athletes were doing so bloody well, how could they possibly criticise? How could they say you should have got stuck into him, when it's the most successful Australian athletics team in history. So they were up against a brick wall.'

Thelma Norman said the Norman family was very proud of Peter's stance on the dais. 'We'd always had black people in the home and they were friends. He didn't look on their colour. He looked on the people themselves.' Neville Sillitoe never discussed his feelings about the ceremony with Peter.

'I knew he was very strong on what was right. It didn't surprise me at all. It was no more than what I would have expected of him.'

Peter believed the approval rating from the Australian athletics team was probably split three ways:

> There were those that approved of what I did. There were those who would have been happier had I not done what I did. And there were those that said you can count on Norman to do something stupid like that. No-one from the team shot me down over it. It wasn't till I got home that I felt the wrath and the tongues of a few senior officials in the sport, both verbally and with a few letters. Even though it wasn't verbal, I'd made a statement by wearing a badge, as I'd made a statement with the tracksuit that I used to wear saying 'God is love' on the back.

Di Burge knew Peter wore a badge on the dais. 'There was no criticism of Peter from the team, but there was a fear that there might be repercussions. Not that he'd lose his medal, but he might get into trouble.' Jenny Lamy, who won a bronze medal in the women's 200 metres, thought what Peter did on the dais was brilliant, 'because as far as I'm concerned everybody is born equal'. Hurdler Pam (Kilborn) Ryan also supported Peter's stance: 'Other people mightn't have provided support, but that was Peter. He was a sympathetic listener when you talked to him and he was "Mr Nice Guy". He had a good sense of humour and was always generous and helping people.'

Ron Clarke opined that it wasn't easy being black in America in those days.

> I appreciated their case. It was something you could really understand. So if they are going to have a medal ceremony at the Olympics, the guy who deserved to get up there is allowed to do anything. If he wants to wave his flag or someone else's flag or a surrender flag or protest, he is entitled to do it. It's his time. He did it. You've given him the stage, so don't complain if he doesn't act the way you wanted him to act.

Greg Lewis had a completely different view: 'The black fist was the Malcolm X salute, which was violence and Black Power. Now it's been watered down to human rights. It was an unfortunate association. That's the reason it had all that publicity.'

John Carlos said that the demonstration on the dais created a lot of dissension in the US team: 'Some people felt what we did on the victory stand took something away from their events.'[33] Carlos's white teammate Larry Questad, who finished sixth in the 200 metres, was sitting with other US athletes in the stands, directly in front of the victory dais. He said he was 'just sick' when he saw what transpired.

> All people talk about are the black fists! People should remember Tommie broke the world record by two-tenths of a second. That was a tremendous event, one of the same calibre as Bob Beamon jumping 29 feet. There haven't been too many such events where someone makes a quantum leap on the world record by taking two-tenths of a second off in one whack and he did! No-one ever thinks about the performance. It was a performance that was really outstanding.

Questad believed that what happened on the victory dais overshadowed the performance. 'That was a hell of a 200 metres.' Forty years on, he still felt that Smith and Carlos made a mistake: 'They paid for it dearly. If they hadn't done that, they would have been probably happier, healthier, wealthier, and been more influential in the community than they have been. This country likes heroes that are winners. It was almost like they won, but lost because of what they did.'[34]

US track coach Payton Jordan strongly disagreed with Questad: 'I said I thought it was a social statement that addressed problems that had to be addressed. It had nothing to do with the Olympics. It had nothing to do with me as a coach, with the sport, but it had everything to do with society.'[35]

Willye White, who won a silver medal in the long jump at the Melbourne Olympics at the age of sixteen, and a second silver in the 4 × 100 metres relay in Tokyo in 1964, competed in the long jump in Mexico. She admired Peter for taking a stance with Smith and Carlos during what she refers to as the 'Black Revolution'. White, who picked cotton and endured blatant racial discrimination as a child in Mississippi, was well-placed to comment on Peter's support: 'To have an Australian do that, when you were having your own problems, was fantastic. He will always be very special!'[36]

Wyomia Tyus held the same view. She won her second successive 100 metres gold medal in Mexico, thereby becoming the first Olympic sprinter, male or female, to retain the blue-ribbon title. She was also a member of the USA's gold medal team in the 4 × 100 metres relay in Mexico. She said, 'By wearing that button, Peter knew it was not going to be easy for him, especially when he got back home. He was going to get a lot of questions like, "How could you do this?" But he took a stand. I can't tell you what he was thinking, but from my perspective, I felt he was in support and understood what was going on and how unfairly people were being treated.'[37]

US sports journalists scoured the Olympic Village seeking opinions on what had taken place on the dais. They found athletes from various nations discussing the 'incident' over dinner and in the village recreation rooms well into the evening. Many of them had been at other venues at the time, but had received detailed accounts from teammates.

> All had opinions. 'I think it's too bad,' said Gary Knoke, an Australian track man who attends the University of Oregon. 'Really politics should not be injected into these Games.' Another Australian, sitting close by, added, 'I can't understand why a black, who takes all the advantages of a country and lets that country send him to the Olympics like this, will refuse to look at the flag. That is what got me, why didn't they look at the flag?' A US fencer said, 'I thought it was terrible. It's too bad. I sympathise with what some of those guys are trying to do, but this is not the time or place.' He is white. A white American coach of another team, who asked that his name not be used commented, 'I'd send those guys packing. It's a disgrace.'[38]

One reporter noted that the reaction around the Olympic Village ranged from 'good show' to 'send 'em home'.

> 'I think it's a shame and a disgrace,' said Bill Toomey, America's decathlon champion. 'There is no place for personal spleen or politics in the Olympic Games.' 'We all thought it was a bloody good show,' commented John Wetton, Great Britain's 1500 metres hope, with a nod of agreement from teammates Andrew Todd and John Davis. 'It's bully that these blokes had nerve enough to express their feelings.' All three are white.[39]

Al Oerter, who achieved an unprecedented fourth consecutive Olympic victory in the discus event in Mexico, told the press, 'It's a free country. Perhaps if I felt as strongly about it as they do, I'd do the same thing.'[40] US

1956 Olympic hammer throw champion Hal Connolly, also competing in Mexico, was in tune with Oerter. 'Connolly indicated that he found the black power action to be a patriotic gesture rather than one of embarrassment to the United States. "Let a Russian try that and see what happens … I know a lot of Russians who don't like what happened in Czechoslovakia, but they can't say a word."'[41]

Sportswriter Jim Murray observed that at the stadium, after the medal presentation, Carlos and Smith were only too willing to speak to radio and television reporters and anyone else within earshot. Murray wrote that the American Olympic Committee leant heavily on the theory that the incident was an insult and a discourtesy to the people of Mexico. He expressed the view that this would come as a distinct surprise to those who could have sworn that it was the US flag Carlos and Smith were clenching their fists at. In the Olympic village courtyard, Murray got what he described as a curious reaction from Harvard crewman, Jacques Feichter. Feichter told Murray that in sponsoring an athlete, you don't only sponsor his performance – you sponsor the whole person, the whole consciousness of the athlete. Feichter believed Carlos and Smith were justified in doing what they did, based on their success on the field. The victory platform was a place they had a right to be, and therefore they could do anything they wanted when they got there.[42]

Jacques Feichter was a member of the all-white Harvard University rowing crew which represented the US men's eight team in Mexico. The majority of the team issued a statement before the Olympics attesting to their moral commitment to support their black teammates in their efforts to dramatise the injustices and inequities which permeated US society.[43] They provided support in several ways, including wearing OPHR badges.

Coxswain Paul Hoffman almost got thrown off the rowing team after he was observed handing Peter his OPHR badge. The night before the eight oar final, Hoffman was ordered to appear before a meeting of high-ranking US Olympic Committee (USOC) officials who accused him of conspiring to violate the Olympic spirit in giving Peter the badge.

> That was blown up into a charge that I had conspired and aided a demonstration, which apparently was an offence in the eyes of some. The next day the rumour went around that they had suspended me and had made provisions to substitute a coxswain.

> At the hearing, I was asked didn't I think Smith and Carlos had dishonoured the Olympics. I said, 'It struck me as pretty clear that the Olympic ideals were represented by people who were talking about equality and brotherhood.'[44]

Even though the charge was dismissed, the committee still threatened to send Hoffman home before the final of the eights. To avoid being expelled from the team, Hoffman was forced to give his word that even if the team didn't win a medal, neither he nor any other crew member would demonstrate in any way. 'After about 30 minutes, the Olympic committee, who frankly were old men, finally decided they'd let me compete the next day.'[45]

Cleve Livingston, also a member of the US men's eight team, fully supported the stand taken by Smith and Carlos and applauded Peter for his support.

> Peter's effort introduced an international dimension. By expressing support for Tommie and John, Peter really sent a message. This was about human rights and human rights are universal rights. South Africa had been excluded from the Olympics because of apartheid. You had the killing of hundreds of students in Mexico City immediately before the Games who were protesting for human rights. This was a very special time in terms of the struggle for human rights all over the world.[46]

The day after the 200 metres final and medal presentation, the International Olympic Committee (IOC) issued a brief statement saying that Smith and Carlos had violated Olympic principles by using the medal presentation ceremony to advertise their domestic political views. The IOC added that any action against both athletes was the responsibility of the USOC. Behind the scenes, however, the IOC put enormous pressure on the USOC to take action. USOC president Douglas Roby told reporters that the IOC threatened to pull the entire US team out of the Games unless action was taken against Smith and Carlos.

The USOC subsequently suspended Smith and Carlos from the US Olympic team and ordered them to leave the Olympic Village. In its official announcement, the USOC expressed

> its profound regrets to the International Olympic Committee, to the Mexican Organising Committee and to the people of Mexico for the discourtesy displayed by two members of its team in

> departing from tradition during a victory ceremony at the Olympic Stadium on October 16. The untypical exhibition of these athletes also violates the basic standards of sportsmanship and good manners, which are so highly regarded in the United States … A repetition of such incidents by other members of the US team can only be considered a wilful disregard of Olympic principles that would warrant the imposition of the severest penalties at the disposal of the United States Olympic Committee.[47]

Pressure was subsequently put on Payton Jordan to take action against the two athletes, as he discussed.

> The IOC told the USOC that these men were through and it filtered down from the top to me. 'You send them home.' I said, 'I will not send them home. They're still part of the team and they did everything they were asked to do.' They were loyal, worked hard, and did tremendous jobs. I said, 'If anyone sends them home it would be up the ladder, not down.' And that's the way it was. I thought too much of those guys to turn on them when they needed me.[48]

Carlos and Smith briefly returned to the Olympic Village shortly after being suspended by the USOC. Carlos and his wife had to force their way through about 50 reporters waiting outside the US building. Newspaper reports noted that Carlos threatened to knock down photographers who bothered him.

> His wife, grim faced, looked straight ahead and refused to acknowledge reporters' questions. At one stage Carlos stopped among the journalists and said, 'Get out of my way. If you don't man, I'm going to start something.' When Carlos reached the Village bus stop, he turned once more and said, 'The next man who puts a camera in my face, I'm going to knock him down and jump on him.' Later Carlos and Smith left the Village by car and drove away to an unknown destination.[49]

Peter had kept a very close eye on what was happening, spending time with Carlos. Peter said the pressure that was brought to bear by IOC president Avery Brundage caused most of the grief as far as the demonstration was concerned.

> The guys weren't actually living in the village at that time. They were with their wives in a hotel in Mexico City. They actually snuck into the village at about five in the morning so that they could borrow a couple of suitcases and be photographed being thrown out of the village. I spent most of the next day with John Carlos up in the grandstand at the Games, and I bumped into him several times between then, and the time that they decided they'd had enough of the Olympics. They were still there on the closing ceremony night I believe but I couldn't find them.

Rumours began to circulate in the Olympic Village that black members of the US team were planning a mass walkout of the Games in protest against disciplinary action being taken against Smith and Carlos.

> The reaction was immediately one of shock, then anger on the part of many US athletes and there were threats of a general boycott. As the day wore on, the situation subsided and the boycott threat faded. 'If the two men are sent home, the whole team may go,' said Lee Evans from the same San José State College that produced Smith and Carlos. 'And some white too,' said Hal Connolly, veteran hammer thrower and former Olympic champion. Jesse Owens, the famous four medal winner of the Hitler era, and Stan Wright, Negro assistant coach, moved in to smooth the waters … In mid-afternoon, the press representative of the US Olympic Committee appeared on the scene and compounded the confusion by announcing the two athletes had 48 hours to get out of the country. It developed that the USOC had no such power. That was strictly up to the Mexican government.[50]

Lee Evans was initially not going to run in the 400 metres. He was one of the original supporters of the OPHR and the movement for a black boycott of the Olympics. He had also been a close friend of Smith's for a number of years, and more recently, a friend of Carlos's. When Evans first heard about their suspension, he was very emotional and decided that he wouldn't run in the 400 metres final unless either Carlos or Smith asked him to compete. Evans's biographer Frank Murphy contends that Bud Winter, who coached Evans, Smith and Carlos at San José State University and was in Mexico for the Games, asked Smith and Carlos to intervene.

Evans ultimately elected to run, after a strong plea from Carlos, in Smith's presence. Murphy writes that Evans decided to use his anger to 'build his normal fire even hotter' for his event. 'For days, he had been concentrating on his race. When Smith and Carlos left, he returned to the task with intensity. He was going to take these people who had struck such a blow at him, and he was going to strike one of his own.'[51]

Evans duly smashed the world record to win the 400 metres (run the day after the suspension) in 43.86 seconds. Larry James was second. Ron Freeman completed a clean sweep for the USA, taking third place. The three medallists staged a variation of Smith and Carlos's protest by wearing black berets, as well as black gloves and OPHR badges, at their presentation ceremony. The three black athletes gave the clenched fist salute several times, but they stood firmly at attention and took off their berets as the US national anthem was played.

> Asked later by reporters why he and his fellow medal winners took off their berets for the raising of the US flag, Evans said, 'We wanted to show respect for the flag.' He added that he hoped 'White people will honour our respect.' Evans said, 'I feel I won this gold medal for black people in the USA and black people all over the world.' Didn't you win it for white people too? Evans was asked. Evans laughed and replied, 'Yes I did. I've got a lot of white friends in San José, here and all over the world.'[52]

The *Sydney Morning Herald* editorial 'Politics at the Games?', published several days after the medal presentations, made it quite clear what that newspaper thought of the Black Power demonstration on the dais and the action taken by the USOC.

> The US Olympic Committee was surely unwise in suspending Tommie Smith and John Carlos and ordering them home because of their 'Black Power' demonstrations. It is true that the exclusion of politics from the Games is a basic Olympic tradition and one that needs to be preserved. But the 'politics' concerned surely means organised nationalistic demonstrations by or on behalf of teams or against teams' activities which, being 'political', can be reasonably expected to offend somebody. Who, apart from racial bigots, could possibly be offended by the harmless exhibition of racial pride

offered by Smith and Carlos in their moment of triumph?

Some Americans may feel that the raising of fists during the playing of the national anthem was in bad taste. If the US Olympic Committee felt this, it should have remonstrated with Smith and Carlos in private ... By suspending Smith and Carlos and threatening their Negro teammates with 'the severest penalties' (presumably the ruining of their athletic careers) if there were repetitions, the committee fairly begged for a walkout which would certainly have introduced 'politics' into the Games and must have humiliated the United States. The fact is that what Smith and Carlos did, in their elation, was not a political demonstration but an intensely human expression by proud representatives of one of the most unjustly treated races in and throughout the world. It was in sympathy with this feeling, presumably, that Australian Peter Norman joined them and we can be glad that he did.[53]

NOTES

1 The plastic badges were approximately 7.5 centimetres wide with the words Olympic Project for Human Rights in black letters outlined by a green laurel wreath.

2 Paul Hoffman, interview footage, *Salute*, 2008.

3 David George Burghley won the 400 metres hurdles at the 1928 Olympics. He also won the 440 yards hurdles at the 1930 British Empire Games.

4 *Sunday Herald Sun*, 17 October 1993.

5 Peter Luck, *This Fabulous Century*, Circus Books, Melbourne, 1979, p. 107.

6 During his 21-year professional cycling career, Hubert Opperman, or 'Oppy' as he was better known, won many events, including three blue ribands for fastest time in Australia's famous Warrnambool to Melbourne road classic, twice winning from scratch. He was three times fastest rider in the prestigious Goulburn to Sydney Classic. He won four Australian Road Championships. Opperman became the world's greatest endurance cyclist by winning the 1931 non-stop Paris–Brest–Paris event (726 miles, 1168 kilometres), breaking all previous records over the distance. He was subsequently hailed a hero throughout France. At 36, Oppy retired in a blaze of glory after setting numerous state, national and world records in an incredible 24

hours of continuous unpaced cycling on the Sydney velodrome. Oppy served in the RAAF during World War II. After the war, he served for seventeen years in the Menzies Liberal federal government.

7 'Fact Sheet 8 – Abolition of the "White Australia" Policy', National Communications Branch, Department of Immigration and Citizenship, Canberra, October 2007.

8 Tommie Smith, interview footage, *Salute*, 2008.

9 Amy Bass, *Not the Triumph but the Struggle*, University of Minnesota Press, 2002, p. 240.

10 Tommie Smith, interview footage, *Salute*, 2008.

11 Alan Trengove, 'A white lift for colour on the dais', *Brisbane Courier Mail*, 18 October 1968.

12 Trengove, 'A white lift for colour on the dais'.

13 Trengove, 'A white lift for colour on the dais'.

14 Robert Gray, 'Australian joins racist protest', *The Australian*, 18 October 1968.

15 Robert Gray, 'Norman hits out at Australian tracks after silver medal win', *The Australian*, 18 October 1968.

16 Gray, 'Norman hits out at Australian tracks after silver medal win'.

17 Gray, 'Norman hits out at Australian tracks after silver medal win'.

18 Brent Musburger, *Chicago American*, 17 October 1968.

19 'The natural right of being a slob', *Chicago Tribune*, 19 October 1968.

20 '2 accept medals wearing black gloves', *The New York Times*, 17 October 1968.

21 'Smith, Carlos level bitter racial blast after triumph', *The Charleston Gazette*, 17 October 1968.

22 'Black-fist protest rocks Olympic world', *The Edwardsville Intelligencer*, 17 October 1968.

23 Peter Norman, 'Grandstand', ABC radio, July 1992.

24 Tommie Smith, interview footage, *Salute*, 2008. Inexplicably, Smith failed to make any mention of Peter's support on the dais in his 2007 autobiography *Silent Gesture*.

25 John Carlos, interview footage, *Salute*, 2008.

26 'The third man in Mexico City', *The New York Times*, 17 September 2000.

27 In his outstanding book *Australia and the Olympic Games* (University of Queensland Press, St Lucia, Queensland, 1994), Australian Sporting Hall of Fame member Harry Gordon described Judy Patching as having a 'rare capacity, probably a legacy of his navy years, to apply strong discipline in a warm, down-to-earth fashion'.

28 Alan Trengove, 'Norman warned over protest', *The Herald*, 18 October 1968.
29 Trengove, 'Norman warned over protest'.
30 Trengove, 'Norman warned over protest'.
31 'Officials rap Australian medallist', *Sunday Telegraph*, 20 October 1968.
32 Nor could the authors find any evidence from newspaper reports at the time to support Peter's comments.
33 John Carlos, interview footage, *Salute*, 2008.
34 Larry Questad, interview footage, *Salute*, 2008.
35 Payton Jordan, interview footage, *Salute*, 2008.
36 Willye White, interview footage, *Salute*, 2008. In all, White competed in five Olympics. She was inducted into the USA Track and Field Hall of Fame in 1981. White, who commented at one time that the Olympic movement taught her not to judge a person by the colour of their skin but by the contents of their heart, passed away on 6 February 2007 from pancreatic cancer.
37 Wyomia Tyus, interview footage, *Salute*, 2008.
38 'Black-fist protest rocks Olympic world', *The Edwardsville Intelligencer*, 17 October 1968.
39 'Smith, Carlos do their thing to scorn, praise of athletes', *The Fresno Bee*, 17 October 1968.
40 'Reactions among athletes', *The New York Times*, 18 October 1968.
41 Bass, *Not the Triumph but the Struggle*, p. 249.
42 See 'The sociological Olympics', *Los Angeles Times*, *c*. October 1968.
43 See 'The spirit of the Olympics', *The New York Times*, 1 August 1968.
44 Paul Hoffman, interview footage, *Salute*, 2008.
45 Paul Hoffman, interview footage, *Salute*, 2008.
46 Cleve Livingston, interview footage, *Salute*, 2008.
47 'Black power men dropped', *The Sydney Morning Herald*, 19 October 1968.
48 Payton Jordan, interview footage, *Salute*, 2008.
49 'We may quit the Games – U.S. blacks', *The Herald*, 19 October 1968.
50 'Threat of boycott fades after black fist incident', *Iowa City Press Citizen*, 19 October 1968.
51 Frank Murphy, *The Last Protest: Lee Evans in Mexico City*, Windsprint Press, Kansas City, 2006, pp. 276–7.
52 'Evans ran 400 for buddy Carlos', *Pacific Stars & Stripes*, 21 October 1968.
53 'Politics at the Games?', *The Sydney Morning Herald*, 21 October 1968.

5

SUNDAYS BELONGED TO THE SALVOS

George and Thelma Norman had taught their oldest child, Peter, and his siblings, Laurie, Heather and Elaine, by example that it was a person's character, not their colour, that really counted. They had also passed their strong Christian faith on to their children, as Peter related:

> Our lives revolved around being part of the Salvation Army for a long time. We went to Sunday School, followed by the church service at 11 o'clock, then home for a roast lunch, then back in the afternoon for more Sunday School, home for leftovers for tea, and then, as we got older, back to the service in the evening.

From a very early age Peter learnt strong values that stayed with him for the rest of his life.

> One of the big things the Salvos taught was total tolerance. William Booth, the founder, once said, 'Go for souls and go for the worst.' So the Salvos mission wasn't just to preach on Sunday. It was also to go out and find people who needed help and bring them to church. There was no such thing as discrimination or quality control or anything like that. It was a matter of all men are created equal. Race or creed or colour didn't come into it. We were taught through the Salvation Army to love everybody.

> Having very loving parents and grandparents contributed somewhere along the line too.

The Salvation Army began its service to the Australian community in September 1880 when two recent army converts arrived in Adelaide from London. Edward Saunders and John Gore led the first Salvation Army meeting in Australia from the back of a greengrocer's cart in Adelaide's Botanic Park. Practical help was identified as an immediate need and so the two Salvationists set about feeding as many of Adelaide's poverty-stricken as best they could. But their mission in life was not only to feed the hungry. It was also to save souls and proclaim the power of God to bring peace to individuals' lives. In short, their mission, and that of the Salvationist movement, could be best described as 'Christianity with its sleeves rolled up'.[1]

In 1940 two young Salvationists met for the first time at the Salvation Army Hall in Thornbury, an inner-northern Melbourne suburb. As individuals, the two young 'Salvos' were fine proponents of the Salvation Army mission. But, in due course as a couple, they were an outstanding example of Christians who were well and truly willing to roll their sleeves up and do whatever they could for their fellow man, regardless of race, colour or creed. At the time of their meeting, George Norman was a member of the Thornbury Salvation Army band and Thelma Stubbings had only recently joined the Thornbury timbrel band. George lived in Thornbury at this time, while Thelma lived in the neighbouring suburb of Northcote.

George William Norman was born on 1 July 1918 in Mullumbimby, New South Wales. His parents, Peter George (born 1888) and Sarah Anne Norman (nee Ford; born 1885), were both Salvation Army officers. George's brother, Herbert Henry (known as Herb), was born in 1920 and his sister, Elsie Jane, was born in 1922. Both Peter and Sarah Norman had attained the rank of major in the Salvation Army and, as such, were qualified to perform all the functions normally carried out by ministers of religion. Both Peter's and Sarah's parents had been pioneering Salvationists in Australia.

Thelma Hettie Stubbings was born on 6 July 1921 in Wonthaggi, Victoria, to Charles Robert William (known as Charlie; born 1884) and Hettie Stubbings (born 1885). Thelma had three older sisters: Florrie Margareta (born 1910), Melva Grace (born 1912) and Eva Lyall (known as Lyall; born 1917). Eira Faith (born 1923) completed the family.[2] Charlie

Stubbings had been a miner in Wonthaggi and subsequently worked in different stone quarries when he and the family moved to Northcote when Thelma was seven. Thelma's mother was kept busy at home looking after the family. Both Charlie and Hettie were soldiers in the Salvation Army. Hettie's parents Solomon and Margaret Lemin had both also been pioneering members of the Salvation Army in Australia.

Thelma wasn't overly impressed with George at first. It wasn't so much that George wasn't friendly – quite the contrary as George was a fun-loving and jovial chap – it was more that she thought George was somewhat lacking in commonsense due to his playing cricket in bare feet with the Salvos in a church competition. Thelma's opinion of George would soon change.

One Sunday night, before the evening service began, George asked Thelma if he could take her home after the service. Thelma agreed but when George was nowhere to be found after the service, she started walking home. Along came George on his motorbike and whisked her up and took her home. A romance began to bloom that night, but for a time Thelma had some opposition. Another young lass had a crush on George and, for a short time, George also continued to see her, but as Thelma said triumphantly, 'I got him!' George and Thelma married on 29 November 1941 at the Thornbury Salvation Army hall. They initially lived with George's mother in Harold St, Thornbury.

George had joined the Australian Citizen Military Force (CMF), also known as the militia, in late 1939. During September 1939 an all-volunteer force was raised for service worldwide. This force became known as the Second Australian Imperial Force or 2nd AIF. The divisions and brigades of the CMF constituted the part-time home defence army and held this role until the start of the war with Japan on 7 December 1941. The CMF was not mobilised until then, but all units, including George's, did a series of brigade camps and additional periods of training for one- to three-month periods, beginning at the outbreak of war in 1939 and ending with full-time service on mobilisation. The militia's purpose was the defence of Australian territory, which also included Papua.[3] This political and geographic restriction led to the CMF troops being ridiculed by the all-volunteer AIF as 'a protected species – not available for export' or 'chocolate soldiers' and other even less polite terms.[4]

When not on CMF duty, George was a painter by trade, while Thelma worked as a dressmaker. Both continued to be heavily involved with Salvation Army activities.

During the war, Australian service personnel fought in campaigns against Germany and Italy in Europe, the Mediterranean and North Africa, before the major focus turned to addressing the huge threats to national safety created by the Japanese forces in South-East Asia and other parts of the Pacific. Australia's Prime Minister John Curtin made a direct declaration of war against Japan without consulting the British war cabinet. This was the first time in Australia's history that the country had acted so independently of Britain. Curtin also introduced a new era of Australian foreign policy when he made it quite clear that Australia would look to America for support, 'free of any pangs as to our traditional links of kinship with the United Kingdom'.[5] For the first time ever there was a very real possibility of a direct threat to Australia's shores.

Japan swiftly achieved a series of victories, resulting in the occupation of most of South-East Asia and large areas of the Pacific by the end of March 1942. Singapore fell in February 1942. The Australian mainland came under direct attack for the first time in February 1942, when Japanese aircraft bombed Darwin and Japanese midget submarines attacked Sydney Harbour. In response to a heightened threat, the Australian government expanded the army and air force and called for an overhaul of economic, domestic and industrial policies to give the government special authority to mount a total war effort at home.

While Australia's major effort from 1942 onwards was directed at defeating Japan, thousands of Australians continued to serve with the RAAF in Europe and the Middle East. In March 1942, after the defeat of the Netherlands East Indies, Japan's southward advance began to lose strength, easing fears of an imminent invasion of Australia. Further relief came when the first AIF veterans of the Mediterranean campaigns began coming home, and when the USA assumed responsibility for the country's defence, providing reinforcements and equipment under the leadership of General Douglas MacArthur, the supreme commander of all Allied forces in the South-West Pacific.

By 1942, pressure was strong on young Australians to enlist in the services. George planned to follow a number of his militia mates in joining the AIF. Herb wanted to join the same battalion as his brother. George was torn, however, between what he saw as his patriotic duty and remaining at home with Thelma, who was expecting their first child. Thelma was living with George's mother and they, along with most Australian families, were struggling to cope with rationing of many household essentials including tea, sugar, butter, meat and clothing.[6]

George and Herb were on a CMF bivouac with the 24th Battalion around Maryborough, Queensland, when the news of Peter George Norman's birth reached them via telegram from Thelma's sister Eira. Peter was born on Monday 15 June 1942 at 7 am at 'The Haven' in Fitzroy. He weighed 7 pounds 5 ounces and was 21 inches at birth.

Throughout 1942, the threat of Japanese invasion receded further as the Allies won a series of decisive battles in the Coral Sea, at Midway, on Imita Ridge and the Kokoda Trail, and at Milne Bay and Buna. Further Allied victories against the Japanese followed in 1943. Australian troops were mainly engaged in land battles in New Guinea, the defeat of the Japanese at Wau and the removal of Japanese soldiers from the Huon Peninsula. This was Australia's largest and most complex offensive of the war and it was not completed until April 1944. The Australian Army also began a new series of campaigns in 1944 against isolated Japanese garrisons stretching from Borneo to Bougainville, involving more Australian troops than at any time in the war. Australian troops were still fighting in Borneo when the war ended in August 1945.[7]

George had transferred to the AIF soon after Peter's birth. He saw his son for the first time when Peter was seven months old, when he and Herb returned to Melbourne on two weeks leave. George and Herb were deployed to New Guinea in early 1943 and were stationed there for 18 months. They returned to Melbourne on six weeks leave in August 1944. Thelma took Peter to Melbourne's Royal Park railway station to meet George. Peter recognised George from the photo of his father that Thelma had attached to his highchair tray. After recognising George out of a crowd of soldiers, Peter called out 'my daddy!' and dropped from Thelma's arms and rushed to meet his father, much to George's elation. The memory of that moment stayed with George for the rest of his life. George was momentarily less than impressed, however, when Peter stood up in his cot one morning during this period of leave and ordered George out of his mother's bed. So much for remembering the face on his highchair tray!

While George served overseas, Thelma looked after their son and worked as a dressmaker, initially in factories but later from home. George wasn't in the best of health on his return from New Guinea and ended up in an army hospital in Ballarat with malaria. 'When we finished the leave,' said Herb, 'George was still convalescing in Ballarat. We went straight back to the Atherton Tablelands for retraining and reinforcements, before going to Bougainville in January 1945. George came about a month later. George and I came back home just before Christmas in 1945.'

During the war, the Salvation Army continued its marvellous work on the home front, but its soldiers also were prominent on the battlefields, offering home comforts, advice, support and spiritual assistance to Australian service personnel. The famous Salvation Army 'hop in' tents and canteens were set up in training camps in Australia, in the deserts of North Africa and in the jungles of New Guinea. Wherever an Australian soldier, sailor or airman served, the Salvation Army endeavoured to be there too.[8]

Like many service personnel, George and Herb, who were very close mates, both found it hard to adjust to life back in Australia. George's first job back was driving a coal truck at the wharves. Herb had malaria so had to rest up for a time, before resuming his apprenticeship with the building company he had been working with before the war. He subsequently began civil engineering studies. George soon tired of driving a truck and got a job as a painter with the Housing Commission. He ultimately rose to be a foreman, then a supervisor and finally became second-in-charge of maintenance.[9]

George and Herb were both motorbike enthusiasts. They bought their first motorbikes before the war to get to and from work. Herb's first bike was a 1928 Harley Davidson, which he paid off at 10 shillings a week. George's first bike was an Indian Scout, complete with sidecar. George and Herb delighted in riding down to Victorian coastline towns, such as Lakes Entrance and Torquay. George traded in his Indian Scout for a Harley Davidson after the war. For years to come Peter would have warm memories of his father's motorbike. 'In those days Harley Davidsons weren't the image they are today. Dad's Harley was a workhorse. It had a sidecar and we used to go lots of places in the old Harley.' Herb upgraded his Harley for a newer model after the war. He had a large box attached to the bike in which he carried timber to do odd jobs with George.

Thelma had taught Peter his name, address and age just in case he ever got lost. It would prove to be a wise move as Peter loved adventure. There were times when Thelma didn't know where she was going to find him.

He would climb over a 1.8-metre-high trellis fence on occasions to go exploring the neighbourhood. The Normans lived two houses down from the railway line. On one such expedition, unbeknown to Thelma, Peter climbed over a locked gate to get a closer look at the 'choo choo' train that he would often watch passing by from a bedroom window. Thelma discovered Peter's adventure when the local baker knocked at the front door to tell Thelma that he had found Peter wandering the streets and, much to his surprise, Peter had been able to tell him his name and address. The baker got an even bigger surprise when Thelma told him that Peter was not quite two years old at the time. Thelma's tuition had paid dividends.

Peter was an imaginative child. At three, he befriended an imaginary person 'Tichee' who went with him everywhere. Peter kept Tichee informed of everything that was going on in his life, but was very quick to blame Tichee rather than himself if he had done something wrong.

Peter's earliest recollection of his father was of him 'sitting around the kitchen table at Nana's house because Mum and Dad and I were living with her at the time at 26 Harold Street, Thornbury. We were having a meal. There was a quarry nearby and there was an explosion over at the quarry. Dad ducked under the table. It was an automatic thing for him to do during the war. I was probably three'.

Peter adored his Nana and loved sleeping in her room.

> Every morning Nana would brush her hair, put it into a plait, then kneel down by her bed and pray for five or ten minutes. At night, she and I would kneel down and say our prayers together. Ours was a very close family with Nana, as the matriarch, Mum and Dad and Uncle Herb all in the one house. Nana was a very big influence on my life. She was a seamstress, dressmaker extraordinaire, as well as being a Salvation Army officer and a saint. She was a very proud Salvo. There were always people in Salvation Army uniform at Nana's. Salvos used to come from all over Melbourne and beyond to get Nana to make clothes for them or to see Dad who was the odd-job handyman and always willing to do anything for anyone. While Nana was sewing, Mum was out working. Nana would make me a sandwich from fresh bread delivered by the horse and cart.

Peter particularly enjoyed his Nana's dripping, and golden syrup sandwiches – it was good nourishing food. 'I also remember going to the grocers with coupons with Nana to get butter, sugar and things like that.'

Peter had been named after his grandfather, Peter George Norman, who had died on 5 September 1939. 'I never knew him but a couple of times a week, Nana would get out his cornet. It was in a little brown case which had my name written down the side of it, Peter George Norman. I'd be allowed to blow this instrument.' Peter's grandfather was a talented musician, as was George, and in time Peter would display musical talent.

While still living in Thornbury, the Normans welcomed the arrival of Laurence William (known as Laurie) Norman on 3 November 1946. Shortly after Laurie's birth, George and Thelma purchased Thelma's parents' family home and the extended family moved to Northcote to take up residence at 72 Andrew Street. The Wells family became very big in Peter's life at this stage. Thelma's sister Melva lived with her husband Bill Wells and their five sons – Jim (born 1935), Billy (1936), Norman (1939), Alan (1941) and Ron (1945) – in Andrew Street, Northcote.

Peter got on well with all the Wells boys, but particularly with Alan, who was a real larrikin and fun to be with, as was Peter. Despite being fourteen months younger, Peter was slightly bigger than Alan, and as Ron Wells recalled, Peter used his additional size to his advantage: 'Peter used to belt the crap out of Alan, even though they were great mates. They liked winning at just about anything they had a crack at, including races in billycarts against Laurence and myself in the laneway at the back of Peter's house and also down Separation Street, Northcote.'[10]

Peter became a Carlton supporter in Australian Rules football as a young child without even knowing what Carlton was, let alone what a supporter was.

> Uncle Bill was a mad Carlton supporter. I knew if I stood with the boys on the front veranda when Uncle Bill came home from work, and we sang the Carlton theme song (the version he'd written) out loud and clear, we'd get a penny each. This was much to Dad's chagrin because he was a Collingwood supporter. Mum was Carlton and some of the aunties and Grandma were Carlton and my cousins all barracked for Carlton. Hawthorn and Foster's Lager were Pa's [Thelma's father, Charlie Stubbings]

> two teams. Right up until we lost Dad, there was still this Carlton versus Collingwood rivalry within the family, which was extended some years ago when Laurie started to barrack for Geelong. The girls also barracked for Carlton so we were a real interracial family as far as football was concerned.

Heather Thelma Norman, the first of Peter's sisters to arrive, was born on 16 May 1948 at Bethesda Hospital, Fitzroy. The Norman family was complete with the birth of Elaine June Norman on 14 April 1951. Peter used to tell Elaine that she was found at the municipal tip during one of their father's regular trips when he would go with a full trailer and return with a full trailer. 'You could get some great stuff at the tip, so it made sense that they got their best kid at the tip,' said Elaine.

By then Peter had started school. He said of his primary school days:

> My first school was Westgarth Central (No. 4177) where we wore a navy-blue uniform. Every morning, all the kids in our street walked around a kilometre or so to school together. You'd go your separate ways in different classes, but at lunchtime you'd meet up and play footy or throw cricket balls at each other or whatever it might be. Come 3.30 in the afternoon we'd all meet at the school gates and go home together. That went on from bubs grade right through to year 8 when I left Westgarth Central.
>
> With the nickname of 'Pansy' I wasn't terribly well-respected for my rough tactics or anything like that at school. I was an asthmatic, so was off school quite a lot through illness, then later on I wagged it a lot because I didn't like school. It wasn't a happy place for me. I just wasn't clever enough, but I had to be a very good actor to be able to convince Mum that I was too sick for school.
>
> I always wanted to play football and wear the green and gold colours of Westgarth Central. At that stage I never ever dreamed of wearing green and gold and representing Australia. Football was the go. I couldn't play cricket as I couldn't master the art of bowling. Other kids could bowl faster and bowl trickier spin than I could.

Peter's situation improved when he had the opportunity to participate in athletics. One day some teachers came to Peter's classroom looking for students to try out for the long jump: 'Anything had to be better than class, so out I went for the long jump. A little while later the same thing happened for the high jump and then the triple jump. I managed to get into the school team in all the events that I tried out for, and it was a pretty good way of cutting classes.'

Peter really enjoyed running and competing in the jumping events in the school sports and he won all events in which he competed. He enjoyed competition so much that he eventually set up a long jump on the nature strip outside his house and a high jump on the front lawn. He also marked out a flat race strip in his street. This meant that all the local children could compete against each other in a range of sporting events.

The Mathwin family lived diagonally opposite the Normans. The children – Beverley (or Bev), Donnie, Geoff and Maureen – were around the same age as the Norman children and they would all play together on the street. Peter recalled:

> We had many football and cricket matches out on Andrew Street, Northcote. The back lane was concreted and had a very neat curve and that's where we'd run and rollerskate. We had our own form of skate hockey. We'd set up goals and we used axe handles and bits of wood. We also rode our bikes around a bit. The Wells family by this time had moved on to another suburb and I didn't see as much of them.

Peter and Donnie were the best of mates. They were in the same year at school. As well as walking to and from school together and hanging out together at lunchtime, they would go to the pictures most Saturday afternoons. Bev, being the oldest, was in charge of the group that included Geoff, Donnie and Peter. She related how

> We'd all walk to the Northcote picture theatre. Sometimes if there wasn't much on at Northcote, we'd go to the Westgarth theatre, which was in High Street, near Rucker's Hill.
>
> There were peppercorn trees on an embankment on the side of Rucker's Hill. Coming home from the pictures, if we'd seen a Tarzan movie, the boys would swing on the branches of the

> peppercorn trees pretending they were Tarzan. We were all fans of Tarzan and Westerns. We'd go to the pictures most Saturday afternoons because we'd get out of our parents' hair. We'd go to the Northcote baths as well. We'd walk back home along High Street and get thruppence worth of chips in newspaper. We'd rush home after that and we'd stand on a chair and listen to 'Superman' on the little mantle radio. We'd also turn our lights out and listen to the horror serial 'Inner Sanctum'.

Donnie, who was more often than not called 'Metho' (a nickname derived from his surname), and Peter, often referred to as 'Pedro' or 'Pete', hung around a lot together in those days. They loved loitering around the local quarry at the end of their street. That the quarry was out of bounds, because it was very deep and still being worked, meant nothing to these two young mischievous lads. Donnie started smoking at an early age, and Bev believed that he might have led Peter astray. She recalled seeing Peter have the odd puff or two at the time. Donnie and Peter also had great fun shooting at anything that moved with shanghais, bamboo pea-shooters and potato guns. They, along with Bev, made their own whistles out of apricot kernels and whiled away countless hours playing with and losing lots of marbles or playing with spinning tops or their pocket-knives.

Donnie was very placid and was always happy to follow Peter's leadership. As a result there was never any ill-feeling between them. Peter, Donnie and Laurie frequently played 'British bulldog'[11] in the street. Bev and Maureen and the Norman girls would play from time to time. Bev said, 'We played in the streets until we were called in when the streetlights came on. We'd complain loudly about having to go in.'

Tom Huntley, another of Peter's mates, often joined Peter, Laurie and Donnie playing British bulldog and kicking a football in Andrew Street. Tom remembered Peter breaking the streetlight in front of the Norman home many times while kicking the footy. Tom, born in October 1941, lived in nearby Separation Street, Northcote. He recalled meeting Peter in grade 5 at Westgarth Central:

> We met while walking the 30 minutes or so from Westgarth to do woodwork at the nearby Fairfield primary school. We were never in the same grades so I only remember seeing him in the school grounds before this. We eventually became mates. We'd hang

> out in the back laneways. Peter and I used to do a lot of target practice with air rifles and my dad's .22. We'd ride our pushbikes down to the river bend at Heidelberg or right up Plenty Rd.

Life for young people was pretty carefree in Australia in the early 1950s, as it was for their parents. The country was more stable than it had been for many years. Robert Menzies' Liberal government had assumed power in 1949, and within a few short years, the worst effects of World War II had diminished. The economy was growing steadily.

> Industrial development, foreign investment (particularly from America) and mineral discoveries were booming. Families were gradually achieving higher standards of living. The US influence became increasingly apparent as Australians drifted away from the old British values of thrift and prudence to the American way of the pursuit of happiness through consumption. Household appliances such as refrigerators and washing machines become a part of every Australian home. Many families purchased such items on hire purchase, that is, on the buying now pay later premise.[12]

The early 1950s also saw a large population increase, resulting from the postwar 'baby boom' and the Menzies government's policy of population growth through immigration. Between 1945 and 1952 some 720 000 immigrants arrived in Australia, including approximately 360 000 British and 170 000 displaced persons, mostly from Eastern Europe.

Employment was high, particularly in the building industry and in light and medium industry. Home ownership increased. Farmers' incomes grew significantly due to high demand for wool and foodstuffs. At first, many were sceptical about the boom lasting. It was all too easy to look back to the war and to the Depression of the 1930s. Australia's recovery from the Depression had been slow and full employment was not achieved until the outbreak of World War II in 1939. But the decade began smoothly and scepticism gradually disappeared.

Peter recalled that the Norman family 'wasn't wealthy by any means'. He described his father as being 'pretty strict, but very loving. We kids never wanted for anything. Come Christmas time, there was always a brand-new second-hand Dad-painted bike or a handmade-by-Dad pram for the girls. A lot of our toys were Dad made. We treasured those bikes and toys as much as anything you could buy from a shop because they were made and given to us with love'.

Peter and Laurie admired their father for many things, particularly his generous spirit. Peter said, 'Dad was very generous with his time and energy and his talents, which ranged from fixing a car to painting houses, plastering and building things. He was multi-talented and that was one of the things that made him a treasure.' Laurie recalled his father working three jobs at times: 'He worked for the Housing Commission during the week. On weekends he'd paint houses with a mate. He also worked at a petrol station. Dad was very generous. He'd do anything for anybody, so at times people took advantage of him.'

Peter first got to know his cousin Kevin Berry through the Thornbury Salvation Army band. Kevin was two years older than Peter, having been born in June 1940. Kevin grew up in Newcastle Street, Preston, on the border of Preston and Thornbury, with his parents Frank and Myrtle, his brother Alan and sisters Margaret and Maureen.

Frank was the bandmaster of the Thornbury Salvation Army band and, as Kevin was a drummer, Peter had to become a drummer too. 'Kevin, Laurie and I played in the band for a long time,' said Peter. 'I had a good sense of rhythm and was fairly proficient as a drummer. From time to time I played full percussion and side drum, and even had a bit of a stint on the second cornet, but drums were my favourite.'

George was also in the band. He played a large deep trombone, and was a fine player, but didn't take his playing too seriously. George was a jovial, larger-than-life character and enjoyed having fun while playing. He kept the congregation constantly amused with his antics on the trombone, whether it be making strange noises or knocking another band member's hat off with his trombone as they marched. Not to be outdone, Peter would at times play a 'really snazzy beat' while the band marched up the street. Laurie recalled that 'the band would be trying to march to it, but they'd be hopping all over the place', much to Peter's amusement.

Thelma made Peter's first Salvation Army uniform. In fact she altered the whole band's uniforms, as she described: 'Because the uniforms were made of navy twill, you could turn it on the other side and it was like new. George's mother used to do all this and I took over from her. The whole band needed their uniforms turned up so I took them apart, washed them, put them back together again, this time inside out, and made new uniforms for them.'

Peter would demonstrate some of Thelma's adeptness later in life.

On Sunday mornings, the band would meet at 9 am for what was called the 'open-air' service. Band member Peter Burke had a Vanguard station wagon with a sound system with a microphone and PA running off his car battery – which, as Peter says, was 'pretty high-tech in those days' – so that the word could be preached from the street corner.

The band would play while the songsters sang the hymns. There would be a period of preaching, then, after being in a circle for the open-air service, the band would group in marching formation and march back to the Thornbury hall. In the afternoon the band would play at one of a number of hospitals in the area. At 6 pm another open-air service was held at which, once again, was a preaching period from the circle. Around 6.45 pm the band would march back to the hall for the evening service, which started at 7 pm and finished around 8.30 pm. As Peter said, 'Sunday's were pretty much taken up with the Salvos.'

With Peter's encouragement, his mate Tom joined the band. 'He would let me play the bass drum,' recalled Tom. 'He was supposed to play it. I got to be pretty good, so I got to carry it in the marching band. Peter would be beside me with the kettle drum.' Tom not only enjoyed playing with Peter, but being in the band also gave him an opportunity to spend time with George. To this day, Tom refers to George as his 'hero'. Tom appreciated George taking a strong interest in him. 'He was a fantastic guy and so much fun to be around. Because I was in the school cadets and going to army camp, I thought Mr Norman was more open with me by talking about his experiences in New Guinea and Bougainville. They had such a hard time.' Tom described Thelma as 'a really sweet, nice lady.' He appreciated her kindness to him during his mid-teens and always looked forward to going back to Peter's after the services because 'Mrs Norman would give you a glass of lemonade, which she used to buy in crates'.

Peter developed asthma at an early age, but it was more than coincidence that an attack would come on at examination time. Peter hated exams.

> I've always had seasonal asthma that comes on at springtime and lasts through till roundabout midsummer and then goes away. Mum and Dad would make sure that I'd get the best possible medical assistance that they could afford. There were all sorts of funny sprays used and little white and pink tablets that either

put you to sleep or at least helped you breathe. Asthma wasn't looked on as life-threatening. I don't think I ever got to that stage in those days.[13]

When Peter was around twelve, he started making puppets with *papier-mâché* heads. He always put a collar on each puppet so that he could attach costumes to the collar. Each puppet had its own name and distinctive face, hair colour and personality, which came out in the shows that Peter put on for his sisters and other neighbourhood children. A few years later, Peter turned his attention to magic after seeing the famed Australian magician 'The Great Levante'.[14] His uncle Alan Cozens was somewhat of a magician and, after much persistence on Peter's part, he taught Peter a range of magic tricks. Later when he started working, Peter bought his own magic materials from Bernard's Magic Shop in the city. Occasionally he'd even delegate his sister Heather to purchase supplies for him, much to her delight.[15]

Kevin and Peter were always competitive. The Thornbury Salvation Army hall was located on the corner of High and Gooch streets. Quite often before Wednesday band practice, or on a Sunday between services, the two cousins would have footraces up and down Gooch Street. But to Peter's great disappointment, Kevin always won. 'It was always his aim to beat me,' said Kevin, 'but at that stage he didn't. I was a mad sportsman as a kid and liked football, basketball and all those things. Peter used to play them too but preferred athletics. Peter was fast but probably didn't like the heavy stuff in football.'

Peter described how Kevin became both a target and a 'big brother' for him: 'We got on pretty well together, but had this love–hate relationship that lasted a long time. Anything he could do, I could do better and vice versa. We both loved football. He played football for the Preston Wanderers and invited me along to play.'

George had been a fine footballer and cricketer in his youth, but couldn't afford a pair of football boots. So, on Friday nights, he'd polish up his work boots. Then he'd take out the leather laces, put in freshly boiled-up white laces and then get out his boot-making blocks. With a couple of wire brads[16] and some scrap leather, he'd make football stops and nail them to the base of his work boots for his football match the next day. 'He did that for me too,' says Peter. 'He made my school boots into footy boots. They worked. They stopped me from slipping over.'

Peter was excited about playing football for the first time as a member of an actual team. Getting to the football oval meant a 5.5 kilometre bike ride from home at 7 am every Saturday, rain, hail or shine.

> I played in the blue and gold of the Preston Wanderers without much success. I ran around a lot, kicked the ball whenever it came near me, but didn't know much about what I was doing. I always went training and was there every Saturday morning and by sheer persistence played a few games and loved every bit of it.

Thelma had the job of washing Peter's muddy shorts and jumper. Peter related: 'If I wasn't playing, the shorts were muddy anyway because you've got to look the part.' George's Saturdays were taken up shopping, going to the market, mowing someone's lawn or shifting their furniture. Quite often he would go past the ground where Peter was playing. When he'd get home, he would tell Peter some of the things that he had done wrong, whether it was running through the middle of the field or the way he threw the ball in as a boundary umpire. Peter enjoyed getting his father's feedback.

As Westgarth Primary finished at grade 8, Peter, Tom and Donnie went to Collingwood Technical School in 1956. 'I wasn't very smart but was very good with my hands,' stated Peter, 'so that seemed a good reason to go to tech school and learn a trade.' They travelled on the same tram every day to the 'tech', as Tom recalled. 'There'd be mobs of us on the tram going to Collingwood from Northcote. Collingwood was cool. You had to wear a uniform at Collingwood otherwise you never got through the gate. We wore a grey jumper with orange and black stripes.'

Unfortunately for his educational prospects, Peter soon discovered that life beyond the Collingwood Tech was far more exciting.

> I discovered that if you had a bus pass you could get all the way into the city instead of getting off at Johnston Street. If you knew the right people – like, for example, Frank Gasper, who had just left school and now worked for a cinema chain – you could get free tickets to the pictures, so wagging school became pretty easy, good fun and much better than education.

Tom recalled Peter missing a lot of school at Collingwood. 'I didn't see much of him there. He'd come and go as he pleased. In our first year at Collingwood, all the Westgarth kids had to repeat grade 8. Peter would have done first year but not a lot of second year. Peter knew what days to be at school. He wouldn't miss excursion days – for example to McRobertson's chocolate factory.'

Peter was now fourteen. He didn't envisage staying at school much longer. Australia was beginning to change and opportunities would soon be knocking for young people such as Peter. It would just be a matter of being open to these opportunities when they presented.

By the mid 1950s, Australians had more money and free time than ever before. Families could afford washing machines with spin-dryers, vacuum cleaners and refrigerators that didn't need constant cleaning. Victa lawnmowers were gaining popularity. Cars were more readily available. By 1955, young school leavers were virtually guaranteed jobs. Supported by strong trade unions, they could earn as much as seven pounds a week, which compared favourably with the adult basic wage of twelve pounds per week.

Australians were listening to the likes of Bing Crosby, Frank Sinatra, Frankie Lane, Johnnie Ray, Doris Day and Patti Page. There was no music specifically catering to adolescent tastes. Radio, the dominant form of home entertainment, broadcast music to a single target audience, namely adults. Young people were essentially clones of their parents. They wore hand-me-down clothing, had the same hairstyles as their parents and shared the same values. There were few, if any, signs that they objected to the lifestyle, the clothing or the music of the day. This was not the case in the USA, however, where films such as Marlon Brando's *The Wild One* in 1954 and James Dean's *East of Eden* the following year expressed the rising discontent among that country's youth. That discontent was not yet apparent in Australia – local audiences enjoyed both as entertaining films rather than as bringing the message that young people should be heard as well as seen.

Similarly, the 1955 film *Blackboard Jungle*, starring Glenn Ford as a dedicated teacher trying to win over a class of juvenile delinquents, failed to have a dramatic impact in Australia except for the song played during the film's opening and closing sequences. 'Rock Around the Clock' changed the face of music as it was arguably the first rock'n'roll record heard in Australia. Its infectious back-beat was perfect for dancing and expressing the feelings of adolescence.

Peter would soon be influenced by rock'n'roll music, as would thousands of teenagers across Australia, but its influence on Peter would be nothing compared to that of a major sporting event about to occur in Melbourne. This event was to have a dramatic and life-changing effect on Peter.

NOTES

1 Historical data obtained from the Salvation Army, '125 Years in Australia', <http://salvos.org.au/about-us/our-history/125-years-in-australia.php, 2008>.

2 Two brothers, Alvin Charles and Albert Arnold Stubbings, died at approximately 4 months of age in 1913 and 1914 respectively.

3 Control of the Territory of Papua was given to Australia by the British in 1906 and was retained until Papua New Guinea gained full independence in 1975.

4 Paul Haseler & Mark McGilchrist, 'Notes on the Australian Army in WW2', <http://au.geocities.com/thefortysecondinww2/level1/line5/the_militia.htm>.

5 Peter Luck, *This Fabulous Century*, Circus Books, Melbourne, 1979, p. 80.

6 Drapery, tobacco, chocolate and petrol were also rationed.

7 Australian War Memorial, 'Official Histories: Second World War', <www.awm.gov.au>.

8 The Salvation Army, '125 Years in Australia'.

9 In all George spent 36 years with the Housing Commission.

10 The Wells family shifted to the bayside suburb of Brighton in 1947, but Alan and Ron maintained regular contact with Peter. Sadly Alan passed away in 2005.

11 The rules for the game varied, depending on how rough the participants were prepared to be. One player (the bulldog) stood in the middle of the playing area, while the other players lined up along one end. These players then tried to run past the bulldog to the other end of the area without getting caught. Those caught stayed in the middle and became extra bulldogs. The winner of the game was the last player not caught.

12 Damian Johnstone, *The Wild One – The Life and Times of Johnny O'Keefe*, Allen & Unwin, Sydney, 2001, p. 7.

13 Peter said the first time he ever went to hospital with asthma was when he was in his 30s 'when you didn't try and fight it yourself'.

14 Born Leslie George Cole in Sydney in 1892, 'Levante' turned professional in 1910, working in country touring shows as an escapologist. He travelled to New Zealand in 1920, performing magic and escapology, before performing extensively throughout Australia. He subsequently performed for many years in England before returning to Australia at the outbreak of World War II. Levante was awarded both the Performing Fellowship and the Masters Fellowship by the

Academy of Magical Arts. He died in 1978.

15 Peter's love of magic continued. He later took great delight in performing tricks for his two daughters Emma and Belinda. He also taught a number of tricks to his nephew Matt Norman, after much persistence on Matt's part.

16 A brad is a small wire nail that holds the leather stops in position on football boots to help a player keep his footing on the oval.

6

YOU'LL NEVER MAKE A RUNNER!

In November 1956 the XVI Olympic Games were staged in Melbourne, Australia. Melbourne had been chosen over Buenos Aires to host the Games by only one vote. Teams from 67 nations, represented by 3184 athletes, took part in the Games' nineteen sports. A number of countries boycotted the Games on political grounds. Egypt, Lebanon and Iraq boycotted in protest at the Franco-British expedition to the Suez Canal, which followed the advance of Israeli troops into the Sinai. Communist China did the same to avoid a meeting in Australia with Formosa (Taiwan). Holland, Switzerland and Spain stayed away in protest at Soviet intervention in Hungary, where an uprising was crushed weeks before the opening of the Games. Subsequently Hungarian delegates were warmly embraced at the Games, unlike Soviet officials who were treated with cold courtesy. Their antagonism would peak when Hungary met the USSR in a water polo tournament that was more of a bloodbath than a sporting contest.[1]

The Games opened in brilliant sunshine on 22 November 1956 before a huge crowd of 103 000 people, packed into the Melbourne Cricket Ground (MCG). His Royal Highness, the Duke of Edinburgh, 'inaugurated the Games by delivering the Opening Speech, a historic pronouncement that was fanfared by trumpets and the thunder of a 21 gun salute'[2]. The Olympic torch, on the final stage of its journey from Olympia in Greece, was borne proudly into the stadium by young up-and-coming Australian athlete Ron

Clarke. A huge ovation greeted Clarke as he ran round the stadium carrying the blazing torch and proceeded to the cauldron to light the Olympic flame. Flag-bearers of all represented nations 'formed a whirl of colour around the dais when, through a profound stillness, came the voice of John Landy, one of Australia's best-loved athletes at the time, who had been given the honour of delivering the all-inspiring vow, the Olympic oath'.[3]

Ron Clarke and Landy became indelibly linked by an event that took place during the 1956 Australian mile championship.[4] Over 20 000 people packed Melbourne's Olympic Park on 10 March 1956 hoping to see Landy break his own world mile record. At the start of the third lap, Landy was well-placed behind New South Wales runners John Plummer and Alex Henderson, and Victorian runner Clarke, then world junior mile record holder. With some 160 yards of lap three to run, Clarke was marginally in the lead. As the four runners bunched on the kerb, Henderson, according to Clarke, tried to wedge his way between him and the kerb, and in doing so accidentally clipped Clarke's heel. Clarke lost his balance and tumbled on to the track. Henderson staggered on to the verge of the arena, recovered and ran on. Meanwhile Landy desperately tried to jump over Clarke, but in doing so spiked Clarke's right arm. In a wonderful display of sportsmanship, Landy ran back to check on the fallen Clarke. Only after being assured that the young miler wasn't badly hurt did Landy resume the race. By now Landy had lost some 60 yards (or roughly seven seconds) to the leader Henderson and there were only some 600 yards in the event left to run.

Henderson took the field through the three-quarter mile in three minutes six seconds, with Landy fourth and still more than fifteen yards back. By the back straight of the last lap he had cut the lead back to within five yards. Landy ran a 56-second last lap, surging past Henderson about 150 yards from the finish line. He won the event by twelve yards from Henderson and Merv Lincoln in four minutes 4.2 seconds. Clarke finished a gallant fifth.[5] It mattered not to the huge crowd that Landy had not broken his world record – they stood as one and applauded Landy for winning one of the most sensational races in Australian athletics history and displaying truly outstanding sportsmanship.[6]

Peter went to the 1956 Olympic Games, as he related.

> I had no idea of the magnitude of the Olympics back then but I wagged school and made something like ten shillings and nine

> pence a day selling pies in the old Southern stand at the MCG. I did that till I got caught. I saw about three days of track and field but didn't sell many pies. I guess that's when I decided I really wanted to have a go at this track-and-field business.
>
> Names didn't mean much, as the Olympic Games weren't promoted like they are today. But everyone knew about the 'Golden Girl' Betty Cuthbert. I saw Betty running down the straight with her mouth wide open and knowing that was the Golden Girl. I remember seeing Chilla Porter when he was still in contention for a gold medal in the high jump, then finding out the next day that he had finished second. He was a bit of a hero of mine because I'd started to have aspirations as a high jumper, not realising that little fat kids don't high jump too well. I saw Vladimir Kuts and I remember thinking how this tough little robot figure just kept on going round and round the track and gradually just chewed the rest of the field to pieces. I remember seeing my idol Hec Hogan. To see Hec in the flesh was quite something! Hec used to enjoy a cigarette and a beer. He once was questioned about this and said if he had to train for an extra couple of hours a week so he could enjoy a cigarette and a beer, then so be it.

Hec Hogan was a Queenslander but competed in Victoria for the majority of his career. He won seven national 100 yard championships in a row, was co-holder of the world record for 100 yards at 9.3 seconds. He ultimately won a bronze medal in the 100 metres behind the USA's Bob Morrow and Walter Baker. Four years later, almost to the day of the final of the 100 metres at the Rome Olympics, Hogan died of leukemia, aged 29 years.

Harry Gordon, one of Australia's finest-ever sportswriters, rated Hogan as the most popular Australian athlete of his time. He described how he spoke with 'a slow, sunny drawl' and had 'a casual amiability that was essentially Australian. He was thoroughly unaffected by his success'[7]. Hogan was 'chunky, with a rather lop-sided running style, a balding head and a highly distinctive taste in headgear; he wore a snug green beanie on cool days, and a floppy white sunhat on hot ones'.[8]

Hogan was ranked as the fastest starter in the track world at the time, and came in for a lot of criticism because of his quick getaway. He missed selection for the 1952 Helsinki Olympics, but by 1956 could not be overlooked after winning five national 100 yard championships in a row, beginning in 1952. Although he rarely trained for the distance, Hogan also won the 220 yards national championships in 1954 and 1956. Gordon says that Hogan gradually lost speed after 1954, probably as a result of the disease that later killed him. 'It was sheer courage, plus his jet starts, which enabled him to finish third against superior runners in the Melbourne Games.'[9]

Peter had much to admire in his idol and much to do if he was to emulate Hogan and others he saw at the Olympics.

> Track and field really caught my eye. I enjoyed it and thought I'd like to have a go at some of those things I saw. I set up a high jump bar on the front lawn and used to jump over a bit of dowel across two nails, that sort of thing. I'd have high jump competitions with Laurie and all the kids in the street. That was all good fun. It was a bit of a kickstart I guess.

Kevin Berry, however, would give Peter his biggest kick along. Kevin had joined Collingwood Harriers as a high jumper so Peter also joined as a high jumper, 'to see if I could beat him'. Kevin and Peter were part of an influx of junior athletes wanting to join the Collingwood Harriers after the 1956 Olympics. Spurred on by having seen Chilla Porter compete in the Olympics, Peter, wanting to be a high jumper, tried out in the club's December 1956 track-and-field trials in the high jump and the hop, step and jump. He didn't do well enough to win selection to compete in either event during the season, but won a last-minute reprieve when he was asked to run in a relay trial. 'They asked me if I'd fill in the last leg. By the time I got the baton, we were well down, but I ran as fast as I could and we won the event.' Peter's disappointment at missing out on the high jump turned to elation when he received a phone call from the club secretary the week after the trials. 'He said, "You're running in the C-grade 100 yards." So I became a sprinter fairly well by accident.'

Kevin spent six months at the Collingwood Harriers, but as soon as the season started, he went back to playing football. Peter, on the other hand, had found his calling. He officially joined the Collingwood Harriers on 10 January 1957. He had his first competitive races for the club on 12 January 1957, the opening day of the Victorian Amateur Athletic Association's 1956–57 interclub track season, which had been delayed due to the Olympics. He debuted as a junior in C-grade at Olympic Park and won the 100 yards event in 11.7 seconds, finished second in the 100 yards hurdles, and was a member of the team that finished second in the 4 × 110 yards relay. A week later, on 19 January 1957, Peter finished third in the Junior B-grade 220 yards event in 25.5 seconds.

Peter desperately wanted a pair of spikes when he took up running. George borrowed a pair for him with the assurance that if he stuck at running long enough, he'd consider buying him the spikes. George later followed through when he saw Peter's dedication to running. 'I finally got some pretty good spikes,' said Peter.

> On Saturdays I'd catch the bus down to Olympic Park. Quite often I'd get home on the bus after a day's competition and Dad would say something like 'You ran very well in the relay today. You looked good.' It was only then that I realised that Dad had taken some time out from what he was doing to come down and have a look, without showing himself there.
>
> That made me feel in a way, peed off, because I really could have done with a ride home. Later on I realised I was learning to stand on my own two feet. I wasn't being driven to the track like some of my competitors. Some of those competitors were perhaps born with a silver spoon in their mouths, got nursed through, driven to training, driven to competition, so perhaps they didn't care quite as much about the competition as I did. I made my own way there and that meant a little more to me. I was encouraged by the family to do it, and I was doing something I wanted to do because I enjoyed it. It's not as if there were crowds there. It was the athletes and not much else. I wasn't a star in the making. I was just one of the kids having a good time.

All too soon Peter's first athletics season had finished. He had enjoyed it and looked forward to learning more about this sprinting caper next season. In the meantime, his attendance record was causing school authorities great concern and Thelma duly received a letter from the principal of Collingwood Technical School asking her to come to the school. There she met not only the principal, but also the Education Department's school inspector. Thelma was just as mystified as they were as to what Peter had been up to. He would leave home at the right time and get home at the right time later that day, so Thelma had no way of telling if Peter planned to wag school on a particular day. Peter was called in to face the principal, the school inspector and his mother and was given a 'right royal' dressing down. He toed the line for a short period, but it wasn't long before he began to truant again.

Peter would always plan something special when he wagged school. 'He went to the police court and to the Old Melbourne Gaol on one occasion,' said Thelma, who only discovered details of Peter's escapades after the fact. 'I thought, one of these days you'll end up in jail if you're not careful.' On other occasions Peter would ride his bike into the country. He always travelled alone on these adventures, presumably because he was less likely to be sprung if he went solo. One day Peter came home from Collingwood Tech with his school clothes carrying a foul odour. Peter told his mother that he had wagged school to help out at the local slaughter yard.

On yet another occasion, Peter wagged and went to the family's local butcher to ask for a sheep's head, with the tongue, brains and everything else still intact. Thelma discovered this on her next visit to the butcher when he asked her why Peter had wanted the sheep's head. Thelma knew that the butcher wasn't 'pulling her leg' when he showed her the bill. Thelma was flabbergasted and confronted Peter when she got home. He initially denied the purchase but had to own up when Thelma related what the butcher had said. She asked Peter why he hadn't given her the tongue and brains to cook. He revealed that after cutting up the sheep's head, he'd buried the 'remains' in the back garden. His trips to the local slaughter yard and to the butcher eventually proved to be an omen.

Peter also wagged school, much to Heather's delight, to accompany his sister and her school class as an extra helper on an excursion to the museum and the art gallery in the city.

Herb described how Peter could put it over George and Thelma: 'He could twist his mother around his little finger.' Herb told them they couldn't have it both ways. Peter would wag school and they'd give him money to buy something up the street, so Herb suggested no pocket money but that didn't last long. Unbeknown to Peter and Herb, Thelma was somewhat relaxed about Peter wagging school because she had, in fact, skipped school on occasions in her youth. But it became a serious matter when Thelma received a second letter from the school principal. Peter continued:

I'd wagged school and gone to the movies in the city. I'd managed to get free tickets from a guy that used to go to school with me but who now worked at the State Theatre. The lights had just started to dim when this lady came in and sat down beside me and said, 'Hello, what sort of job do you wanna get?' It was Mum. She'd gone into town for a medical appointment, which had been cancelled, so she decided to go the pictures. She thought the movie she wanted to see was on at the State Theatre. When she got to the State, it wasn't that movie at all. They were showing *The Court Jester* starring Danny Kaye, so she thought she might as well see it. This wasn't the first time I'd been sprung wagging school and forging notes to try and avoid getting caught. We watched *The Court Jester* and then on the way out Mum said, 'We'll go to the Commonwealth Employment Service and see what sort of job we can get you.'

So we watched the movie together. It's still one of my very favourite movies. It's a real classic! We went straight from the theatre around to the corner of Johnston and Smith Streets to the Commonwealth Employment Office to find out what sort of employment you could get for a wayward 14 year old. We had a choice of two jobs that I was qualified to take on. One was in the boot-making industry for which there was plenty of work around the Northcote area. I was also qualified to be an apprentice butcher. Kevin Berry had already left school and was an apprentice butcher. I thought, 'Well if he can do it, so can I.' So I became an apprentice butcher.

Peter got a job in a large wholesale butcher's shop in Clifton Hill, not far from the Collingwood Harriers track. But Peter often cut himself and would be sent home. Eventually he was put off for having too much time off work. Kevin told Peter that a vacancy for an apprentice had come up with the Angliss meat company where he was working. As Peter was already an apprentice, he was able to transfer across. Kevin said it was a better opportunity for Peter because 'they moved you around and you got a lot of experience. At that stage Peter would have been fifteen. But he didn't finish his apprenticeship with us. He was probably only there six months'.

Peter lay around at home for some time before Thelma told him to find a job or else he wouldn't eat. That threat didn't bother Peter, so, in desperation, George and Thelma sent Peter to work for a few months on a farm owned by family friends and fellow Salvationists Vern and Ruby Williamson. Vern was a musician and he and George had quickly become close friends after their first meeting. Vern often travelled with George and the Thornbury Salvos band over a period of some fifteen years. The Williamsons had first met Peter when he was three years old when George and Thelma started travelling up every year to the Williamson farm, which was just outside Ballarat. George loved working in the fresh country air with Vern, and Thelma and Ruby got on well together.

As a young person, Peter referred to Vern as 'Uncle Vern' and continued to do so all his life. 'We eventually decided to go into pigs,' says Vern, 'so I needed stacks of galvanised iron. George would come up with a great trailer load of stuff that he had picked up at the Northcote tip. Peter would help us knock the sheds together.' Ruby Williamson recalled George's trips to the tip saved them a great deal of money.

Eventually the whole Norman family would holiday on the Williamson farm, with the exception of Laurie, who preferred spending time on the farm at Mundoona (a small town north-east of Melbourne) owned by the family of his Uncle Herb's wife Una. Over the years Herb and George spent several holidays together on the Mundoona farm with their families, as Herb recalled: 'We used to go there at Christmas and Easter. The kids, including Peter, would get into the horse and cart and ride round the farm collecting mushrooms. They'd go fishing in the creek and spend time feeding the pigs and sheep, feeding lambs with the bottle, and watching over the dairy cattle and horses.' When Peter eventually got his driver's licence, he and Laurie would periodically drive up to the farm. They'd help milk the cows and go rabbiting. Laurie recalled Peter shooting a wasps' nest on one occasion: 'That had dire consequences for all concerned.'

Peter enjoyed working with Vern during the winter of 1957, but with the athletics season due to start it was time to head back to Melbourne. Peter duly returned to the butchery trade. Tom Elmi had purchased a small butcher shop at 204 Lygon Street, East Brunswick, early in 1957 and later that year he advertised for an apprentice. Peter and Thelma visited Tom in the shop and Tom liked Peter immediately and decided to give him a trial run. If Peter worked well, Tom would arrange the transfer of his apprenticeship. Peter readily agreed and set out to impress Tom. A few weeks later Tom was only too pleased to arrange all the necessary paperwork. Peter formally became Tom's first apprentice.

Tom was an ex-serviceman and had done some running in his army days. He took a keen interest in Peter's performances for Collingwood Harriers, and Peter kept him apprised of what grades he was running in and his times. Unbeknown to Peter, Tom, who was 34 at the time, fancied that he still had a bit of pace, albeit over no more than 50 yards. He challenged Peter to a sprint race one lunchtime. Tom insisted that Peter give him a two yards start, given that he was some eighteen years older than Peter and hadn't competed for several years. 'I beat him by about two yards over the 50 yard race,' says Tom. Not wanting to be cruel, but also not wanting to see his young apprentice ultimately get hurt, Tom told Peter that, given he couldn't beat a 34 year old, he should give running away: 'I said to him, "You will never make a runner because you just can't get out of the blocks quick enough."' Undeterred Peter soldiered on and was soon telling Tom that he had progressed with the Harriers since his last report. Tom, thinking it was time to put the matter to rest once and for all, challenged Peter to another lunchtime 50 yards sprint. Once again, Tom won the race by about two yards and repeated his advice to Peter.

Peter knew that Tom was only trying to help, but he was really enjoying the running so he put Tom's well-meaning advice aside. A few weeks later, much to Tom's amazement, Peter told him that he had been selected to run in the A-grade for the Harriers. It was only then that Tom realised he had never asked Peter what distances he had been running. Peter told him his best distance was 220 yards. The penny finally dropped for Tom – Peter might be slow out of the blocks, but he was really only getting warmed up by the 50 yard mark, whereas Tom had reached his limit. Tom decided it was time he retired gracefully. There would be no more challenges. Rather he would actively encourage Peter in his athletics career because obviously he was progressing well at sixteen years of age.[10]

Peter worked for Tom for the next two years, but Peter was never punctual. 'We got very close during that period,' said Tom, 'but he was ten minutes late every day that I can remember. On Friday mornings we'd start at six o'clock, but he would bowl up at ten past six. He caught me one Friday morning when I was in a bad mood. I said, "Look Peter I'll have to let you go. I'll get you a job but you'll have to promise that you'll be on time."

I got him a job at the Coburg Meat Supply under Les Leckie, the manager.' Peter eventually completed his apprenticeship under Leckie, but would always look back on his time with Tom as being his happiest in the butchery trade. In ensuing years he worked for short periods for Tom on a relief basis if Tom's butchers needed a Saturday morning off or were taking holidays.

Peter discussed the impact that Tom had on his life:

> From working in retail sales in a small shop like that, where every customer has to be a customer who comes back, Tom taught me more about people management than you could ever learn at school, university or in a book. It was a beautiful education and I was getting paid for it and enjoying it, apart from all the hours. I can't think of my life panning out the way it has if it hadn't been for that butcher shop and Tom Elmi. A lot of things would have been very different. I don't see how I could have learnt the skills that I've learnt.[11]

Elaine recalled that the Norman family ate well when Peter became a butcher and that Peter became a good cook after Tom sent him along to cooking school.

George and Thelma bought Peter a new pushbike for his sixteenth birthday so that he could ride to work and get to and from athletics training safely. Peter soon put the bike through its paces and, much to his delight, it came through with flying colours. But it was a rather sheepish son who told his parents over the tea table that night that he had been caught speeding by the police when coming down Rucker's Hill, under the railway overpass at Clifton Hill. George and Thelma struggled to keep a straight face as Peter told the sad tale, particularly when, with a very serious look on his face, he reassured them that he had escaped the clutches of the law with just a caution! In years to come, Peter would take great delight in retelling the tale, but unlike on the first occasion, he would always add a fair degree of embellishment.

The annual Salvos athletics carnival at Royal Park on Melbourne Cup Day was a highlight of the Salvation Army social calendar for many years. Thornbury would always enter a team, as would most Melbourne Army corps. Competitors faced off against each other in running, jumping and throwing events, while non-competitors barracked fiercely for their respective teams. Peter participated in the annual event from his early teens to around the age of seventeen. He recalled such carnivals:

> I didn't find out that I could really run well until going to Sunday school picnics and Salvation Army sports carnivals. You'd go in everything, the 100, 200, 400, the long jump and the high jump. Thornbury used to do very well because I could hold my own with most of the guys my age and I used to win most of my events. Kevin Berry was in another age group and used to win most of his events, so that gave us a pretty good start.

By the late 1950s, advertisers were aware that teenagers wielded considerable buying power, particularly in clothes and music. Initially forced to buy from second-hand clothing shops and modify the clothing – for example, pegging up their pants – teenagers now welcomed the growth in clothing outlets. Many teenage males favoured long jackets, pointed-toe shoes, bright shirts or white T-shirts, luminous socks in a variety of colours, stovepipe trousers, string ties and greasy duck-tailed hair. Their female counterparts wore flared skirts with rope petticoats, wide belts, white blouses and high heels. Denim jeans or tight matador pants were also popular, as were ponytails.

Dances and milkbars became favourite haunts for these so-called 'bodgies' and 'widgies'.[12] Television's arrival in Australia in September 1956 opened up a whole new world, not only in its programming but also with its advertising, much of which was aimed at the teenage pay-packet. In context and message, television portrayed America as the centre of the universe. Commercial television, in particular, was very much focused on America.

By his mid teens, Peter had developed strong friendships with several female members of the Thornbury youth group. He was also starting to take a strong interest in rock'n'roll and in the latest fashions for teenagers, although he was mindful that some of the music and clothing of the day wasn't necessarily popular in the Salvation Army community, or the general community for that matter.

The Thornbury Salvos had a vibrant youth group. Helen Pletzer was one of some 60 teenagers who participated in youth group functions every Friday night. Helen was born in Estonia in February 1943. Her parents divorced when she was four, and she and her mother came to Australia as postwar immigrants when she was six. They ultimately settled in Woolton Avenue, Thornbury. A friend of Helen's mother suggested that Helen should join the Thornbury Salvos. Helen was around thirteen at the time. She was soon playing the timbrel in the band and attending youth group, and over a period of time developed friendships with a number of teenagers, including Peter.

Helen looked back on those times: 'Sometimes on Friday nights the youth group went tenpin bowling, or had games nights or played table tennis. Other nights we'd go to the pictures. I went to the Normans' home in Andrew Street. Peter and I used to watch "Ringside with the wrestlers" with Gorgeous George on the television. I also went to Olympic Park with Peter a few times to see him run.'

In time Helen fancied that she was in love with Peter. She was sixteen, but she said it was just hormones: 'He and I were friends. I liked Peter because we had things to talk about. He was handsome, a nice guy, and easy to talk to.' Helen appreciated the fact that Peter would listen to her. Peter enjoyed Helen's company: 'Helen Pletzer was one of my girlfriends at the Thornbury Salvos. A bunch of us, boys and girls, would go off and have a milkshake or play the pinball machine after the youth club on Friday night. Bad things like that! Helen was a part of that.'

Peter had by now fallen for one of Helen's girlfriends: 'My first girlfriend and [early] love of my life was Helen Swan from Thornbury Salvos. We went steady for about eighteen months. Things were getting pretty serious after she stayed over at my house one night and she cleaned my shoes. I thought that was pretty serious stuff. She was proving to be homely and worthy of homely duties perhaps.'

Helen Pletzer and Helen Swan used to 'dag around' together. Helen Pletzer recalled:

> The Swans lived at 16 Ryan Street, East Brunswick. Helen was a bit of a wild one, a bit of a nutcase and a lot more out there than the rest of us. I think she only came to the Army because of family pressure. I don't think she liked it all that much. She had other items on the agenda. Helen wasn't picture gorgeous but had a certain something. She was outgoing and friendly. She and Peter terminated abruptly but I don't know why. I thought they were a bit of an odd couple anyhow. I didn't think they had a great deal in common except the Salvation Army. Maybe it was the fact that she was perhaps a little older than Peter. He maybe was bulldozed into the relationship by Helen. She was dominating. It was a case of whatever Helen wants, Helen gets.

> She wasn't particularly subtle. Peter, being a nice guy, possibly saw it as a case of it being easier to give in, than battle.[13]

Elaine was upset when Peter and Helen Swan broke up. 'Helen used to take Heather and I to the pictures. She was voluptuous, had a round beaming smiling face and a laughing personality. We lost this beaming fair Viking-type girl who we pretty well much loved.'

Margaret Shewan was also a member of the Thornbury youth group. She, like her girlfriend Helen Pletzer, was born in 1943. Margaret got to know Peter well during a nine-year period from 1955 to 1964. She recalled Peter falling heavily for Glenys McLean from the youth group following his break-up with Helen Swan. Glenys lived in Darebin Road, Thornbury, which was within walking distance of the Thornbury Salvation Army hall. 'Peter was crazy about Glenys. She was very pretty, blond, blue-eyed and tiny. She went with him before Peter had a car, so he used to walk to her house, then run home.'[14]

Margaret's sister Helen Shewan was also in the youth group. She recalled Peter's romance with her close girlfriend Glenys, who was instrumental in Helen joining the Salvation Army. 'Glenys was born in 1944, so would have been about eighteen months younger than Peter. She was quietish, but very pretty and very appealing to the guys. Peter was very keen on her, whereas she liked him, but wasn't madly in love with him. They went out together for maybe six months.' Helen Shewan was somewhat jealous of Glenys going with Peter because she thought Peter was a good-looking young man at the time.

Peter and Glenys, and indeed any other young couple going together at the time, would always participate in Friday night outings with the youth group. On other occasions, neighbouring youth groups would get together for outings. The group would go to the pictures at the local Regent Theatre in High Street, Thornbury, or tenpin bowling or ice-skating at St Kilda's St Moritz rink. George Norman was one of a small number of regular volunteer drivers who would transport group members on such occasions, giving generously of his time to help out, regardless of the cost.

Once a year, the Thornbury youth group would get together with other Melbourne Salvation Army youth groups at a large Army-owned facility in the bayside suburb of Parkdale. It was a great opportunity for young Salvationists to learn more about their faith, but also to enjoy plenty of good food cooked by volunteer parents and have fun participating in a range of activities, including volleyball, table tennis, singing, lying on the beach or boating. Margaret recalled Helen Pletzer and Peter boating in the Mordialloc Creek and their canoe getting stuck: 'Peter got out to push it, not realising that the banks dropped away, and before he knew it he was underwater. It was very funny seeing him trying to get out on the water.'

Quite often either the Thornbury Salvation Army congregation, or other neighbouring congregations such as Preston and Fairfield, held what were then referred to as musical programs on Saturday nights. Soloists or groups of various sizes would play and/or sing. Peter would perform on some of these programs as part of a musical group called the KS Trio, which Peter says stood for 'Kan't count and Kan't spell'. The trio – brothers Ray Downs (tea-chest bass), Gary Downs (guitar and main vocalist) and Peter (drums and occasional vocals) – sang mainly religious songs such as 'Wings of a Dove'. 'We had a good time with that, but it was only in Salvation Army circles. It wasn't a band you took out on the road. It was all "Michael Rowed the Boat Ashore"–type stuff and Negro spirituals and that sort of gear but it was good fun.' The trio wore blue-clad jerkin costumes made by Thelma, which they complemented with pink shirts.

Heather and Elaine always looked forward to the trio rehearsing at home. 'While rehearsing and mucking around,' said Heather, 'they'd do "Tom Dooley" because Elaine and I used to sing that.' Elaine remembered they also sang the 'Banana Boat Song' and performed comedy skits, much to Heather's and her amusement.

Peter developed a love of music from a very early age. He listened to the wireless as a child, not only for the radio serials, but also for the music. Once he started working, he began to accumulate a collection of tapes and records and in later years CDs. He particularly enjoyed big-band music and jazz as a young person. Louis Armstrong, Gene Krupa and Harry James were real favourites. He retained his interest in these performers as he got older, but continued to expand his list of favourites.

The birth of rock'n'roll in Australia excited thousands of Australian teenagers, including cousins Kevin and Peter. The release of the movie *Rock Around the Clock* in October 1956 did much to bolster rock'n'roll in Australia. The movie loosely covered the so-called rags to riches rise of Bill Haley and featured nine of Haley's best recordings. Its success encouraged other film studios to turn out similar films for teenagers. The title tune had sold in excess of 200 000 copies in Australia since its release a year earlier, after being included in the movie *Blackboard Jungle*. Kevin stopped counting the number of times he saw *Rock Around the Clock* after the twelfth time. Peter saw it with him several times.

Australian teenagers soon had their very own rocker to cheer on when Johnny O'Keefe and his group, the Dee Jays, exploded onto the music scene. In January 1958, O'Keefe and the Dee Jays recorded 'Wild One', which not only became the first Australian recording to make the Top-40 music charts but also provided O'Keefe with the nickname that became synonymous with him. From that time on, wherever he went throughout Australia, it was always Johnny O'Keefe, the Wild One.

Peter soon became a fan of the Wild One, especially because of O'Keefe's July 1959 recording of the 'call and response' gospel-style song 'Shout'. Peter loved it from the moment he heard it and it became one of his all-time favourite records. Heather ended up with many of Peter's records when he later left home, this record among them. Elaine recalled Peter often singing 'Shout' during the KS Trio practice sessions. She loved eavesdropping during Peter's music sessions at home, not just with the KS Trio, but also when Peter and a few mates, including Tom Huntley, Gary Cronin, Alan Day and 'Manly' Moorcroft, gathered around the piano in the front room for singalongs. Heather and Elaine would be in their pyjamas in the passageway bopping along, and much to Elaine's delight, Tom would always dance with them.

Ken McBride shared Peter's passion for rock'n'roll. Ken (who was eight months older than Peter) met Peter in early 1958. The two got on well from this first meeting, especially when the conversation turned to music by the likes of Buddy Holly and Johnny O'Keefe. Peter soon talked Ken into joining the Thornbury Salvos. The two 'rockers' became such good mates that Ken travelled from his Heidelberg home to stay with the Norman family every weekend for the next two years. Ken would go to Northcote every Friday night in time for the youth group. He'd return home Sunday night after the services and after he and Peter had enjoyed Thelma's homemade 'Nana's pumpkin pie', which was a hit every Sunday.

Peter and Ken often went to the pictures to see either one of the latest rock'n'roll movies or a 'Cowboy' or something like James Dean in *Rebel Without a Cause*. Peter tried (but failed) to teach Ken to play the drums. They wiled away countless hours playing with Peter's train set.

During his teens, Peter developed a keen interest in clothing. Heather recalled Peter's zest for looking good and keeping up with the fashions. 'Appearance was always very important. He liked to dress well but wasn't afraid to wear things that perhaps others wouldn't, such as bright fluorescent socks, ming-blue ties, dark shirts with thin white ties with a glittery-type emblem, or a white tie with a red emblem, or a black tie with white glitter.' As with his musical tastes, Peter's fashion sense remained important to him for the rest of his life.

Each child in the family had a nickname, except Heather, much to her disgust. 'I was just Heather. How boring is that?' Peter was Pedro, Laurie was Onyx, to reflect his interest in 'material stuff', and Elaine was Stinky because, according to Heather, she had a 'stinking temper and Peter knew what buttons to press with her'. Elaine counteracts that by suggesting that Peter 'used to tease the living daylights out of us' so it was only natural that she would fire up at times.

Heather and Elaine were not particularly interested in sport, but Laurie was a really good Australian Rules footballer. Before Peter focused primarily on athletics, he and Laurie played a few games of footy together in the same open-age team. Peter described Laurie as a pretty good forward: 'He used his spring to good effect and he could kick a ball very nicely too. He came into track and field later on and could have been a very good triple jumper, but hurt his knee rather badly when he was showing promise.'

Peter and Laurie got on well together, but like many brothers were very competitive, as Peter related:

> Competition was always pretty harsh and rife. We've got a trophy that's like the Davis Cup of the Norman family. It's a little China lion that I won for throwing tennis balls at Coke bottles at a carnival when I was about twelve. It didn't matter whether it was a game of chess, darts, table tennis or tennis, we'd play a few social games then 'Okay this one's for the Lion!' That lion was nearly the death of both of us. We used to do some terrible things to each other for the sake of the lion. After we married, we played tennis, squash and badminton for the lion. Whoever won the lion match, got to take the lion home. Sometimes we'd run contests over a weekend and beat the hell out of each other to see who won the lion.

Peter was always generous with his siblings. Elaine says that when Peter's mates came to the house, and Peter might have been doing something with Laurie, 'They'd want him to leave Laurie home, but Peter's attitude was "If he doesn't come, I'm not going".' Peter gave good presents too, as Elaine recalled.

> He gave Heather and I an Easter casket full of chocolates and an Easter egg when I was eight. I've still got the casket. He also gave me my very first grown-up box of chocolates, apart from the Easter chocolates. For my twelfth birthday, he gave me turtle oil soap and bath cubes that were very grown-up and luxurious. I still have a gold heart locket on a very fine chain, which he also gave me. He put a lot of thought into those presents. These things made me feel grown-up and special.

Peter had been given a model train set as a young boy. He added to the set over the years and enjoyed playing with it. Peter gave the set to Laurie when he married.

Heather recalled riding on Peter's back down the passageway at their home when she was young. 'We played "Bucking Broncos". He'd write down different rides on pieces of paper and Elaine and I had to pull a paper out of a hat and we'd get that particular ride.'

Heather described Peter as a born teacher. He taught Heather how to ride a bike. He even taught her how to walk properly in high heels. He'd say to her 'you have to walk properly now if you're going to be a lady'. He also expressed his opinion on what clothes he thought suited her. 'He made you feel that he was interested in you and in what you were asking,' said Heather.

NOTES

1 L'Equipe & Jacques Rogge, *The Olympics: Athens to Athens 1896–2004*, Weidenfeld & Nicolson, London, 2004, p. 137.

2 *The Olympic Games, Melbourne 1956*, Colorgravure (*The Herald & Weekly Times*), Melbourne, 1957, p. 3.

3 *The Olympic Games, Melbourne 1956*, p. 3.

4 Metric distances have always been used in the Olympics. At this time, however, the USA and Commonwealth countries, including Australia, competed over imperial distances.

5 Ron Clarke went on to compete in two Commonwealth Games and two Olympic Games, and to set many long-distance world records during a long and illustrious career. Despite this, he said that 'most people today remember me as either the torchbearer at the 1956 Olympics or the guy who fell over in front of John Landy'.

6 The description of the race is based in part on 'A milestone for Clarke', *The Herald*, 16 February 1965; Ron Clarke & Alan Trengove, *The Unforgiving Minute*, Pelham Books, London, 1966; Paul Jenes, *Fields of Green, Lanes of Gold – The Story of Athletics in Australia*, Playwright Publishing, Sydney, 2001, p. 114.

7 Harry Gordon, *Young Men in a Hurry*, Lansdowne Press, Melbourne, 1961, p. 15.

8 Gordon, *Young Men in a Hurry*, p. 15.

9 Gordon, *Young Men in a Hurry*, p. 16.

10 Tom followed Peter's career with great interest in the years ahead and was delighted with Peter's silver medal win in Mexico.

11 Peter very much doubted whether he would ever have become a teacher had it not been for the skills he learnt 'from handling the Mrs Smiths and Mrs Browns in the butcher shop. It was a very good, very meaningful part of my overall development and education'.

12 The term 'bodgie' applied to male youths in Australia and New Zealand, who during the 1950s distinguished themselves by their outlandish fashions. A 'widgie' was the female counterpart. Their British and American counterparts were the 'teddy boys' and the 'greasers'.

13 All efforts to locate and interview Helen Swan for this biography proved fruitless. Helen was last known to have married (assuming the new surname of Hart) and moved to Queensland in the early 1980s.

14 All efforts to locate and interview Glenys McLean for this biography also proved fruitless.

7
WINNING A PREMIERSHIP AND A BET

The 1957–58 athletics season was Peter's first full one with Collingwood Harriers. While he didn't set the world on fire, Peter found that he was a lot fitter this time than he had been the previous year. His biggest achievement for the season was winning the club's under-17 100 yards championship in March 1958 in 10.5 seconds. Peter's increased fitness was due to playing a full season of football during the winter with his mate Ken McBride in the Thornbury 'Redlegs' team, and also having taken up competitive basketball.

By now the Thornbury Salvos had started a basketball team, as Peter related.

> We had a meeting to decide what we were going to be. Kevin Berry wanted black and white because he was a Collingwood supporter. Someone else wanted black and red because they were Essendon supporters. So to hurry up the process I suggested pink and black, so we had pink tops with black numbers and pink satin shorts with black piping. We looked absolutely stunning. We won some games playing in an open-age tournament. We got as far as A-grade but this was when basketball was in its infancy in Melbourne so we were relegated to playing in the dog pavilion at the Royal Melbourne Showgrounds.

Peter's off-season sporting activities paid handsome dividends in the 1958–59 interclub competitions. He had his first win for the season in a C-grade 100 yards event. He won his first two 220 yards events in December 1958, his fastest time being 23.1 seconds. In January 1959, Peter was promoted to run in an A-grade 100 yards event. He finished fifth in 10.6 seconds. Peter's burning ambition when he started running was to run for the club's A-grade team, and proudly stated: 'I managed to get in the A-grade team when I was sixteen.' Two weeks later, he again ran in an A-grade 100 yards event, this time finishing third in 10.6 seconds. On 7 February 1959, Peter finished second in the Victorian under-17 220 yards championship in 23.5 seconds. He won the club's under-19 100 yards championship on 28 February 1959 in 10.2 seconds. In winning this, Peter simultaneously set new club under-17 and under-19 records. That same day he also won the club's under-17 100 yards championship.

On the basis of his excellent form, Peter was again promoted from C-grade to A-grade for the interclub grand final on 14 March 1959 against Melbourne University at Olympic Park. Peter finished sixth in the 100 yards in 10.5 seconds. He then teamed up with Jim Shand, Kevin Coffey and Harold Burridge to win the 4 × 110 yards relay. Much to his, the club's and his family's delight, Collingwood Harriers defeated Melbourne University to win the A-grade premiership for the 1958–59 season. Peter would always savour this premiership. Not only was it the first premiership team he'd participated in, but also it would prove to be the only premiership team of which he was ever a part.

But there was still more to come. On 21 March 1959, Peter finished second in the Harriers's senior 100 yards championship and he won the club's senior 220 yards championship that same day. He also finished second in the club's under-17 long jump championship, jumping eighteen feet.

Peter began the 1959–60 athletics season on 25 October 1959 by winning the Harriers's senior 100 yards trial in 10.4 seconds. On 14 November 1959, Peter ran his first 440 yards event in an interclub competition for the Harriers, clocking 52.3 seconds. He would periodically run the 'gut-busting' event during his career, but he never enjoyed it. On 16 January 1960, Peter equalled the club's senior 100 yards record of 9.9 seconds, simultaneously setting a new club under-19 100 yards record. In late January 1960, Peter represented Victoria in a two-day Victoria versus New South Wales competition. Peter was unplaced in an invitation junior 100 yards event, but took second place in the 220 yards event.

On 20 February 1960, Peter won the Victorian junior 220 yards championship in 22.2 seconds, thereby equalling the Harriers's senior 220 yards record and setting a new club under-19 220 yards record. During February and March 1960, Peter won the club's senior 100 yards championship in 10.1 seconds. He also won the club's senior 220 yards championship in 22.9 seconds, and finished second in the senior 440 yards championship. He won the junior 100 and 220 yards championships and finished third in the junior long jump championship. Overall, Peter was satisfied with his fourth interclub season achievements.

Off the track Peter continued to hang out with his mates, including Donnie Mathwin. Donnie had never been into sport, but he and Peter had remained close, even after the Mathwin family moved to nearby West Heidelberg in 1954. Peter and Donnie would spend hours listening to rock'n'roll on the radio. They both liked Elvis, Johnny O'Keefe and Bill Haley, who with his roundish face, Donnie resembled. By now Donnie had his own 'set of wheels'. Helen Pletzer recalled that she, Peter and Donnie and his girlfriend, Susan Shuttleworth, used to hang around the local milkbar, 'Des's', in High Street, Thornbury. 'We'd play the pinball machine and keep the poor old proprietor up till the wee small hours, till he finally threw us out and then we'd hoon around in Donnie's FJ Holden and do stupid things like drive to Seymour [then a small country town some 96 kilometres north of Melbourne] for a hamburger.' The foursome also went to the local Preston drive-in on a couple of occasions. Donnie's FJ had a big boot (trunk) and, as was the custom at the time, Susan and Helen hid 'cuddled up' in the boot, while the two boys sat in the front seat until they had paid their entry fee and found a suitable spot for watching the double feature. Once settled, Susan and Helen were able to get out of the boot.[1]

Donnie and Peter were known to have the odd drop or two of alcohol. Donnie's younger brother Geoff remembered seeing them on one particular occasion: 'They were drinking a large bottle of beer. It just astounded me that they could drink beer straight out of the bottle like that.' Tom Huntley recalled being with Peter and Donnie during another drinking session: 'We were behind Peter's house in the laneway smoking cigarettes and drinking alcohol with a couple of girls from the hamburger shop.' The Salvation Army did not condone smoking and drinking alcohol, but Laurie Norman said Peter accepted the Salvation Army's strictness only when he wanted to: 'When he didn't, he didn't. I don't think it affected him a lot. He played it as he wanted to.'

Peter's life changed significantly on 7 June 1960 when he met Ruth Newnham during the Melbourne Metropolitan Division Crusaders trip to Queensland. He related how

> Ruth was playing netball for a Salvation Army team and I was playing basketball in a similar team in a Victoria versus Queensland tournament. A bunch of us were heading out to dinner one night. I was rather attracted to this cute, pretty little centre player from Altona. We had to walk across a railway crossing and someone commented on the narrowness of the railway lines. Being full of knowledge I said the Queensland rails were three feet six inches apart, unlike the Victorian rails which were 5 feet 3 inches apart. Ruth said something along the lines of 'Five feet three inches! That's ridiculous! Train lines aren't that wide apart.' I said I'd bet her that they were. If I was right, she had to come out to dinner with me the week after we got back. I don't think we ever checked the width of the gauge, but we went to dinner and that started our relationship.

Marie Ruth Newnham, known as Ruth, was born 18 July 1944. She was the eldest of five children. She had two brothers, John and Richard, and two sisters, Jennifer and Barbara. Her father, Verdun, was an accountant with ICI in Deer Park, an outer-western suburb of Melbourne, before he set up his own accountancy business in the 1950s. He was also a builder. Later on Ruth worked for him for several years. The Newnhams were Salvationists and lived in Queen Street, Altona, also in Melbourne's west.

Ruth, who was one month off her sixteenth birthday when she met Peter, was very quiet and shy. Peter was eighteen but didn't have a car, so he and Ruth would frequently travel into the city by train where they would work out what they were going to do. As both enjoyed seeing live musicals, they would invariably search out something in that vein. Peter was Ruth's first boyfriend. 'We became constant companions each weekend,' said Ruth. 'We attended many athletics meetings, church groups and youth groups. We also stayed with family and friends. We were great theatregoers, which was wonderful because you could dress up. Live theatre was really our passion.' After they had seen a live show, Peter often would buy the music soundtrack. Among the soundtracks he bought were 'Irma la Duce', 'Westside Story' and 'The Pyjama Game'. 'He'd play them and sing along while playing drums,' said Elaine Norman. 'Heather and I would sing along too. When he wasn't home we'd play his records.'[2]

The Norman and Newnham families soon became close. 'Because we lived at the beach at Altona, when we'd go away, the Normans would come and live in our house and have a holiday by the beach,' said Ruth. Both Heather and Elaine quickly adopted Ruth as another sister.

Ruth was soon playing netball with the Moreland Salvation Army team on a weekly basis. Peter took an interest in the netball, as did Ruth in Peter playing football for the Thornbury 'Redlegs' with Laurie. Peter and Laurie also played basketball competitively in a church competition. Laurie's future wife Jill described how in those days the girls sat and watched and held the boys' watches while they played. She said, somewhat tongue in cheek, 'That was a sign of devotion! Almost like a friendship ring.'

Once eighteen, Peter was eager to get his driver's licence and a car. Elaine remembered Peter driving a 1928 Chev at one time. 'I don't know where he got it from, but he was driving Heather and I to netball one time. There was no floor in the back and we had to sit with our feet up and watch the road go past underneath us. Then he had "Susie", the little blue coop. He sold that and got a Honda fastback.'

Through Ruth, Peter met Robin and Rhonda Kidney in March 1961 when he competed in the South Australian championships. Ruth and Rhonda had first met in 1959 during a Salvation Army netball tournament and quickly developed a friendship that continues to this day. Robin, a talented Australian Rules footballer and surf lifesaver, warmed to Peter at their first meeting. In December 1961 Ruth and Peter went to Adelaide during the Christmas holidays with George and Thelma and stayed with the Kidneys. 'From that point onwards,' said Robin, 'we became part of the Norman family. Whenever Peter came to Adelaide to compete, he stayed with us. We were also going over and staying with them.'

Rhonda came from a family of six girls so immediately adopted Peter as her brother. 'I'd always wanted a brother but didn't have one. He just seemed to fit the bill. Peter and I had something special right away and over the years, even though I didn't see him a great deal, it was always there.' Robin was impressed with Peter from the outset because he said Peter wasn't swayed easily: 'He was a man of his word. He wouldn't keep his mouth shut if there was a wrong done. He had a very strong sense of fair play and honesty. If Peter said he was going to be with you, he was with you, no doubt about that.' Robin and Rhonda would prove to be loyal and supportive friends to Peter, none more so than in the last months of his life.

Peter was on the verge of making a momentous decision – one that would ultimately lead to success at the highest level of athletics. He started the 1960–61 interclub athletics season in good form, setting a new Collingwood Harriers club senior and under-19 220 yards record (21.9 seconds) on 10 December 1960. In late January 1961 he set a new club under-19 record for 440 yards. On 4 February 1961, he finished fifth in the Victorian senior 220 yards championship. The event was won by a future teammate Gary Holdsworth. Later that month, Peter won the club's senior 100 yards championship in 10.1 seconds and the club's senior 220 yards championship in 22.9 for the second season in a row. Peter also won the club's under-19 100 yards championship in 10.1 seconds.

Midway through the 1960–61 season Peter met a man who was to change his life. Neville Sillitoe had competed for the Coburg Harriers during the 1940s, over 100 and 440 yards. He was no slouch over these distances; his fastest times being 9.9 seconds and 48.9 seconds respectively. Sillitoe transferred to East Melbourne Harriers as an athlete, before becoming the club's coach in 1956. He remembered meeting Peter: 'We were training on what was then known as the "Women's Oval" at Royal Park. On the ground next to us I saw this kid running around on his own.' Neville described Peter as being 'just a club runner' at the Harriers when they met – 'he hadn't achieved any notoriety at that time'.[3]

Peter continued the story:

> I didn't have a coach as Collingwood Harriers didn't have a sprint coach. I was just training and running with the other guys. I used to watch a few of the club's very good sprinters at training, including Harold Burridge, who was a fantastic 100 yard sprinter, and Jim Shand who was the club's top 200 man. I'd try and copy them and do some of the work they were doing. Neville invited me to train with his group. No strings attached. I didn't have to join his club, East Melbourne Harriers. It was just a matter of going along and seeing what I could do.
>
> It didn't take very long to show up that what I'd been lacking in was the racing that I got by training with Neville's guys. My sprint time came down, in a matter of something like two

> months, from 22.1 seconds for 220 yards as it was then, down to 21.2 seconds. That was just through Neville's tutelage and his ability to read the type of training I required. Plus of course the racing I got against these other guys in training. I went over to South Australia with Neville and won [on 18 March 1961] their junior 220 yards championship in 21.4 seconds and broke the South Australian open record.[4] It was a pretty good indication that Neville was doing the right thing by me. So very soon after that I decided to move from Collingwood Harriers and join Neville's club.
>
> Neville had the happy knack of being able to identify talent in sprinters. Neville's group included Gary Holdsworth, who was already winning senior events. He won a national championship at the age of nineteen and, in doing so, set a new Australian record of 20.9 seconds for the 220 yards. I thought he was worth having as a hero. The squad also included Mickey Wirt, Terry Moore, Cliff Bastow and Ray McLeod. EMH had a bunch of sprinters that were to be feared by any club that they ever raced against. In state titles, there'd be four of them in a six-man final for both 100 and 200. And I was being invited to go along and be part of this group!

Gary Holdsworth, born in August 1941, was a sixteen-year-old student at Coburg Technical School when Sillitoe found him. Holdsworth recalled first setting eyes on Peter late in the 1960–61 season.

> Neville had seen Peter run in relays. Neville saw potential so said he was going to try and get Peter to EMH. I couldn't see Peter's potential, but I was just an athlete, not a coach. Neville has the uncanny ability to pick talent. Peter began training with us from then on, doing our winter build-up for the 1961–62 season.

Holdsworth said he learnt one thing that day, 'namely never doubt the word of a master coach. We all know how Peter became the best-performed Australian sprinter ever'.

John Francisco, now the history/archives officer at the Collingwood Harriers athletics club, was then competing for the club in the shot-put, discus and occasionally javelin. His father, Norm Francisco, had co-founded the club in 1926, was secretary for many years and then president of the club between 1949 and 1960. He became the club's first life member.[5] Francisco recalled the club receiving a letter from Peter requesting clearance to go to East Melbourne Harriers: 'That letter was tabled at a committee meeting on 6 November 1961. In line with club policy, Peter was asked to meet with members of the committee, to discuss his clearance request, on 14 November 1961.' Francisco said the club understood that Peter wanted to move to EMH so as to have a specialist coach and to train with athletes of his own level.

> That was okay. It was the sneaky way it was done. While the club was unhappy with the events that led to Peter's clearance request, we were not going to stand in his way, so reluctantly the application was approved at a committee meeting on 4 December 1961.
>
> We were disappointed to lose our top sprinter. Peter was a young, likeable and dedicated athlete. Over the five years he was with the club, Peter scored many points in interclub competition, competed with distinction in club and Victorian championships, winning many first placings in senior and junior events. In the process he set many club records. He won the club's 100 yard championship on two occasions. This event is the club's 'blue ribbon' event, with a blue sash being awarded and the winner's name being added to the club's honour board. Peter had also run in an A-grade premiership with the club.'

Graham Young, a friend of Peter's at the Collingwood Harriers, was a member of the committee that considered Peter's clearance application. He agreed there was certainly controversy over Peter's departure.

> Good sprinters were hard to come by. There was a lot of rivalry between EMH and Collingwood at the time. There was a feeling that EMH was poaching Peter. I was the same age as Peter and I was in favour of Peter going because his future was more assured with EMH and Neville Sillitoe. Neville didn't have the greatest reputation with other clubs, but I got to know Neville very well and I found he was a fantastic guy. He was just so switched on and knew every rule in the book and knew how to manipulate them.

Peter had enjoyed his time at the Collingwood Harriers. The club had been good to him, having taken him on as a fourteen-year-old untried athlete and given him the opportunity to develop as a sprinter. He had appreciated the friendship of his teammates and club officials, but knew that it was time to move on. Collingwood's grass track did not suit his running style as well as the cinder tracks on which he would be running for EMH. And the opportunity to train and compete under Sillitoe was too good an opportunity to pass up. Ray Harbert, a distance runner with Collingwood at the time, agrees that Collingwood couldn't match the level of coaching that Peter would get at EMH under Sillitoe. 'We didn't want to lose our best athlete, so were a bit crook on it, especially the way it was done. But certainly it was the best move for Peter.'[6]

Peter had been the Collingwood Harriers' top sprinter when he left the club. When he joined EMH for the 1961–62 season, he was just one of a number of sprinters in what was essentially a sprint club. He had plenty of hard work ahead of him if he was ever to become one of the club's top sprinters. Maurie Drew, who was a very fine triple jumper for EMH and at state and national level, and also competed for the club in the high jump and pole vault, said that the 'guts' of the EMH team, all the way down from B-grade to under-17, was the sprinters. 'There were sprinters everywhere and they were talented. Neville was always bringing young kids along in the junior grades and there were some super runners among them.'

Drew recalled that Peter didn't show up as a brilliant sprinter when he first went to EMH. 'He was an ordinary athlete when he joined the club, but you'd see the improvement from one winter's training to the next. He was desperate to beat Gary Holdsworth. It was his lifetime ambition. But first he had to learn his craft and work his way through the grades.' One aspect of Peter's lifestyle really surprised Drew: 'Peter was the only kid I knew in athletics who smoked back then.'

Peter enjoyed his first season at EMH. Not only did he hone his sprinting skills, but he also got to compete in other events, as then new teammate Holdsworth related.

> In the early days Peter would do the high jump. You only had to start to get points. He did a lot of other events. Initially in the first few years we were doing everything. It was good fun. EMH was a prolific winner of premierships from E-grade to B-grade

> but we always struggled in A-grade, mainly because of our lack of depth in the field events. Peter often did the high jump and I became the shot-putter at times. Both of us had difficulty in reaching the qualifying A-grade standard in those events, but we enjoyed it just the same.

Sillitoe prepared training programs to suit each individual and realised during the season that Peter did a lot better on less work. He found this out only by trial and error. 'We worked a lot on his bend running. When he started with us, this was not all that crash hot.'

Now a fully qualified butcher, Peter had a very busy timetable during the athletics season. He worked from 6 am through the week until 5 pm. He would generally be on the training track by 5.30 pm. On Saturdays he would start at 5 am and be out of the shop and on his way to the track by 12.30, changing as he went in the car, ready to run at 1.30 p.m. While she didn't see Peter every Saturday morning, given his early start, Elaine described how you didn't talk to Peter on race mornings or touch his stuff: 'He would be psyching himself up and he didn't have time for daily nuances. You just kept out of his way. If you didn't, he could be quite sharp with you. As a kid, I didn't understand. I just thought this was the shitty side of Peter.'

Peter finished the 1961–62 season strongly, being a member of the EMH 4 × 110 yards relay team – consisting of Holdsworth, Mick Wirt, Terry Moore and Peter – that won the Victorian championship on 10 March 1962. Peter would win many Victorian titles in the coming seasons, but his first title win would always remain special. The next athletics season would, however, see Peter reach out beyond the state level.

NOTES

1 Donnie and Susan later married and had three daughters. Sadly Donnie died on 20 February 1998, at the relatively young age of 56, having suffered poor health for some time.

2 Peter had eclectic taste in music. His record collection ranged from Liszt; Hungarian rhapsodies; waltzes; Strauss; Gilbert and Sullivan; band music, especially army bands; through to rock'n'roll. He loved soft ballads by the likes of Ray Charles and Jimmy Webb. Richard Harris's 'MacArthur Park' was a real favourite. He also loved musical comedies and light opera.

3 Sillitoe's comments are somewhat dismissive of then eighteen-year-old Peter. Certainly Peter's best performances lay ahead, but he wasn't a hack runner by any means. By this time he had run in an A-grade club premiership team, won four club senior championships and set club records. He had also won a Victorian junior championship.

4 Peter also set a new Collingwood Harriers senior and under-19 record.

5 The Collingwood Harriers now awards the Norm Francisco medal to life members who have made a major contribution to the club.

6 Ray Harbert is a club stalwart at the Collingwood Harriers. He has competed for the club for the past 52 seasons and served the club in a number of capacities. He and 1968 Olympian Bob Gardiner were awarded Norm Francisco medals in June 2002.

8
GOD IS LOVE

Peter trained with Gary Holdsworth during the 1962 winter, thinking he was there to help Holdsworth make the Australian team for the upcoming British Empire and Commonwealth Games to be held in Perth later that year. 'One day when I was working,' said Peter, 'I got word to say there was an event on at Melbourne University that day. They needed runners to fill up the 200 metres field. I ran and lo and behold I beat Gary in a time that then equalled the state record held by Hec Hogan. People then started to think that maybe I had a shot of getting to Perth for the Games.'

Peter ran in the Victorian trials on 7 October 1962 and performed well enough to compete in the national trials – held at Olympic Park, Melbourne, on 21 and 22 October 1962 – for selection to the Games team. Peter competed in the 220 yards event at the trials and ran second to New South Wales's Bob Lay in 22.0 seconds. Both Holdsworth and the precocious talent Gary Eddy were eliminated in Peter's heat. Lay won the final in 21.8 seconds from Mike Cleary (21.9) and Dennis Tipping (22.0). Peter was fourth in 22.2 seconds. At that time, countries were permitted to select four athletes to compete in an event, so all four runners were selected to run for Australia in the 220 yards at the British Empire and Commonwealth Games. 'I made an Australian team,' said Peter, 'before I represented my state [at senior level], which was something of an unusual thing.'

Holdsworth, who was the top 220 yards runner in the Commonwealth at the time, admitted to running badly in the 220 yards national trials: 'I should have been in it but I stuffed up.' Holdsworth won selection, however, to compete in the 100 yards, so Peter was able to have his East Melbourne Harriers (EMH) teammate with him in Perth.

Western Australia's capital city, Perth, was the setting for the seventh British Empire and Commonwealth Games.[1] For the first time since the inception of the Games, South Africa did not compete. It had been excluded from the Commonwealth in 1961 because of its apartheid policies. India did not compete, as its government was preoccupied with resolving a border dispute with China, nor did Nigeria. But British Honduras, Dominica, Papua and New Guinea and St Lucia competed for the first time. In all, 35 countries were represented by 1041 competitors.

The Australian athletics team arrived early at the Games Village. Peter was impressed with the facilities and took great delight in telling his family about them in a letter dated 9 November 1962 in which he described the village homes as being 'terrific'. There were nine athletes in his home: Nick Devlin, Nick Dawes, Byron Williams, Kevin Rule, John Blackmore, John Randle, Lawrie Peckham, Gary Holdsworth and himself. Peter wrote

> The meals are way out of this world. You just couldn't imagine what they feed us athletes on. We had a chicken dinner last night … There is so much to tell you I don't know where to start … You can sit where you like and eat what you like. The meals are served buffet style like in Myers where everyone takes a tray and puts what they like on it … There is a bar for Ovaltine, which is served hot and cold and all for nothing which is beaut. There is also free Coca-Cola. On arrival we each received a package of soaps … They must have thought we were dirty … Your loving son, Peter G. Norman 220 Aust.
>
> PS Please keep this letter as I would like it as a sort of diary.

The Games were held between 21 November and 1 December 1962 during a Perth heatwave. Temperatures rose over the 38° Celsius mark on most days. The newly built Perry Lakes stadium was jammed to capacity with 51 000 people for the opening ceremony. More than 300 people were treated for heat exhaustion as the temperature soared past 40° Celsius. It wasn't only the general public who felt the heat. Games historian Cleve

Dheensaw noted that 'soldiers took water out to athletes who had to stand in the middle of the field in the searing heat of the hottest November day in Perth in twenty years'.[2] The extreme heat continued to be a problem throughout the Games, and crowds dropped to around 18 000 at the main stadium on some days. Much to Peter's delight, his girlfriend, Ruth Newnham, travelled by train to Perth for the Games with a large group of Salvationists. Ruth saw Peter compete and visited him in the Games Village.

Peter finished third in 21.6 seconds in heat 3 of the 220 yards event. He again ran third in heat 2 of the second round in 22.0 seconds, and then sixth in 21.8 seconds in his semi-final, thereby missing the final of the event, which was won by Kenya's Seraphino Antao. The Kenyan also won the 100 yards event. Holdsworth was initially awarded third place in the 100 yards final, ahead of Australian teammate Mike Cleary, and was duly presented with a bronze medal. A few days later, after re-examining the photo finish, officials reversed their decision and Cleary was awarded the bronze medal. Holdsworth was relegated to fourth place but officials allowed him to keep his bronze medal.

Neville Sillitoe was satisfied with Peter's performance, given that Peter hadn't been running that long. Peter was delighted to make the semi-finals, seeing it as a step forward.

Australia finished with a record haul of 105 medals, including 38 gold.[3] This was 25 more medals than the previous best at Auckland in 1950, and almost 39 more than the 66 won at the 1958 British Empire and Commonwealth Games in Cardiff, Wales. Triple gold medallist at the 1956 Olympics, Betty Cuthbert provided one of the great highlights for Australia in the 4 × 110 yards relay[4] on the last day of the Games. Cuthbert took the baton five yards behind the Australian-born English anchor runner Betty Moore. Some 40 000 spectators were on the edge of their seats as Cuthbert set off after Moore: 'With every stride I started pegging her back,' said Cuthbert, 'and with every stride that old drive and enthusiasm flooded back. This was how I felt in Melbourne. Then I was almost up to her with the line only yards away and nothing was going to stop me now. I squeezed out every drop of speed I had in me and hauled myself right up alongside her. We were shoulder to shoulder for a fleeting moment and then I gave one last desperate kick and sped over the line just a stride in front. Australia had won!'[5]

Peter made the semi-finals in the Victorian 100 yards championship on 16 February 1963. The final was won by Holdsworth from Seraphino

Antao, who competed by invitation. Peter ran third in the Victorian 220 yards championship behind Holdsworth and Antao. He also competed in the Victorian 440 yards championship, finishing third behind Sandringham's John Randall and Old Scotch's David Evans. He was also a member of the EMH 4 × 220 yards relay team, which won the Victorian title.

In March 1963, Peter ran in his first Australian championships at Adelaide's Thebarton Oval, finishing fifth in the 220 yards final behind Holdsworth, Peter Vassella, Cleary and Lay.

A number of major athletics events were being held on Sundays. The Salvation Army believed that on Sunday, being the Sabbath, sport shouldn't be played. Peter said they were very strict on this: 'We weren't even allowed as kids to kick a football on the street on Sundays. Sundays were set aside for spiritual things.' Peter couldn't understand why on Sundays he couldn't use his talent for running fast, when someone who could play a musical instrument could use that talent all day long. 'My gift was running, so it was only right for me to make the most of the gift that I had been born with.' But Peter had been thinking of ways in which he could spread the word of God after the Perth Games in 1962.

Peter ultimately came up with the idea of wearing a tracksuit with the words 'God is love' emblazoned on the back. Ruth sewed on the letters. Peter recalled:

> While the Salvation Army band was marching around the streets on Sunday, or playing inside using their talent to promote the Lord, I felt I could do the same thing by wearing my tracksuit to track meets. While I don't think they agreed with it, they didn't exactly try and stop me. Wearing the 'God is love' tracksuit caused a bit of a stir. It was something of a political statement for me to make in those days. Because of my upbringing, I believed what it said. The tracksuit got comment from teammates, but more from the opposition who used it as a weapon. Stuff like, 'God won't help you today, you're running against me.'

Peter's sister Elaine remembered that while Peter had his detractors in the Army, some progressive people understood that running on Sundays was something Peter had to do if he was to succeed in the sport: 'Some of the old time officers argued that while he might not be in church, he was certainly still giving his testimony on the athletics field. Rather than sitting in church testifying to people who had already found God, he was out there spreading the word.'

Thelma fully supported her son's stance: 'Peter spread the word and thousands saw it. Whereas if he was going to church, only a handful of people would have seen him. He still taught Sunday school and ran in the afternoon. Then the Athletics Association told him to take his tracksuit off because it was advertising! He could wear it at training but not in competition. So he had it from both sides. Peter was annoyed by all this.'

Thelma and George had encouraged their family to stand up for their principles. Peter and his siblings had also been raised to respect all people, regardless of colour or creed. They were taught to believe that it was what was inside a person that counted the most. This belief came right down the family line, beginning with their grandparents. Peter said:

> We're very lucky in Australia that, for the most part, people are more tolerant than they are in many parts of the world. We've been through a number of eras where people that were different came to our shores. The Chinese back in the goldrush days were given racial names. Then there were the Greeks and the Italians and, of course, they were 'wogs'. More recently it's been the Vietnamese and, latterly, people from the African countries, and they have had to put up with similar racial taunts.
>
> I just can't see how anyone can dislike someone simply because they are different. Who isn't different? That old song says, 'Red and yellow, black and white, all are precious in his sight'. It doesn't matter whether you're black, green, brindle, fat, slim, tall, short – everyone's got their place. And everyone's got a personality. If you don't like someone because you don't like their personality or you don't like their views then okay, but tolerance is the beautiful thing.

Elaine said her brother was accepting of all people.

> He always had that capacity to accept, with a sense of fun, people who were disabled or who were a little slow. In the Salvation Army, we had a few kids who were a little backward and Peter would always tease them and make a fuss of them and they just loved him. He never considered them less than him.

Elaine also felt that Peter was a perfectionist and loved to be right, and liked to be best at what he did – 'not specifically better than other people, but the best that he could be. If you said he couldn't do it, he just had to prove you wrong'.

Having made an Australian championship final the previous season, Peter set his sights on gaining selection in the 1964 Tokyo Olympic squad. He started the 1963–64 season in fine style. By mid January 1964 he had beaten Holdsworth three times over 220 yards in interclub competition. Peter had asked his sister Heather at the beginning of the previous season to help out the EMH by taking statistics.[6] She did so during the 1963–64 season. She would sit with Thelma in the press box every meet, but each had a different motive for being there. Thelma said that, while being track-and-field fans, they mainly went because of Peter, whereas Heather suggested that it also offered her the opportunity to watch Peter's fellow athletes.

Sitting in the press box every Saturday also gave Thelma the chance to make sure that sportswriters concentrated on the job at hand. Melbourne *Herald*'s Steve Hayward felt Thelma's wrath on one occasion in January 1964. 'We used to sit near him in the press box every week,' recalled Thelma, 'but he never took any notice of us. He was always too busy studying the horse-racing guide, then he'd write up his column.' By this stage, Peter had beaten Holdsworth for the third time, but each time Hayward's headline referred to Holdsworth being beaten, rather than Norman winning. Thelma considered that Hayward wasn't giving due credit to her son and her patience finally ran out when she saw Hayward's headline after Peter's third win: 'Holdsworth down again'.[7]

Rather than wait till the following Saturday's competition, Thelma decided to take immediate action. She caught the train into the city and visited Hayward at the *Herald*'s offices. She had the element of surprise on her side. Hayward barely knew that he shared the press box every week, let alone that the two women were closely related to Peter Norman or that the woman about to give him a tongue-lashing was in fact Peter's mother.

Thelma said to Hayward:

> What's with these headlines? You sit there every Saturday afternoon and look through the racing guide. You've got no idea what's going on out on the track and you come out with headlines like 'Holdsworth beaten by Norman' or 'Holdsworth

> down again'. Why not turn it around the other way and say 'Norman beats Holdsworth'. Give them the same amount of headline, because they're both good.

Before Hayward had a chance to speak, Thelma finished by saying that she wanted to see him watching what was happening on the track the following Saturday. Finally, Hayward was able to find his voice and asked Thelma how she knew about the form guide. Thelma explained who she was and that she sat next to him every Saturday: 'So Steve Hayward got to know that I was one to be reckoned with!'

Sports journalist Jim Blake could have considered himself fortunate to have escaped similar treatment from Thelma. Blake also witnessed Peter's defeat of Holdsworth for the third time that season and his report was published under the headline 'Holdsworth beaten'.[8]

Peter defeated Holdsworth for the fourth time that season over 220 yards on 22 January 1964, but in doing so he aggravated an ankle injury that had been plaguing him through the season. This was a major setback for Peter, who had impressed all and sundry with his form. Many sportswriters, including the *Age*'s Ron Carter, rated Peter as one of the top contenders for the 1964 Australian 220 yards championship.

Peter was not able to compete in interclub competition on 25 January 1964, and the injury continued to plague him, leaving him unable to compete in the Victorian 220 yards championship in mid February. By mid March, his ankle had improved with intensive treatment and Peter looked forward to competing in the 1964 national championships in Melbourne later that month. Selection for the Olympic team was based on an athlete's results in the championships, but Peter's Olympic dream was shattered when he severely injured his ankle in rather unusual circumstances just before the national championships.

> I'd never had a major argument with Neville [Sillitoe] until the Tuesday night before the selection trials [21–24 March 1964] for the Olympics. I'd been playing in a basketball match the night before and someone came down on my ankle, stepped on me sideways and snapped my ankle. I turned up at training on crutches. We argued that night. He'd already heard what had happened. He said, 'Come on, do three laps, 3 × 100 run-throughs and half a dozen starts.' 'Come on!' I said. 'Don't look to me for

> sympathy. That's not gonna happen. You've got convenient pain so you can get out of training tonight.' Neville was almost in tears. It would have been Gary and I going to Tokyo, but it was not to be.

Peter would not make it to Tokyo, but he was determined to help his mate get there, no matter what it took. Peter knew he couldn't run because of his ankle, but there was no way that he was going to withdraw from the 220 yards event. He intended to make things as tough as possible for Holdsworth's opponents. Holdsworth had run second in the 100 yards at the championships, so he needed to win the 220 yards event to guarantee selection. He related how, 'Peter was in the heat of my main opposition Bob Lay. Neville sent Peter out there just to fool around and keep Bob on the track as long as he could. Peter broke once, sauntered back, put as much pressure on Bob as possible, then broke a second time.' Peter was duly disqualified and left the track with a wry smile on his face. He had done as much as he could. It was now up to Holdsworth to deliver the goods. Holdsworth didn't let Peter down, winning the event in 21.5 seconds ahead of Lay. Holdsworth was on his way to Tokyo, as too was Lay.

The Australian athletics team had mixed success at the Tokyo Olympics in October 1964. Betty Cuthbert defied her critics who said she was finished by achieving her fourth Olympic gold medal with a stunning win in the inaugural women's 400 metres event. Her winning time was just one-tenth of a second outside the world record. Judy Amoore won bronze in the same race. Pam Kilborn won bronze in the 80 metres hurdles, Michele Mason won silver in the high jump, Marilyn Black won bronze in the 200 metres and Ron Clarke won bronze in the 10 000 metres. Of Peter's sprinting compatriots, Bob Lay was the best performer, making the semi-finals of the 100 metres where he came face to face with the eventual gold medallist, the powerfully built American Bob Hayes. Holdsworth and Lay were eliminated in the quarter-finals of the 200 metres.

Peter's disappointment at missing Olympic selection was softened by his wedding to Ruth in a ceremony officiated by Brigadier Ray Everitt at Thornbury Salvation Army Hall on 18 July 1964. Ruth also celebrated her twentieth birthday that same day. The wedding party consisted of Alan Wells (Peter's cousin and best man), Laurie Norman, Ruth's sister Jennifer Newnham and girlfriend Elaine Davies. Thelma made Ruth's wedding dress and the bridesmaids' dresses. Approximately 100 guests attended the reception at the Thornbury Methodist church hall.

Peter was calm the morning of the wedding. He spent some time dressed in his 'wedding gear' kicking the footy out in the street with some of his cousins. Elaine was upset that she wasn't able to join Peter in the impromptu football session: 'Mum said I couldn't go out because I had just had my hair done for the wedding. I was really ticked off because I'm sure Peter would have let me play.'

Peter and Ruth initially rented then purchased the former Salvation Army hall in North Road, Newport, in Melbourne's western suburbs, as their family home. The large room at the front of the building, which had previously served as a meeting place for Salvationists, became the perfect venue for family Christmas parties. Peter had always enjoyed those spent with his mother's family during childhood and took great delight in organising such functions at Newport. The room also housed three large fish tanks in which Peter bred black Oscar fish and other varieties of fish. He also grew bonsai there. He added a large slot-car track to the room. Having his own home afforded Peter the opportunity to build on his culinary skills. He did much of the cooking at home and developed into a fine cook in the years ahead.

Peter couldn't train during the winter of 1964 as he was still recovering from his ankle injury. As a result, he began the 1964–65 season slowly. Holdsworth did not compete that season, so Peter assumed the mantle of number-one sprinter for EMH. By the fourth week of interclub competition, Peter had dispelled all doubts about his fitness and was starting to prove himself a worthy replacement for Holdsworth. Sillitoe was pleased with Peter's progress after his ten-month lay-off. Peter appeared to be returning to the form he'd displayed two years earlier when he made the Perth British Empire and Commonwealth Games team.

By mid January 1965 Peter was in top form. He defeated 1964 Olympic sprinter Bill Earle to win the Victorian 200 metres championship on 18 January 1965. His time of 21.6 seconds was one of the fastest times run in Australia to that point. Peter then finished second in the Victorian 100 metres behind Roger Halliday. Sportswriters now rated Peter as the greatest threat to Gary Eddy for the Victorian 220 yards title to be run on 30 January 1965, and the 220 yards Australian championship in Hobart on 20 February. Peter continued his good form in interclub competition against his old club, the Collingwood Harriers, the week before the first big clash with Eddy, clocking 22 seconds flat for the 220 yards, running into a slight headwind. Sillitoe was happy with Peter's performance, believing he had struck top form at the right time. He believed Peter could now take out the Victorian 220 yards championship. It was not to be, however, as Peter finished second (21.7 seconds) behind Eddy (21.6 seconds) in the final.

By the time of the 1964–65 Australian championships, at Tasmania's North Hobart oval in late February 1965, Peter was showing signs of not having had a strong pre-season preparation. He finished second in his heat of the 100 yards championship and ran in the final, but did not finish the race. He pulled off to the side of the track part way through the race in an endeavour to save energy for the 220 yards event. He finished second in his heat, and fourth in the final of the 220 yards race behind Eddy (Victoria), Eric Bigby (Queensland) and Alan Cardy (NSW). He was a member of the Victorian 4 × 110 yards relay team, which ran third behind New South Wales and Queensland. Overall, Peter was happy with his progress during the season, particularly given his lack of pre-season training. But there was much work to be done in preparation for the 1965–66 season and for his bid to win selection in the Australian team for the forthcoming eighth British Commonwealth Games in August 1966 in Jamaica.

After his season's layoff, Holdsworth was focused on returning to competition in the 1965–66 season. He was also intent on winning selection for the 1966 Games, and so joined Peter in a tough winter training program before the start of the season. Peter described the training:

> Neville had a reputation for being as shifty as they come when it came to preparing and getting his athletes on to the track in the best possible condition. For instance, he had Gary and I running boundary for the under-13 Paramount Football Club that he coached out in Broadmeadows. Every Saturday morning, Gary and I had to be out in the Broadmeadows area at eight o'clock to run the boundary. This was part of our winter training. In the summer it was down to hard, fast track training.

Peter ran well for EMH in interclub competition during the early part of the season, but had mixed success at the Victorian championships in early 1966. He finished second behind Holdsworth in the 100 metres final, third behind Holdsworth and newcomer Greg Lewis in the final of the 220 yards event, and won the 200 metres. But all season, Peter had been focused on winning the Australian championship. He was desperate to prove himself on the big stage and win his first national title. It was now or never. Success would guarantee selection for the forthcoming Jamaican Games.

On 27 March 1966, in extreme heat, with the temperature hovering around 40° Celsius, Peter won his first Australian 200 metres title in 20.9 seconds at the Perry Lakes stadium in Perth. Holdsworth finished second in 21.2 seconds, ahead of Queensland's Stuart Laing. Peter set up his win with a brilliant start and cruised over the line 2.5 metres ahead of Holdsworth. His time was only 0.1 seconds outside the Australian record of 20.8 seconds, held jointly by Lay and Lewis, who had equalled the time in winning his heat. Lewis and Lay finished fourth and fifth respectively in the final. The Victorian team of Allan Crawley, Lewis, Holdsworth and Peter in turn won the Australian 4 × 100 metres championship. Both Peter and Holdsworth could now look forward to competing in Jamaica in August.

Sillitoe said about Peter that, although generally quiet by nature, he could occasionally see red.

> In his first championship win in Perth, I talked to him between the heat and the final. In his heat Peter ran out one of the favourites. I happened to overhear an athlete remark, 'I don't care who wins the final as long as it's not that Norman!' I passed on the conversation to Peter with perhaps a little exaggeration. I don't think I've ever seen him madder, but he went on to a convincing win.

Sillitoe has since admitted that this never happened. 'I don't think Peter ever knew that. It wasn't hard to fire Peter up, but he probably didn't need it.'[9] Greg Lewis, born in December 1946, was spotted by Sillitoe while running as a junior with the Frankston Athletic Club. Peter suggested that

> Neville could see potential in this young tearaway, who ran probably more like a bulldozer than even I did. He was strong as an absolute bull and just as headstrong, but very fast. He had a start which, at that time, was second only to Bob Lay in Australia and against most opposition he could usually hold them off. Unfortunately Greg came along at a time when Gary Holdsworth was running extremely well and it took a long time for Greg to break through.

Lewis's arrival added sting to EMH's sprinting team in more ways than one, as Holdsworth described: 'That's when the fun really began. It became an instant arm wrestle between the two for mental supremacy. Training became a verbal battlefield between Peter and Greg. It was mostly good-humoured, but sometimes the barbs really became heated.' Holdsworth related that you couldn't say anything to Peter; he wouldn't let you get away with it. He always had to have a comment coming back at you and he usually came out on top.

> Peter had a sharp tongue, a tongue which wasn't saved only for Greg. The more senior an athlete he became, the more cutting the remarks were. I was the only one who ever escaped it. Even the juniors in interclub would cop it sometimes. He'd talk to them when they were running sometimes. He'd say, 'Come on, can't you run faster than that.' Often pre-race opponents were made to feel very insecure with a few well-chosen words. Peter and Greg usually teamed up with their banter at this point.

Sillitoe was never a technical coach – his athletes ran very naturally. He didn't interfere with style unless it was absolutely necessary, believing that the more naturally you ran, the better you ran. Lewis said that Sillitoe didn't espouse any philosophy. He was there to make them as strong as they could be and, very rarely, did he ever interfere. 'I've never heard him once talk about technique. He was only interested in making you tough.'

Peter and Lewis were both power sprinters, but there were differences in their styles as Holdsworth described: 'Peter's running compared to Greg Lewis's was totally different. Peter was more of a long striding hustle-bustle runner, whereas Gary was chop, chop, chop. He was very clipped, whereas Peter had more length in his stride.' Lewis added that Peter ran from the front of the body, so was over his legs all the time: 'That requires some considerable strength. Put him on a soft track, he was useless and I wasn't far behind him. We both relied on power, so when the revolution of hard tracks came, it suited us right down to the ground.'

Peter believed that athletes had to accept their coach's techniques and training regime unconditionally. This didn't mean that you couldn't question them, but they had the last say. He described how 'you would argue with Neville sometimes if he told you to do an extra 300 metre sprint. But after the argument finished and you hadn't convinced him, you'd go out and do the 300. You knew you couldn't afford not to do it, because he was always right'.

> Neville was such a great coach, probably because of the closeness he had with his athletes. He could read us like a book. Prior to championships, on the odd occasion you'd turn up expecting a rugged night of training and you'd warm up and he'd say, 'Right that's it, warm down and go home. That's all you need now.' He timed it to the nth degree. He juggled Greg, Gary and I in the same team, racing against each other every week, and he would tell you that he didn't ever know which one was going to win when we started. But he knew that the three of us were the best prepared we could possibly be. That instils a tremendous amount of confidence in the athlete to know that there's nothing else you can do.

Sillitoe's athletes trained every night except Friday. Peter never trained as hard as Holdsworth or Lewis: 'I seemed to come up much quicker than they did, but I didn't put it down to anything like natural talent. It was more the coach being able to read what was required to make me run fast.'

Sillitoe understood that his athletes had different make-ups. Holdsworth had to train very hard and needed a lot of training, the advantage being that when he got to his peak he could hold it. Peter came to head very quickly so didn't need a lot of work. It was a balancing act for Peter, who would get to his peak quickly but to maintain it was hard. 'Peter only needed three nights a week,' said Holdsworth. 'He might have been there five nights a week but some nights he wouldn't do much at all, which annoyed me no end.'

The work the three athletes did together helped each of them. There was no way Peter would refuse to run on the inside of Holdsworth around the bend to make Holdsworth work harder. He'd do it because he knew it would benefit Holdsworth and, in turn, benefit him when it came time for Holdsworth to run on the inside of him. Peter would have to run further and harder to keep up with Holdsworth. 'Everything you did was flat chat,' recalled Peter. 'There were no half measures. Once you'd done a couple of laps to warm up, you'd come out to do what we called run-throughs. The first one would be just a stroll. The second one would be a stride to about half way, then you'd accelerate through to the finish. The third one would be absolutely flat out from the first step and you'd gradually increase your speed.' Peter said from that point during a training session, if you made one mistake, you would be two metres behind the other two runners and so you would learn to concentrate on not making mistakes. You learnt what pressure was all about. 'You knew when it came to the state titles, the other two guys were going to be in the final with you and they were going to be the ones you had to beat. It was the same when you got to the national championships. So to learn to run under that pressure and not make mistakes was tremendous grounding.'

Lewis agreed that it was a pitched battle at training. 'The intensity that we would train at was everything.' He said, however, that he and Peter didn't always warm up in the traditional manner – they had a trick up their sleeve: 'We did away with the long warm up, the jog, the casual stretching and all that crap. We'd turn the car heater on down at the legs on the way to training, then jump out of the car and catch up with the young blokes from the third run through.'

Sillitoe was always looking at ways of adding variety to their training. He developed different activities and Holdsworth, Peter or Lewis never questioned him. They would do a lot of work through the winter, including running a relay at the Sandown racecourse in which each sprinter had to run two laps of the track. This was in addition to the boundary-umpiring Peter and Holdsworth did for the West Brunswick amateur Australian Rules football club for some five years. Holdsworth suggests that Peter might have been having a good time running the boundary, but he needed to do the work.

Sillitoe was seen as somewhat of a 'wizard' by his athletes. His sea-salt baths on the Thursday night before a major event were a tradition, as Peter described: 'You'd get into this bath of sea salt which he'd gradually heat up until you could hardly bear it. You'd lay in it for exactly 15 minutes. Not a second more. You'd leap out, rub down with a rough towel, always rubbing towards the heart, while you dried yourself. That was the magic touch. I guess physically it was no more magic than his lucky socks that he always wore, but it worked.' Holdsworth said, 'We liked having sea baths because we knew when we had them there wasn't much more training to go. You never had them before any old meet, only the ones that really counted.'

Sillitoe taught his runners that the way to learn to run fast was to run fast. Every training session was a competition. The runners believed in Sillitoe's ability to give them exactly the right work necessary to bring them to their top on championship days. He left the rest up to their will to succeed against their competitors. Sillitoe knew exactly what type of training would bring each runner to his peak, and he was the needle that goaded them into the razor-sharp state of mind necessary for success in big races.

Holdsworth contended that Sillitoe would rather be critical than complimentary to get the best out of you: 'You just had to accept that.' He hastened to add that the criticism wasn't to put you down: 'We wouldn't have been anything without Neville. He was the crux of the whole thing.'

Peter's early starting times, and long hours as a butcher over six days, combined with training and competition, were beginning to wear him down physically and mentally. He began work between 5 and 6 am every morning and would work until 5.30 pm Monday to Friday, then Saturday until 1 pm. In the early 1960s, Peter was working for Murray and Norma Lawson as a butcher at M & N Hygienic Meats in Werribee in Melbourne's outer-west. The Lawsons liked Peter and he felt the same about them, appreciating the interest they showed in his athletics career. They would regularly drive across Melbourne to see Peter compete with EMH. Peter subsequently took over management of a small one-man butcher shop at the rear of a supermarket in central Werribee. He and Ruth talked about what he could do to free up his time. Teaching loomed as a possibility.

Peter enjoyed working in a butcher shop and interacting with customers but knew that it wasn't all there was to life:

> I was 22 and managing a shop down in Werribee. It was something like five o'clock in the morning and I'd cut all the orders. I had a window display in place and I was sitting down having a cup of coffee and I thought, "Hell I'm going to be doing this till I'm 60. I don't want to do this till 60." I handed in my resignation that day and set myself on the track to become a physical education (PE) teacher.
>
> At that time the Victorian Education Department was offering teaching positions in the technical division to qualified trades people. I had some physical education experience because I had represented Australia in track and field. I'd had experience in running youth clubs and boys club for the Salvos, so I wasn't without contact experience with kids. I did what they then called the tech teacher-training course out at Glenbervie Tech Teacher's College. That gave me the qualifications to get through for quite some time.

By the time he got to the British Commonwealth Games in Jamaica, Peter was a physical education teacher. He taught three days a week at Williamstown Technical School and at Coburg Technical School another two. 'Within eighteen months, the head of the physical education department at Williamstown Tech School was called up for national service training. That left them without a head of department so I became a full-time head of department and within another twelve months became sports master, union delegate and God knows whatever else.'

Alec Gardiner had responsibility for staffing at all technical schools in Victoria at this time. Alec and Peter hit it off from their first meeting and soon became friends. Peter related to Alec's down-to-earth approach. Sport was also a strong common interest, particularly Australian Rules football. Alec, born in January 1935, had been a speedy and clever winger for Footscray in the Victorian Football League, then the premier football competition in the nation. In his day, Alec could match any player of his era for speed. He ultimately played 91 games for Footscray, including the club's losing 1961 grand final match at the Melbourne Cricket Ground.

Alec remembered Peter starting teaching during 1965. 'Peter became one of the first Phys. Ed. teachers Williamstown Tech ever had. I ran into him at sports-master meetings. His organisational abilities were pretty good because he had to organise buses, events etc. for the whole school as sports master.'

Steven Tupper, a PE student of Peter's at Coburg, recalled that Peter was very strong on discipline. 'He was fair but he always made sure that everyone was doing their bit. If someone didn't do what they were told, Peter's look was enough to scare the hell out of you. He was quite nice, but when it came to discipline, phew. He'd give you that look. You knew he was fair dinkum.' Raymond Threlfall, a student at Williamstown, agreed with Tupper:

> A lot of kids feared him. He wanted to develop muscles for kids who didn't have muscles. He would ride you pretty hard. You didn't forget him. He was a no-nonsense teacher. He had a sense of humour, as macabre as it might have been. He would stand you up with a medicine ball on top of your head and laugh about it. And he got the rest of the class to enjoy it too. I was hopeless at PE. I was a fat chubby bloke. That's probably why he rode me so hard.

By now Peter and Ruth were actively involved in the Salvation Army in Altona. Peter was the young people's sergeant major, while Ruth led the girls' primary and timbrel divisions. Peter and Ruth were officially 'commissioned' to these positions on the basis of their standing in the Salvation Army community. Peter also captained the Altona Salvation Army men's basketball team, which played in an interchurch competition.

Peter rarely, if ever, missed a church service at this time, even when interstate for athletics competitions, such as the regular EMH team trip to Adelaide to compete in the South Australian championships. Graham Johnston roomed with Peter on two such trips.

> We'd compete on the Saturday, then on the Sunday Peter would insist we go to church. He didn't ram religion down my throat, but he would say that I'd had a pretty good weekend and had done very well. He'd add that I was getting help from above, whereas I thought I was doing it on my own.
>
> Off we'd trot. Peter would introduce himself to the Salvation Army officer as being from Victoria. The officer would in turn introduce us to the congregation and ask us to stand up. He'd ask would one of us like to read from the Bible. That frightened me. Fortunately Peter would do it.

Johnston wasn't worried about going to church – it was the thought of having to front the congregation. But fortunately, on both occasions, Peter did the Bible readings. It was something he was very comfortable doing, given his years of practice.

NOTES

1 From 1930 to 1950 the Games were known as the British Empire Games, then the British Empire and Commonwealth Games until 1962. Fron 1966 to 1974 they were known as the British Commonwealth Games. From 1978 onwards they have been known as the Commonwealth Games.

2 Cleve Dheensaw, *The Commonwealth Games – The First 60 Years, 1930–1990*, ABC Books, Sydney, 1994, p. 72.

3 Swimmers Dawn Fraser and Murray Rose each won four gold medals. Ken Roche (440 yards hurdles), Trevor Vincent (3000 metres steeplechase), Percy Hobson (high

jump), Trevor Bickle (pole vault), Ian Tomlinson (triple jump), Warwick Selvey (discus) and Alf Mitchell (javelin) won gold, as did several Australian women. Pam Kilborn easily won the 80 metres hurdles and Dixie Willis won the inaugural 880 yards event. Australia won the trifecta in the women's long jump and in the high jump. The long jump was won by Pam Kilborn ahead of Helen Frith and Janet Knee, while Robyn Woodhouse won the high jump ahead of Frith and Michele Mason.

4 The Australian team consisted of Joyce Bennett, Glenys Beasley, Brenda Cox and Betty Cuthbert.

5 Betty Cuthbert & Jim Webster, *Golden Girl*, Pelham Books, London, 1966, p. 107.

6 Ruth also helped the club out in this regard at certain times.

7 *The Herald*, 20 January 1964.

8 *The Sporting Globe*, 18 January 1964.

9 *Australian Amateur Athletics* magazine, December 1968 – January 1969.

9

C'EST MOI! ('TIS I)

By 1966 Peter had been wearing his blue 'God is love' tracksuit for two years. The tracksuit was threadbare at the knees and elbows, and he told a reporter that he might have to pay $20 for a new one with a different message for the Jamaican Commonwealth Games. 'I can't put too much on, but could decide on "Jesus saves".' His purpose in wearing a 'slogan' was to create discussion: 'I've had many people come up to me and ask what it stands for. It gives me the opportunity to tell them what I believe in.'[1] Peter subsequently purchased another tracksuit and had Ruth sew the words 'Jesus saves' on the back.

Peter was excited to be going to Jamaica with his close mate Gary Holdsworth. He and Holdsworth had more than just athletics in common – both were very keen on musical comedies.

> We'd been to see *Camelot* and there's a song in that show called 'C'est moi' ['Tis I]. We used to take great delight in singing it at the top of our voices under the shower. While we sang it for our own pleasure, it was also to get up Greg Lewis's nose just a bit because we were coming around to state titles time. Greg used to nearly always break out into this rash as part of expending nervous energy. It might have upset Greg as here we were singing 'I've never lost in battle or game, I'm simply the best by far.'

Holdsworth shared similar memories.

> Peter and I were rivals but good friends, which is very unusual. I don't think we ever had a cross word with each other. Peter and Ruth, and Glenda and I, from our late teens on, were always together. We used to do lots of things together. Peter and I were both mad on *Camelot*. We used to sing 'C'est moi' in the car.

Holdsworth and Peter traditionally grew goatees during the off-season. 'We'd have them from November through to the end of January,' said Peter. 'At the start of February, the big races started to happen and we'd shave off the bottom part and leave the moustache. Everyone knew we were in business then. When we'd get to the national championships, the moustaches would come off too.' According to Holdsworth, he and Peter were just young blokes trying to look like Richard Harris in *Camelot*.

The decision to hold the eighth British Commonwealth Games[2] in Kingston, Jamaica, was momentous. The Games had never before been held outside of Britain, Canada, Australia or New Zealand. There was a strong degree of scepticism as to whether Kingston could pull off the Games. This was not the only burning issue in the Commonwealth, however. As was the case four years earlier, relationships between India and China were tense. Indian authorities also had concerns about India's relationship with neighbouring Pakistan over the future of Kashmir, and its ability to provide support to some 30 000 villagers left homeless when the Jumna River broke its banks and flooded villages in the New Delhi region. But, unlike in 1962, India would be represented at the Games. Rhodesia and Cyprus were also major trouble spots. Neighbouring countries such as Kenya were imploring Britain to use force rather than economic sanctions against Rhodesia, while United Nations troops expected to be deployed in Cyprus for quite some time.

Australia's team left Sydney on 19 July 1966 in a chartered jet bound for Los Angeles, where a combined Australian and New Zealand team was scheduled to oppose the USA in a two-day track meeting. Triple jumper Phil May described how it came about.

> At that time they had a track meet running between Russia and the USA. The Russians pulled out at the last minute. The Americans had booked the Coliseum and had spent a shit-load of money getting

Above: *Despite the photographer's efforts to make him smile, two-year-old Peter flatly refused. His first words to his mother after the photo shoot were 'Isn't that man silly Mum!'*

Above right: *Peter at four-and-a-half proudly escorts his mother and brother Laurie down High Street, Northcote, in Melbourne.*

Right: *Peter stands tall outside the Norman family home at 69 Andrew St, Northcote, January 1947.*

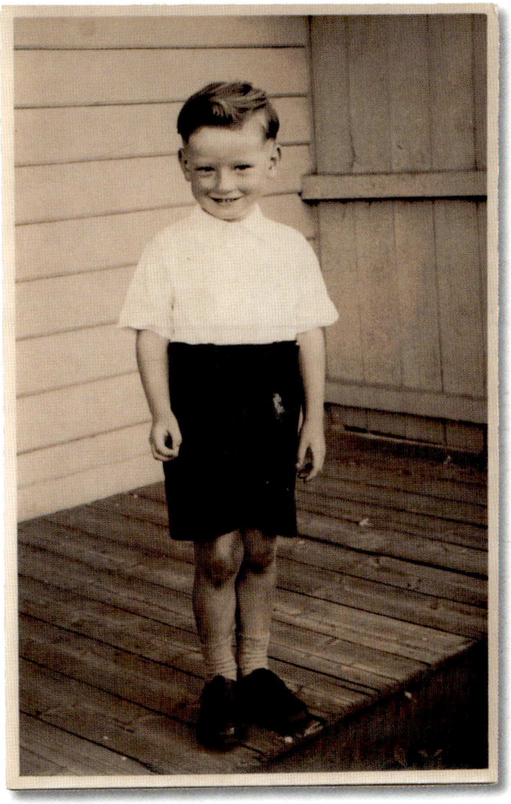

Left: *The three Norman children: Laurie (three-and-a-half), Heather (one) and Peter (six-and-a-half).*

Middle: *The Thornbury Salvation Army Sunday school group circa 1955. Peter (thirteen) is fourth from left in the middle row. His cousin Kevin Berry is third from left in the same row. Peter's future girlfriend Glenys McLean is far right in the front row.*

Right: *Six-year-old Peter with (left to right) Thelma holding Heather (18 months), George holding Laurie (three), a family friend and Peter's much-loved Nana, Sarah Norman.*

Above: *Thornbury Salvation Army band members Peter (drums), George Norman (trombone) and Athol Graham (trumpet) with a fellow parishioner, 5 May 1957. George created havoc with his antics on the trombone.*

Middle: *A delighted Peter (sixteen) poses on 5 April 1959 with fellow members of the 1958–59 Collingwood Harriers A-grade premiership team. This would prove to be Peter's only interclub premiership team.*

Left: *Young and in love – Peter and Ruth Newnham relax at a Salvation Army youth camp, 1961.*

Main: *Peter training in the mid 1960s.*

Top: *East Melbourne Harriers master coach Neville Sillitoe passes on some tips to Peter and Gary Holdsworth, December 1963.*

Bottom: *Peter wearing a favourite item of clothing: a University of Southern California sweater purchased during the USA versus Commonwealth athletic event held in Los Angeles in July 1966.*

Above: *The wedding party – Laurie Norman, Jenny Newnham (Ruth's sister), Peter and Ruth, Elaine Davies, and Alan Wells – outside the Thornbury Salvation Army hall. Thelma Norman made the dresses for the bride and bridesmaids.*

Middle: *Peter and Ruth pose with their delighted parents George and Thelma Norman (at left) and Edith and Verdun Newnham (at right).*

Right: *A dual cause for celebration – the newly married Mr and Mrs Norman on Ruth's 20th birthday, 18 July 1964.*

Main: *Peter in his 'Jesus saves' tracksuit, which he wore for the first time during training at the 1966 Commonwealth Games in Jamaica.*

Above right: *Peter proudly displays his 'God is love' tracksuit top in May 1966.*

Top left: *Peter powers home to win for East Melbourne Harriers during an interclub event in the mid 1960s.*

Top right: *Part of the East Melbourne Harriers team circa 1967: Peter is far left and Gary Holdsworth is far right in the front row; Greg Lewis is third from left in the second row.*

Left: *On top of the world, Peter returns to Melbourne after winning the 1968 Australian 200 metres championship in Sydney in record time. The win cemented his place in the team for Mexico.*

Next page: *The concentration of a champion.*

> everything organised. American ingenuity triumphed again. They said there is a Commonwealth team coming down to Jamaica. It's got to go through Los Angeles. Why don't we get them down earlier and have a track meet and call it 'USA versus Commonwealth', which they did. The whole track and field team was dropped off in Los Angeles on the way to Jamaica. We ended up staying in Birnkrant Hall at the University of Southern California.

Peter was excited at the prospect of competing against a number of top US athletes at the Coliseum, which had been the venue for the 1932 Olympic Games. He would finally see some of the athletes he had only read about, such as young college student Tommie Smith. 'He could run like the wind, and he had what he called his "Tommie jet gear". Tommie, in similar fashion to myself, wasn't known for his fast starting, but had this mid-race acceleration that used to rip through fields and just tear people apart.'

Peter was not pleased with his performance in the 200 metres race, suggesting that he had run 'absolutely miserably'. He also wasn't overly thrilled when told he had to run in the 4 × 400 relay as a substitute for Gary Eddy, who, according to Peter, got 'horribly whipped up' in the flat 400 metres race, so didn't want to run in the relay. Peter didn't want to run either. He hated 400s, only agreeing to run after hearing about 'these marvellous rose-bowl trophies for the winners, second and third'. As there were only three teams in the relay, and as he loved trophies, Peter thought he might as well 'go for a stroll around 400 metres'. The Australian team, in running order, consisted of Ken Roche, Noel Clough, Peter and Gary Knoke.

It was suggested that Peter run the third leg against Smith because they were both 200 metre runners and with his strength Peter would be able to hold Smith. 'I believed all that of course!' When Peter took the baton he was about 10 metres behind. He held Smith through the first 200 metres and then made his move. As Peter made his big push, Smith disappeared over the horizon and beat him by nearly 30 metres. Peter went over and lay down behind the judge's stand, as was his want after a 400 metres run. It was tantamount to passing out.

> Ken Roche came and towered over me while I was lying there. He said, 'You let us down badly out there. I never thought I'd see the day when you threw in the towel like that.' I started to feel pretty bad. Then we got up for the victory ceremony and it

> was announced that the Americans had broken the world record. It was the first time three minutes had ever been broken for 4 × 400. Tommie had run inside the world record for 400 metres and had run 43.8. I had run 46.2 and Ken Roche had run 47.3. When the times were announced Ken turned around and said, 'Oh well, it wasn't too bad I guess!'

The American team of Bob Frey, Lee Evans, Tommie Smith and Theron Lewis had run the phenomenal time of 2 minutes 59.6 seconds to smash the world record previously set by the USA in the 4 × 400 final at the 1964 Olympics.

May said Peter had done his best and did not warrant Roche's verbal attack: 'Normie was on his hands and knees, spewing his guts out. Roche came up and said, "You weak bastard. You let him get away." But Normie ran what was then the fastest-ever leg for an Australian team in that event. Normie got up and showed Rochie his tracksuit and said, "Mate I did my best!"'

Despite being only twenty-four, Peter was regarded by some journalists as being too old for selection for the Games. 'I'd been around a long time without ever really making much of a mark. One journalist said I was selected for a second Commonwealth Games, although I supposedly had little chance of success. He said I was a very good baton handler and I might be handy for both relays. That really stuck in my craw.'

David Prince, the NSW hurdler, was the athletics team captain in Jamaica. Soon after the team arrived in Kingston, the Australian team manager, Fred Humphreys, fell ill. Humphreys requested that Prince, as near as was practical, act as manager and guide the team rather than the coaches who, in Peter's opinion, were 'for the most part there for their long service to the sport, rather than anything they could offer the athletes'. Prince issued the athletics team with three rules in Jamaica. First, to justify their selection, they had to repeat the form on which they had been selected. Second, under no circumstances were they to finish last in any round, whether it be heats, second round, semi-final or final. Third, under no circumstances were they to ever get beaten by a Pom![3]

Prince welded the 1966 team into what Peter described as being virtually the family that went to Mexico in 1968.

> He would never organise anything for the team without involving all the team. The girls were treated like our sisters. It created

> this wonderful caring attitude for each other that I hadn't seen in track and field before. That continued on through Mexico right up as far as the 1970 Commonwealth Games and there were quite a few international meetings in between where that same attitude was carried on because of the standards David Prince set for that team. I tried to copy in some way, shape or form David's leadership skills.

On a flight to Jamaica Peter had the most frightening experience of his life. Having competed at the Coliseum in Los Angeles, the Australian team boarded a flight to Mexico City in a Comet aircraft and then a DC-3 in Mexico City for the flight to Jamaica. 'Taking off at a small airport in Mexico on our way to Jamaica,' said Peter, 'we couldn't get off the ground and most of us were singing hymns.' Holdsworth added:

> The plane flew at telegraph-pole height for about the first five miles. As it was only a small plane, we had pole-vaulting poles laid down in the middle of the aisle. It was an unbelievable experience. Some of us were really, really scared, so much so that David Prince got everyone singing 'Onward Christian Soldiers'.

For the first time ever, female athletes had to undergo sex tests before being cleared to compete in the Games. Sex testing or gender verification was introduced primarily to squash press speculation about some female athletes, whose external appearance and muscular development (from the vigorous training programs) were considered more masculine then feminine. There were also concerns that some males might be masquerading as females in order to gain an unfair advantage. In short, women who excelled at sport were pressured to prove that they were, in fact, biologically female.

Sprinter Di Burge described the testing:

> We had to strip and be examined by one male and two female doctors. Males didn't have to be examined. We weren't racist but being examined by this big, black Jamaican doctor, who looked terrifying, added to the fear. But with Australians being Australians, it still had a funny ending. The boys found out that we had to pass a sex test and they were lined up outside our guarded gates. When we came out from having our tests, we'd give the thumbs up if we passed. There'd be wild cheers from the boys.

Australian athletes found Kingston to be a very unfriendly city, which wasn't overly surprising given that it was reputedly one of the most dangerous cities in the world at the time. 'We very rarely strayed from the village, which was protected by armed guards,' said Phil May. 'We used to go down to the bar in the village and have a swim and a beer, but that was as far as we went.' High jumper Lawrie Peckham added that Kingston wasn't friendly to white people: 'There was a distinct colour problem. It was very hostile towards white people.'

Holdsworth roomed with Peter. He said there was no pleasure in being in Jamaica: 'We had cold showers. The athletics events were held in a half-lit stadium. Even down the back straight it was a bit dark. They swept the track before the 220 event. They swept everything out into the outside lane. Guess who ran in the outside lane. This was before the final! Most of the rough stuff was swept into my lane.'

Burge and a number of other Australian athletes lost a lot of weight. She described the food in the village, when you could get some, as being atrocious. Because of the intense heat – temperatures hovered around 40.5° Celsius with humidity heavy at around 95 per cent – all athletics sessions were held at night. This meant athletes had to leave for the track about 5 pm, so they weren't able to eat before they left the village. It was more often than not early the next morning before athletes got back to the village after competition, by which time the meal areas would be closed. 'You just kept missing meals,' said Burge. 'And the food in the village wasn't the sort you'd pack up and take with you. Even with salads, you'd get a piece of tomato one day, cucumber the next day and lettuce the following day. You'd never get it all together. The safest thing to eat was ice cream.' It wasn't surprising that a number of athletes picked up stomach bugs. Burge got severely ill between the 100 yards and 220 yards events and considered herself lucky that she had a day's rest, otherwise she would not have been able to compete in the 220 yards.

Australian journalist Alan Trengove wrote, 'It may seem unfair to a small country trying to do its best, but I am convinced the Keystone Cops could have done a better job of organising the Commonwealth Games athletics.'[4] His comments were borne out by events experienced by several Australian athletes. Burge won the sprint double and a third gold medal in the relay. It took officials three attempts to get the Australian national anthem right for her first gold medal, the first track medal awarded at the

Games. The one saving grace was that Burge got to stand on the victory dais for a long time. One of her finals was an hour-and-a-half late because cyclists were competing on the cycling track, which went around the outside of the athletics track.

Peckham won the high jump in a competition that ran late into the night, mainly because the Nigerian athlete he was battling against for gold was permitted to take upwards of 30 minutes between each jump. When the competition finally concluded, officials did not acknowledge the place-getters that night. 'We just wandered off and that was it,' said Peckham. Medals were presented the following day.

Dick Leffler, who at this point had won eight national hammer-throw championships in a row, was less than impressed when he discovered that the hammer-throw competition was to be held in the car park instead of the main stadium. Leffler was so disgusted that he considered proposing that the term 'track and field' be replaced by 'track, field and car park'. Leffler, who had won a silver medal in the previous Games, ultimately finished fourth in Jamaica.[5]

Pam Kilborn, who won the 80 metres hurdles,[6] and was also a member of the gold-medal-winning 4 × 110 yards relay team (along with Burge, Jenny Lamy and Joyce Bennett) agreed the Games were a shambles. Kilborn had the hurdles, long jump and relay finals all on within half an hour of each other. 'You were expected to go outside the stadium and walk around to the check-in point to re-enter the stadium with the other competitors before each event.' Kilborn refused to leave the stadium between events because she feared for her safety outside the venue. This was understandable given that, on average, there were 300 stabbings every night in Kingston during the Games.

Notwithstanding her two gold medals, Kilborn experienced her most memorable moment in Kingston on her birthday on 12 August. 'Peter and two or three other members of the team came down to the dining room that evening and Peter said, "I've got a present for you". They sang seven verses of "My dog Sandy has flees". You don't need to learn the words, because they are the words. That was most exciting!'

Peter finished fourth in heat five, then sixth in the quarter-finals of the 100 yards, thereby missing the final, which was won by Canada's Harry Jerome. He then finished sixth in the first semi-final of the 220 yards, again missing the final, which was won by Ghana's Sam Allotey. He collapsed after his semi-final and was taken to hospital. Australia's general manager, Bill Young, told the *Sun* newspaper that Peter had been taken to hospital after spending an hour in a first-aid post as a precautionary measure. 'Norman was up most of Sunday night [the previous night] with stomach trouble but was determined to run,' said Young.[7]

Sillitoe was certain that stomach troubles affected Peter's performance in the Games: 'I fully expected him to make the final and that was a disappointment. That certainly played a part. No shadow of a doubt.' Holdsworth went with Peter in an ambulance to the hospital and he agreed these problems certainly had a bearing on Peter's performance.

Peter recovered in sufficient time to run in two relay events. The team of Eddy, Holdsworth, Allan Crawley and Peter won a bronze medal behind Ghana and Jamaica in the 4 × 110 yards relay. Then the team of Gary Knoke, Noel Clough, Ken Roche and Peter, who was replacing the injured Eddy, finished fifth in the final of the 4 × 440 yards relay won by Trinidad and Tobago.

Overall the Australian athletics team won 21 medals at the Games, including eleven gold.[8] Noel Clough finally won gold with a stunning victory over a star-packed field in the 880 yards, setting a new Commonwealth Games record in the process. Three of his opponents – Bill Crothers (Canada), George Kerr (Jamaica) and Wilson Kiprugut (Kenya) – had been finalists in the 800 metres at the Tokyo Olympics two years before. That in itself would have made Clough's victory special, but coupled with this, Clough had been a borderline selection for the Games, having never won an Australian title or having ever been away from Australia on an overseas athletics trip.

Clough's win gave Peter and Holdsworth enormous satisfaction because they had witnessed the hard work Clough had put in over the previous two years. Clough did not compete for the East Melbourne Harriers, but he had been coached by Sillitoe in the two years before the Games.

Peter was disappointed with his efforts in Jamaica. He hadn't performed to the level that had given him his first Australian championship win a few months earlier. He returned to Melbourne more determined than ever to succeed in the upcoming interclub competitions, and to stamp his authority over his national rivals.

Melbourne always had a very strong interclub athletics competition, and the 1960s was no different. EMH was a B-grade team at this time because the club had no depth. It had great sprinters, but didn't have specialist shot-putters, discus and javelin throwers and the like. EMH's top sprinters – Holdsworth, Peter and Greg Lewis – would compete against three sprinters from another B-grade club in the 100 and 200 metres on alternate weeks. Points would be allocated to first, second and third. The teams would then compete later that same day in what were known as 'invitation events', which gave no points to clubs, but afforded the opportunity for the best athletes to run against each other. Most invitation events were run over 100 metres after all other events had finished.

Since EMH was essentially a team full of sprinters, Peter, Holdsworth and Lewis and others would often find themselves competing in some of the field events, often with interesting outcomes. Peter's former Collingwood Harriers teammate Bob Gardiner[9] recalled meeting Peter occasionally when EMH entered Lewis, Holdsworth and Peter in walking events when they really needed points approaching the finals. 'I'd be matched against Peter and Greg or Greg and Gary. So I can say I'm one of the few people who were faster over 50 metres than the best Australian sprinters because they'd walk about 50 metres, then pull out. You could do that then. You'd get points for starting.'

Interclub competition also threw up some fierce rivalries, such as that between EMH and Box Hill. According to Holdsworth, Box Hill was EMH's most hated opponent.

> We had a good team, good milers, good sprinters, good throwers, but Box Hill was better because they had a good all-round team. We struggled against Box Hill. They had sprinters like Gary Eddy and Byron Williams. Neville would stir us up by coming up with stories on special race days. 'I just heard that bloody Gary Eddy say …'.

By now Peter had discovered a powerful weapon – his finish.

> I first discovered that I was a fast finisher when running against Gary Eddy. Gary was an arch-rival, my nemesis you might say. It was once written that we didn't exactly see eye to eye off the track and didn't have much time for each other on the track either and that was true. I didn't like Gary because he was everything I wanted to be. He was tall, graceful, built like a greyhound and

> could run everything from 100 to 400 and win all three events. Gary was the best sprinter from another club in Victoria and one of the best-looking runners Australia has ever produced. He had more ability in his little finger than I had in my whole body.
>
> He'd get a lot of wins under his belt right up to Christmas, then Holdsworth, Lewis and I would take over and beat him up. I used to like beating him. That made my day. Whenever we raced, I always made sure I ran him down. It wouldn't matter how far behind I was, I'd throw my body all over the place to try and catch him. In most of the big races we ever had, it worked. Getting over the top of him at the fast end of a season was always a very good feeling.

Eddy was certainly a runner to be feared. Born in 1945, Eddy burst on to the athletics scene in 1962 as a schoolboy champion. He competed in the national 220 yards selection trials, but missed selection for that year's British Empire and Commonwealth Games. He was a quarter-finalist in the 400 metres at the 1964 Olympics. He won the 220 yards Australian championship in 1965 and followed that up by winning the 400 metres Australian championship in 1966. He ran fifth in the 100 yards and fourth in the 220 yards events at the 1966 Jamaican Games.

Eddy didn't like Peter: 'At one stage he was the only guy who could beat me and I was the only guy who could beat him. I got on with all the other guys, but for some strange reason Peter and I never got on. We never spoke or socialised. Even when we were away in teams, we never hung out together.' Much was made over the years of the fact that Eddy had been a schoolboy champion from a public school. Moreover, he could appear aloof to those who didn't know him well, but, in reality, he was somewhat introverted. He dismissed the public schoolboy theory.

> I went to a public school but I don't think that made any difference. It wasn't like my parents were particularly rich. In fact my father, being a real estate agent in the early 1960s, struggled to keep me at school because the credit squeeze was sending him broke. So it wasn't anything like that. I think it [Peter and Eddy's mutual dislike] was purely a personality-driven thing.

Eddy had great respect for Peter as an opponent and agreed that the rivalry was intense.

> Peter was a fantastic finisher. I've never seen an athlete who could pull out the last 30 or 40 metres of a race like he could. It was quite amazing. In the 100 he could also come home really quickly, but he just wasn't fast enough in the early part of the race to be in contention at the end. In the 200, he could really bring it home. He was incredibly good. When we came together in the 200 we had a really strong rivalry because in the end we never knew who was going to be the winner.
>
> Peter was very strong and something about his technique enabled him to really shift into another gear towards the end of the 200 metres. Where everyone else was slowing down, he could suddenly pick it up.

In trying to combat Peter's finishing burst, Eddy suggested, all you could do was hope that you were far enough in front at the finish: 'But Peter was a very stocky, strong and driving runner right to the very end. The 200 was perfect for him. When he was in form or in shape he was a very hard guy to beat.'

Eddy admitted that he and Peter most likely shook hands after a race because in those days it was the accepted thing to do, but hastened to add that it wasn't done in a friendly manner. Peter's 'God is love' tracksuit annoyed Eddy, who described himself as an agnostic.

> I've never really been religious. When Peter walked around with 'God is love' on his tracksuit, I thought that was ridiculous. It got up my nose. In those days you had to be reasonably extreme to do that. I sometimes think that those who say one thing and do other things are slightly hypocritical. How could Peter be a Salvation Army representative and have 'God is love' on his tracksuit and yet have such an attitude towards me.

Eddy did not deny that his attitude toward Peter was the same, but he expected someone who promoted such a message to be friendly to everybody.

Lewis rated Eddy as a brilliant runner, but believed that Eddy underachieved in his career. 'We never saw the best of Gary. Because he was so good and we recognised the talent he had, he came under a great deal of undue influence from all of us, basically because we feared his brilliance.' Through competing in interclub events and national championships, and from being teammates during the 1966 Games, Phil May knew Peter and Eddy well. Peter told him that Eddy was the only person in Australian track and field he was scared of: 'Normie was scared shitless of him. We all were because of his unbelievable ability.'

EMH's Graham Johnston incurred the wrath of Eddy's father on one occasion. Johnston remembered Peter springing to his defence at the time.

> Quite often, most of the EMH guys, particularly Peter, would go down to the finish line to watch my races. At the metric championships at Sandringham, I beat Gary over 100 metres and I was pretty pleased with the run. Gary's father was very competitive and always had a cheap shot at you. When I was running I must have wobbled my head a bit. Anyway Gary's father said to me something like, 'If you wobble your head any more, it will drop off.' I didn't say anything but Peter turned around and said, 'With the competition around here, he'd have enough time to go back and pick it up and still win.'

Notwithstanding the rivalry, one-time Box Hill captain Jeff Westlake always enjoyed competing against Peter in both interclub and Victorian championships. 'You could be at the start of a major meet, and even though you were serious and getting psyched up, Peter would wink at you. I'd nod to him and give him a wink and then we'd have a few words to say to each other.' Westlake said Peter was quite a personality out on the track: 'If you were running a 200 metres in the lane next to him, in the last few yards, when he knew he had us, he'd make little comments like, "Jeff, I'm afraid I'm going to have to go now." We'd all fall in a heap after the race.'

Westlake believed you could be strong rivals on the track, but friends off it. He was friendly with a number of EMH runners, probably more so than anyone at the Box Hill club. One particular event highlighted that friendship. He related the story:

> Just before the trials for the 1964 Tokyo Olympics, I had a very bad car smash near Kyabram [in rural Victoria]. I had several athletes in my car. There were about six soldiers in a Holden,

> which hit us head-on. The police were chasing them and I just happened to be in the wrong place at the wrong time. I got knocked around quite a bit. After I left hospital, Peter, Gary Holdsworth and Neville Sillitoe were the first to visit me at my home. You can be opponents, but you can be good friends too. I found Peter to be extremely generous and a lot of fun. He was never stand-offish. What you saw was what you got in a genuine way.

During this period of athletics in Australia, athletes were expected to run on all surfaces ranging from grass to bitumen rubber to cinder tracks. Some tracks were in very poor condition. Transferable spikes were not available at the time, so an athlete would have to own three or four pairs of running shoes. 'You couldn't get away with one pair,' said Holdsworth, 'because we'd run on grass one week, cinders the next, and something else the next. So we'd screw our spikes out and put on longer or shorter depending on the tracks we were running on.' Melbourne-based runners, such as Peter and Holdsworth, bought their running shoes from Hope Sweeney, who serviced both amateur and professional athletes at his premises at 246 Little Bourke Street, Melbourne. Sweeney's spikes were handmade from the very best kangaroo leather. They were tight-fitting, moulded to the athlete's feet, had no padding and had the appearance of a pair of ballet slippers. They were far from comfortable and were very expensive, but Sweeney did a roaring trade. His store was seen as the 'mecca'.

Peter finally won his first Victorian 220 yards championship on 4 February 1967. He had been chasing this state title for six seasons. In a particularly well-judged race, Peter finished two yards ahead of the favourite, Eddy, with Lewis third. Peter's time of 21.0 seconds equalled the Victorian open record shared by Eddy and 1956 Olympic Games sprint champion Bob Morrow. Three specially placed timekeepers clocked Peter at 20.8 seconds at the 200 metres mark. This equalled the Australian record held by Lay and Lewis.

Peter hit top form at the right time. At the Australian championships at Adelaide's Olympic sports field on 25 February 1967, Peter finished fourth in the final of the 100 metres behind Holdsworth, Lay and Lewis. The following day, he won the final of the 200 metres ahead of Eddy and Holdsworth. That same day, the Victorian team of Eddy, Holdsworth, Peter and Lewis won the 4 × 100 metres relay national title.

By far the biggest event in 1967 was the birth of Janita Maree Norman on 11 February at Williamstown Hospital. Janita's birth was an exciting time for Peter and Ruth. 'Janita was the first grandchild on the Norman side,' said Ruth. 'Peter chose the name after a Spanish song "Juanita" but we changed it to Janita because it was easier to spell.' In between working, training and competing, Peter tried to spend as much time as possible getting to know his daughter. This wasn't easy in the early weeks of her life as he had to keep focused on the forthcoming Australian championships. It wasn't easy on Ruth either. Money was tight, so she had to go back to her job as a secretary for an engineering firm six weeks after Janita's birth.

Peter had enjoyed most aspects of athletics up to this time.

> I enjoyed the company of teammates, the competition, the travel and seeing my name in the paper. There were no monetary gains, but it was all just for the thrill of the chase and the small amount of adulation you were able to get from performing well. There was a little bit of newsprint and television, but most of that adulation came from family, friends, teammates and competitors alike.

Training during winter was the one aspect Peter never enjoyed. He chose not to train during the winter of 1967 – the thought of it was hard enough, without even taking into consideration Janita's arrival. By the time the 1967–68 athletics season started, Peter was not in any shape to compete.

By mid November, it looked unlikely that Peter would compete that season, but two events fired him into action. In late November, Sillitoe invited Peter to act as a projectionist showing a film about the 1956 Olympics to children at the Tally Ho Boys' Home. 'The cunning blighter knew exactly what he was doing,' said Peter.

> He knew the way I'd react. After watching Betty [Cuthbert], Marlene [Matthews], John Landy, Hec Hogan and all the great track-and-field stars of 1956, we drove home without even saying a word to each other. As I pulled up outside his place to let him out, I just said to him, 'Nev, do you think I could make it back?' It was as if he was expecting it. He just said, 'Well you wouldn't want to miss another night's training between now and the nationals. And we start at four o'clock tomorrow.'

So began the long, hard road back. Peter was barely back in training when the second event occurred. Tommie Smith came to Australia in December 1967 to run in a series of meets in Melbourne, Adelaide and Brisbane. Even though listed as a definite starter in 'The Recordbreakers' souvenir program, Peter was in no shape to compete against Smith in the meet held at Melbourne's Olympic Park on 13 December 1967. Nevertheless, Peter attended and it really got up his nose to see arch-rival Eddy defeat Smith over 220 yards. Eddy won by a foot in 21.2 seconds, with Lewis a yard behind in third place. Eddy rightly described the win as one of his greatest thrills in athletics. Smith told sportswriter Jack Dunn that it was only the second time he had been beaten over 220 yards. 'That guy [Eddy] was way out there from the time we left the blocks,' said Smith, 'and I could not make up the ground to him. The soft track was a worry, but I could not blame that for my defeat. I am below my best form, and I really tired over the last ten yards.'[10]

Before the meeting was over, the fire had ignited in Peter. 'I'd missed running against Tommie, but I told him that I'd see him in Mexico, half jokingly … I was down in the mouth that night because I wasn't fit enough to run against him.' The *Sun* newspaper's front-page photo the following day showing Eddy flashing over the line to beat Smith was the final straw. Peter was now fiercely determined to do whatever it would take to race Smith for gold in the 1968 Mexico City Olympics. Peter's win in the Australian 200 metres national championship in March 1968 cemented his Olympic selection.

NOTES

1 'Runner with a message', *The Sun*, 31 May 1966.

2 The Games were held from 4–13 August 1966.

3 Sport in Australia has been characterised by a long-standing and intense rivalry with the British, affectionately known as Poms.

4 '5 Australians in shambles', *The Sun*, 9 August 1966.

5 Dick Leffler won four more national titles, as well as finishing second and third on two other occasions. He, Peter and Phil May developed a very strong friendship on the Jamaica trip. Leffler took great delight in watching Peter and May imitate his voice and his mannerisms. 'We would send him up,' said May, 'and he would laugh his head off. He was a beautiful man!'

6 Pam Kilborn had previously won the 80 metres hurdles and the long jump at the 1962 Games.

7 'Three in hospital', *The Sun*, 10 August 1966.

8 Some notable wins were Judy Pollock for the inaugural 440 yards event, Michele Mason-Brown the high jump and Margaret Parker the javelin. Ken Roche retained his 440 yard hurdles title, as did Trevor Bickle in the pole vault.

9 Bob Gardiner was one of Australia's finest-ever walkers, winning eight national titles and finishing in second or third place in eight other championships. He finished fifth in the 50 kilometre walk in the 1964 Olympics and won a silver medal in the 20 mile walk in the 1970 Commonwealth Games.

10 'Smith beaten in sprint sensation', *The Sun*, 14 December 1967.

10

PAYING THE PRICE

The Mexico City Games closed on 27 October 1968 with a streamlined ceremony in an attempt to avoid a repetition of what officials described, at the time, as the 'shambles' at the end of the 1964 Tokyo Games. In Mexico City, a maximum of six team members, plus a flag standard bearer, from each competing nation were permitted to enter the Olympic stadium infield to take part in the closing ceremony. All other competitors and officials watched the ceremony from the stands. But as cannons roared and fireworks blazed, athletes from all nations 'not in the official party of six from each nation jumped the fence and ran on to the infield' to join in the celebrations.[1]

Australia won seventeen medals – five gold, seven silver and five bronze – at the Games. Three gold medals were won in swimming: Michael Wenden, the 100 and 200 metres freestyle events; and Lyn McClements, the women's 100 metres butterfly. Two gold medals were won in athletics. Ralph Doubell won the first, defeating Kenya's pre-race favourite, Wilson Kiprugut, to take out the 800 metres. At the 600 metres mark, Kiprugut had a 6 metre lead, which Doubell gradually pulled back drawing level with the Kenyan shortly after entering the home straight. He went on to win by a metre. His time of 1 minute 44.3 seconds equalled Peter Snell's world record at the time and still stands as the Australian record. Seventeen-year-old Maureen Caird defeated her Australian teammate Pam Kilborn to take out gold in the 80 metres hurdles. In winning gold, Caird became the last 80 metres hurdles Olympic champion, as the event was replaced at the 1972 Olympics.

Kilborn should not even have been at the Games, let alone have won a silver medal. While training the day before the team left for Mexico, she fell face first on to the cinder track at Melbourne's Olympic Park, fracturing a shoulder and losing a great deal of skin from her face, arms and legs. She required injections in both arms and legs before having cinders removed from her body. She refused an X-ray on her shoulder, knowing that officials would drop her from the team once the full extent of her injuries became known. She was 'as sick as a dog' on the plane to Sydney later that same day. She did not sleep that night and continued to suffer intense pain on the plane trip to Mexico the following day. On the day of the hurdles final, Kilborn was still unable to put her injured arm down on the track for the set position, let alone hurdle at the standard that had made her the best hurdler in the world for the previous four years. Her efforts to compete in Mexico, winning a silver medal in the driving rain that fell through the event, can only be described as one of the most courageous and gutsy performances in Australian Olympic history.

Australia's other silver medals were won by Raelene Boyle (200 metres sprint), the men's hockey team, the men's rowing eights, the men's 4 × 200 metres freestyle relay swimming team and the women's 4 × 100 metres medley relay swimming team. Bronze medals were won by Jenny Lamy (200 metres sprint), Karen Moras (400 metres freestyle), Greg Brough (1500 metres freestyle), the men's 4 × 100 metres freestyle swimming relay team and the three-day equestrian team.

Judy Patching, general manager of the Australian Olympic team, said the team did their country proud in more ways than one.

> Apart from visiting the team in the village on a number of occasions, Australia's first ambassador to Mexico, Dudley McCarthy, invited [AOF secretary] Sir Edgar Tanner and I to his home for lunch. He told us that our success in Mexico had made his job so much easier. It had opened so many doors for him and our nation had benefited accordingly. He'd also informed the prime minister, John Gorton, on that score. So the team's success not only reflected on their ability athletically, but diplomatically

> and trade-wise as well. I ultimately got a cable from the prime minister complimenting the team on its achievements. They're the sorts of things that far outweigh the American 'political' interference that we received in Mexico!

Peter enjoyed the success of all his teammates, but would always have a soft spot for Boyle.

> Raelene was a blond-headed ragamuffin who trained at Royal Park where we used to train. It was fascinating to watch Raelene go through her paces, this lithe young kid who could run like the wind, but seemed to spend a lot of time jogging or walking around talking to her girlfriends. Raelene originally got into the team for Mexico more for experience than anything else, but she proved everybody wrong when she won herself a silver medal. She is probably the best-credentialed short sprinter that Australia has ever produced on the international scene.

Boyle said the fact that Peter was a schoolteacher and she was a schoolgirl, both from Melbourne, and that they both won silver medals in the 200 metres, created a bond between them.

> He wasn't expected to win a medal. I was only sent to Mexico to get experience and I came away with a silver medal and a fourth place. He was a great personality. He laughed a lot. He was one of the key figures that pulled the team together as a unit. It stands out in my memory, because I was so young and impressionable, as one of the best teams that ever went away in my era because of this bonding, because of the success. It was a very tight team. The older members were very protective of the younger members and guided us through, even though in many instances they hadn't had much experience either.

Boyle contended that Mexico was Peter's moment in the sun.

> It was the tartan track, the atmosphere, rising to the challenge, all of that. Not every athlete that goes to the Olympic Games has the right moment. It was just perfect for Peter and he loved the atmosphere and the elevated altitude obviously made a difference to him. And not only from the running point of view, but also from

> the lifelong friendships he made with Tommie and John. John Carlos is a very big personality. Tommie is a quite conservative gentleman, whereas John was full of bullshit and jigged and bobbed around. John was a rough nut. He always seemed to be bopping to the music and tracking as they called it. They were just worlds-apart characters who created the universal storm.
>
> By beating John and by taking the actions he did after the race, Peter gained John's respect. Knowing Peter, he would have been friendly after the race. He would have congratulated everyone and he would have been really excited. It was a major breakthrough for an Australian male sprinter to win a medal.

Boyle not only admired Peter as a person, but also as an athlete.

> I loved watching Peter run because, unlike many of Neville Sillitoe's group, Peter actually had a very fine running style. I loved watching people run that had classic styles. Even though he wasn't a big man, he had a beautiful high knee lift and a great arm action that complemented that and he worked his whole body. Not everybody did that. Peter was a classical runner. I used to love watching him come off the turn in the 200 metres because he looked like he was going to blow a valve. It was like he was holding his breath and he was going red in the face. In his peak days, he was driving so hard. After coming second in Mexico, I used to watch him with great interest, expecting one day that he'd have a major breakthrough again where he'd come through with a 20-and-a-bit [seconds] run again.

As predicted, Mexico City's high altitude led to world records in the women's 100 and 200 metres and the 4 × 100 metres relay[2] and the men's 100, 200 and 400 metres (the 800 metres time was equalled) and both relays. New records were also set in the women's and men's long jump and the men's triple jump. Bob Beamon's phenomenal leap of 8.90 metres absolutely destroyed the previous record. By contrast, the rarefied air proved disastrous for many leading athletes competing in endurance events from 1500 metres up to the marathon. These events were won by African athletes in times significantly slower than those achieved at lower altitude.

Australia's Ron Clarke was the world-record holder for both the 5000 and 10 000 metres, and was seen as a strong chance for both events by many sportswriters. Clarke, however, rated his chances in both events as slim at best. He had visited Mexico City previously and knew the effect altitude would have on him and other athletes based at sea level. Nevertheless, with some 600 metres to run in the 10 000 metres race, on the opening day of track-and-field competition, Clarke was up with the race leaders, Naftali Temu (Kenya), Mamo Wolde (Ethiopa) and Mohamed Gammoudi (Tunisia).

A few metres later, however, Clarke was in big trouble. Australian team doctor Brian Corrigan described how Clarke had run out of oxygen and was semiconscious at that point: 'How he ever managed to finish the race remains a mystery,' said Corrigan. 'But finish he did. It took an incredible effort of will on the part of Clarke to complete the race in sixth place, the first non-altitude runner to finish. His willpower was greater than I could ever imagine.' Clarke dramatically collapsed right under the IOC sign at the finish line. He later told Corrigan, 'I had to finish. It was a question of pride'. Corrigan rushed to Clarke's side. By this time Clarke was completely unconscious and remained so for over an hour. Corrigan pumped oxygen into Clarke's unconscious body and cradled him in his arms trackside.

> I burst into tears. I couldn't help it and I realised that courage alone would never be sufficient to overcome the problems caused by the stupidity of the IOC. Here in my arms was this great athlete who virtually had to kill himself in order to prove that these Olympics should never have been held here.[3]

Alan Trengove subsequently described Corrigan's embrace of Clarke as 'one of the most definitive moments in the history of Australian sport'.[4]

Although still in bad shape from his heroic run in the 10 000 metres, Clarke ran in a heat of the 5000 metres two days later, then a day later ran in the final of that event. Ron bravely fought on to finish in fifth place behind Gammoudi, Kip Keino and Temu (Kenya), and Mexico's Juan Martínez. Clarke's Olympic career was then over.[5]

Australia's efforts in Mexico saw it finish in sixth place among the nations competing in track-and-field athletics. The only small nation to finish higher than Australia was Kenya. Mexico's high altitude was certainly a factor in Kenya's success in distance events. Finishing ahead of

Australia were the USA (first), Russia (second), East Germany (third) and West Germany (fourth), all major athletic powers at the time.

Peter asserted

> It's been proved since that this was the best track-and-field team that's ever left these shores. Fifteen of the twenty-four athletes finished in the top ten in their events. A lot of that has to be put down to the support everyone gave each other for the whole time we were away, and part of our success is certainly owed to Ray Weinberg [the coach of the 1968 Australian Olympic athletics team].

As for his own performances in Mexico, Peter said that every run he had there was better than his personal best, so he came away very happy.[6]

> Cordner Nelson wrote in *Track and Field News*[7] that there was a sub-20 in me. He said that with the improvement I showed in Mexico, there's no doubt had I stayed for another three weeks I would have gone away the world-record holder. I found that to be perhaps a long bow, but it's nice of someone of that stature to say that.

Nelson actually said that if Peter had stayed in Mexico City much longer, he might have gone home a world-record holder.

Peter believed he could have run under 20 seconds had he again had conditions similar to Mexico.

> By conditions I don't mean altitude. I mean the same type of competition, the atmosphere of the Olympics and the type of track that was there. We came back from Mexico to cinder tracks and didn't see another synthetic track till the following year when I was in the States again. But we didn't have any tartan tracks at home for a long time. The best I could manage back on cinders I think was 20.4 on several occasions. I just couldn't get the lifts out of the tracks.

Notwithstanding his great delight and pride in winning the silver medal, Peter would often express his views about the Olympics in years to come.

> On one day every four years you get your chance to put your performance down the line. Some of us get lucky and get our

> greatest performance ever out on that one day. On the 16th of October 1968, I was the second fastest man in the world over 200 metres at 5.50 in the afternoon. Run it two hours later, two hours before, the next day, the day before and maybe I wouldn't have been.

Sillitoe contended that Peter was never given the credit that he deserved for his consistent performances in Mexico, especially in Australia.

> Peter's performance against such classy athletes to win the silver medal was never recognised as it should have been by people in Australia. It's more recognised in the States than here. Hec Hogan won a bronze medal in Melbourne and that was great, but Peter's were the best performances by any sprinter that Australia has ever had.

Sillitoe will never forget catching up with Peter on his return from Mexico: 'The first time I saw him, he said, "You've changed my life". I said, "I hope for the better!"'

On his return, Peter received a 'lot of lovely letters' that agreed with what Tommie Smith and John Carlos had done on the dais. A number of writers even pointed out that these men were heroes of their country.

> I agreed with these letter writers. I also got quite a few letters that suggested that if I wanted to do something like wearing an Olympic Project for Human Rights badge, and agreed with these two guys, then why don't I go over and live with them. Letters, notes and a few phone calls came in on a fairly regular basis for probably six months and then on an intermittent basis for the next twelve months.

Peter contended that it was good that the threatened boycott of the Olympic Games by African-American athletes never came to pass.

> Had it been carried out, it would have taken away one platform they had to make a stand. It was proved in a very real way with what Tommie and John did on the dais. If the boycott had gone ahead, white America would have said such things as those black guys won't represent their country, they're scared to get beaten, they don't deserve to be Americans, when you need them

> they're not there, they run away from a fight; all that sort of thing would have been pointed at them. By going to the Games and succeeding as they did, white America sat up and took notice. They were American sporting heroes. Had they not performed as well, they would have just been nobodies and treated like dirt.

He hastened to add that parts of white America despised them for what they did. 'White America was being shown up in a bad way because of statements that they made. Strangely enough some African-Americans didn't think much of the act either for quite a long time.' Peter believed that the 'statement' that they made hurt only Carlos and Smith.

> It had a pretty big impact on them. John and his wife split up because of the pressure brought to bear on them. Tommie's marriage broke up as well. Tommie and John had hate mail, and they and their families had death threats for years afterwards. They went through a living hell for many years.

Smith recalled receiving many threats and having rocks thrown into the windows of his home.

> People also heckled me as I drove down the street, and heckled my wife as she went down town to shop with the little money we did have. In classes where the instructors sometimes wouldn't even look in my direction, you can feel the negative awe around one and I always thought about dying.[8]

Carlos feared first and foremost for his family during the years of death threats. He sheltered his kids. He didn't let them know what was happening outside.

> My first wife took her life 'cause she couldn't deal with it no more. It was tough for them to see their mother take the back door and leave this world saying I can't handle this no more. I had to embrace my kids, protect them in school. Once a teacher found out John Carlos was their father, the teacher turned very negative towards my kids merely because I was their father. I had to deal with the teacher and tell my kids it's not your fault.[9]

In comparison, Peter was never really threatened in any way and wasn't hurt by the statement made by Smith and Carlos. 'I was damn proud to be part of it. I felt the repercussions a little further down the track when it was considered that I probably wasn't the right person to take away on Games trips any more.'

Ruth didn't think at the time that Peter's success in Mexico altered him as a person. Looking back 40 years later, however, she believed that Peter became a more worldly person after his Olympic experiences. He was a seasoned traveller and he was taking a far greater interest in what was happening in the world, particularly with respect to civil rights issues. He was in demand to give interviews to media. He also began to do a lot of public speaking, particularly to church groups to whom he spoke about Mexico and leading the life of a Christian athlete. 'Our lives weren't our own,' said Ruth. 'It became a way of life. We accepted it, but it was a pretty full-on lifestyle. We both worked full-time, and we did these things at weekends and on weeknights. We just took it a day at a time. As things happened, you just did it.'

Ruth recalled that after Mexico she and others in the Norman family lost their identities to some degree: 'You were always introduced as Peter's wife, or Peter's mother, or Peter's sister or Peter's brother. Not by your own name.'

Peter didn't talk to Ruth in great detail about Mexico or what transpired on the dais or the background to the protest. 'I don't think we knew a lot about all that happened in Mexico. I certainly had no idea. I'm not sure how he coped.' Ruth saw it as her role to support Peter in whatever he did.

> I never put any constraints on him. He was his own person. All the years that he was running, it was quite full-on. It wasn't a normal-type marriage. I always stayed with the Normans if he went away, unless I had an opportunity to go with him. There was no money in those days. There were no sponsorships or incentives. If he went to a meet and won, you'd get a towel or a breadknife or breadboard.

It was expensive to travel to athletics events and to the various speaking engagements, many of which were in country regions some distance from Melbourne. Ruth recalled, 'Going to all these places was quite expensive. I continued to work. I had to, because of Peter's lifestyle. Money was always a concern, but we always somehow got by in the end.'

NOTES

1 'Olympic closing changes', *Cairns Post*, 28 October 1968.

2 The USA's Wyomia Tyus told a press conference that the team dedicated their relay win to John Carlos and Tommie Smith; 'Black power solidarity', *Adelaide Advertiser*, 23 October 1968.

3 Brian Corrigan, *The Life of Brian – Confessions of an Olympic Doctor*, ABC Books, Sydney, 2001, pp. 7, 90.

4 Corrigan, *The Life of Brian – Confessions of an Olympic Doctor*, p. 7.

5 Ron Clarke may never have won an Olympic gold medal on the track, but he was awarded one off the track in 1966 by Emil Zátopek, the great Czech distance runner. Zátopek presented Clarke with the gold medal he had won in the 1952 Helsinki Olympic 10 000 metres event because he strongly believed Clarke deserved to have won an Olympic gold medal. Clarke's string of world records – including the three miles, six miles, 5000 and 10 000 metres – set in the mid 1960s, ensure that he is long-remembered as one of the finest distance runners of all time. He is also revered for his fine sportsmanship, both on and off the track, as is Zátopek.

6 Peter's electronic times in Mexico were as follows: first heat 20.23, second heat 20.44, semi-final 20.22 and final 20.06. At the time of writing, Peter's time remains the Australian record for the 200 metres, and his silver medal win is still the best achievement by an Australian male sprinter at the Olympics. His time in the final in Mexico would have won him gold at the 2000 Sydney Olympics.

7 October–November 1968.

8 'Seasons', Channel 7, Melbourne, 1993.

9 John Carlos, interview footage, *Salute*, 2008.

11

THE BIG SHOE SCANDAL

Shortly before the 1968 Olympic Games closing ceremony, rumours spread throughout the Olympic Village that three US athletes had accepted money from an unnamed sporting-goods manufacturer to wear their gear. The Australian press speculated that Tommie Smith was one of the athletes and that he could be stripped of his 200 metres gold medal.

> Peter Norman, Australia's 200 metres silver medallist, could be awarded the gold medal in a startling sequel to the Olympic 'payola' scandal now raging over the heads of several US track stars. One of the American athletes expected to face charges of professionalism is Tommie Smith, the negro 'Black Power' flash who beat Norman in the 200 metres final last week.[1]

According to the press, the allegations of payments were under investigation by the US Olympic Committee, the International Olympic Committee and the International Amateur Athletic Federation. It was said that the investigation started when an athlete reported he had found a $500 'gift' in his track shoe.

> If the investigation reveals evidence to show Smith broke the rules of amateurism, he could be asked to hand back his medal.[2] Norman, as second-place-getter, would receive the gold. 'It's an awful way

> to get a gold medal,' Norman said. 'As far as I'm concerned I ran second, whether they give me gold, silver or a bottle top.'
>
> The payola scandal centres around two European sports shoe manufacturers. It is suggested one company has been paying some track stars to use their shoes. Claims that two men are receiving $400 a month for their athletic life to race exclusively in one brand of shoes, while another man is on a $6000 a year contract, have been circulating for some weeks. One of the athletes in the American relay team is reportedly involved in the scandal and was under suspicion at the time he received his gold medal.[3]

Larry Questad, who finished sixth in the 200 metres final, was the athlete reported to have found money in his track shoe. Questad described how, between the semi-final and the final, he went back to the Olympic Village because he had some problems with his running shoes. He took them to the Adidas tent for attention. He later picked them up and returned to his room in the village, psyching himself up for the 200 metres final later that evening. 'I noticed there was a wad of money in the toe of my shoe. I was still a naive Montana kid to think, "What in the world is going on here? What's this money mean?"' Questad said he panicked and went to coach Payton Jordan and gave him the money.

> I was basically terrified. Here I was gonna win a medal and I'm going to lose it 'cause someone's going to find out I've got this money. I can only surmise it came from the Adidas people for me wearing Adidas shoes. I found out later after my race that other people were taking significantly more money than what I was given in this pair of shoes.[4]

Unbeknown to many at the time, Peter had already received payment from Adidas, thereby violating Olympic and amateur rules and regulations, as he related.

> In the pre-Games event I ran 20.3, which equalled the Olympic record, although it didn't count because it was outside the Olympics. One of the first to congratulate me was David Jones, the Puma rep who was a mate of mine.[5] He said if I'd been wearing the right shoes I would have broken the Olympic record,

> not just equalled it. With that, Horst Dassler [son of Adidas's founder Adi Dassler] came storming across the track and asked what had Jones said to me. I told him. He then said, 'Whatever he offers you is covered.' I went back to David Jones and told him. He said, 'Okay let's say you're on $500 to change shoes.' But he knew I was not going to change. Adidas covered it, so I got $500 to keep wearing Adidas.
>
> Just before the semi-finals, Jones came up and said, 'It's not a joke any more. We're serious. You're on a grand to wear the shoes and you're on $1500 if you run a place.' So I told Adidas. Covered! After the semi-final, it became very serious. Jones came to me and said, 'Mate, if you run first or second you're on double.' I couldn't find Horst to tell him. I had Puma shoes in my bag that I had worn in training, just in case, but when push came to shove, I stayed with Adidas. So Adidas split Puma. It was nothing more than loyalty because Adidas had looked after me. They'd given me shoes and stuff up until then. Tommie and John wore Puma, but being able to say we got first and third wasn't worth a lot of coin to Puma. But can you imagine the pulling power there would have been for Puma if I'd worn Puma shoes! That photo with the three of us with Puma, how much would that have been worth?
>
> Adi Dassler recognised that I'd done the right thing by the firm, and after the final he came over and said, 'You are on gold for life. Whatever you need any time, just let us know.' Two days before Christmas that year, this big parcel arrived by courier. It contained a crystal decanter and six glasses and a beautiful mohair rug with Adidas all over it. This was a Christmas present from Adi Dassler, which I was pretty rapt in.[6]

Peter's room-mate, high jumper Lawrie Peckham, witnessed Peter receiving money from Adidas: 'Before the final, a pair of Adidas shoes stuffed with a wad of money was delivered to Peter. I would have thought it was more than US $1000, but that would be the minimum. It was a real eye-opener.'

Greg Lewis recalled going out to celebrate with Peter and a small group of Australian athletes, including Peckham, May and boxer Ray Maguire after the 200 metres final.

> A select few of us went down to our favourite haunt, the Sanbourne bar in Mexico City, which was attached to a reasonable restaurant. We've gone down with this $1000 American. We've never seen $100 bills before, let alone spent it. You can get a terrific round of drinks with that! I was drinking brandy. We had a ball being served by 'Peanuts Charlie', our favourite waiter. That was a most memorable thing, spending money from athletics!

Peckham recalled going to the Sanbourne that night: 'We didn't get pissed but I certainly had a few. I remember how important the medal was to Peter. He won it before I competed [in the high jump on 19 October]. I couldn't sleep. Each time I opened my eyes, he was sitting up in bed looking at the medal. All night he just looked at it.'

Gary Holdsworth said Peter told him on his return to Australia that he received ten US $100 bills from Adidas. 'Peter told us, in hushed whispers and in strictest confidence, about the money. That was a secret. He would have been branded a professional had it been discovered.' Ruth recalled that when Peter arrived home from Mexico, he had his silver medal in a presentation box. 'Underneath the medal was the money, the $1000, which he gave to me. I hadn't seen American money before that, nor had I ever seen that much money in my life. We didn't have a television, so we bought a black-and-white television set with the money, as well as a cooling fan ... you weren't allowed to be paid in those days. So it was given as "a gift" from Adi Dassler.' Ruth said this was the first time she had ever spoken about the money.

An article in the *Nation* magazine put, what became known as 'the big shoe scandal', into proper perspective.

> The as yet unsubstantiated rumours of money improperly distributed to allegedly amateur contestants, in themselves disagreeable, emphasise once again the hypocrisy of the Olympic rules. All athletes of Olympic calibre are subsidised in one way or another; the standards which must be met in modern world competition are so high that no one can train for them after hours. The antiquated notion of amateurism should be scrapped, and a superb performer should be acknowledged worthy of his hire.[7]

Commonsense prevailed and the controversy gradually died down.

NOTES

1 'Payola claim shocks Mexico', unsourced press clipping, 20 October 1968.

2 There was a precedent for the returning of medals. In the 1912 Olympics, Native American Jim Thorpe was forced to return the gold medals he won in the pentathlon and decathlon events after it was revealed that he had accepted a small amount of money for playing baseball.

3 'Payola claim shocks Mexico', unsourced press clipping, 20 October 1968.

4 Larry Questad, interview footage, *Salute*, 2008.

5 Peter told his wife, Ruth, in a postcard written the night before what he described as 'the big day' [the 200 metres final], 'the shoe war is still going on. I have now got three pairs of Puma and three pairs of /// [signifying Adidas], that's about even so far …'.

6 Peter received Christmas presents from Dassler for the next two years after the Olympics. 'Then Adi went to God and things changed, but that still didn't take away my loyalty to the firm. If I needed a pair of track shoes after I stopped running, I'd call Ted Whitten or Bob Lay and I could go out and pick up a pair of shoes and a pair of shorts or whatever. Bob was always there to help out, along with the great EJ Whitten, who was an Australian Rules footballer known as "Mr Football". He was also known as "Mr Adidas" at the time. I never ever abused it. The only stuff I ever got was what I needed personally.'

7 *The Nation*, 11 November 1968.

12

HOW ARE YOU GONNA GET DOWN THAT HILL?

On 7 January 1969 Peter won his first Victorian 100 metres sprint title at the John Landy Field in Geelong, a city south of Melbourne. Greg Lewis and Gary Holdsworth came second and third. All three place-getters clocked 10.4 seconds, only 0.1 seconds outside the state record and 0.2 seconds slower than the national record. Peter told reporters that he was 'tickled pink' with his win. His good form continued through January and February. He won the Victorian 220 yards title on 15 January 1969, and then narrowly won against Lewis the Victorian 200 metres title six days later. Lewis charged past Peter around the bend and hung on in the straight until the last nine metres, when Peter slowly pegged him back and passed him to win by half a metre.

Peter won the New South Wales 200 metres championship on 22 February 1969 on the newly laid tartan track at Sydney's ES Marks Field. He was now outright favourite for the national title. 'No one will beat Peter Norman at this distance for a long time if one can judge by his running at the New South Wales championships … His seasonal best time of 20.5 seconds is shown to be so far ahead of the rest of the country by the fact that no one else has yet broken 21 seconds.'[1] At the 'Courage Olympian' athletics meeting at Olympic Park in Melbourne on 26 February 1969 Peter took out both the 100 and 200 metres events. His 10.3 seconds in the 100 metres equalled the Victorian residential record,[2] but the time was disallowed because of wind assistance.

Peter's outstanding season continued at the Australian championships at Melbourne's Olympic Park in late March 1969. He finished second to Lewis in the final of the 100 metres, both runners clocking 10.6 seconds. Peter turned the tables in the 200 metres, winning in 21.3 seconds. Peter then teamed with Victorian teammates Lewis, Gary Eddy and Holdsworth to win the national 4 × 100 metres relay title.

On 18 May 1969 Peter competed, by special invitation, against John Carlos, Bill Gaines, Ronnie Ray Smith, Lionel Urgan and Charlie Greene in the inaugural Martin Luther King International Freedom Games in Philadelphia, USA. Peter was deeply honoured to be the only non-African-American to compete in the Games, which were established in memory of the civil rights leader. Peter was also pleased to have the opportunity to spend time getting to know John Carlos.

Peter was back on US soil two months later, having been selected to compete in the Commonwealth versus USA meet in Los Angeles. The Australian members of the Commonwealth team trained at the University of Hawaii en route to Los Angeles. While in Hawaii, Peter and Phil May went for a stroll one evening to have what they thought would be the odd beer or two. 'We were walking back to our quarters,' said May, 'and there's "Los" (Carlos) sitting outside the Coral Reef hotel. We all exchanged hugs and greetings and then we went to the bar next door and drank buckets of beer! It was so good. Two days later we had to run. Not so good!'

It was on this trip that some Australians developed the catchphrase – 'How are you gonna get down that hill?' – that they used when in 'combat'. The catchphrase was a line used during a fierce gunfight in the Paul Newman and Richard Boone movie *Hombre*, which Peter, May, Lewis, Lawrie Peckham and Billy Hooker had seen at the University of Southern California campus where they were quartered. 'We would be in situations on the track,' recalled May, 'and we'd eyeball each other and say, "How are you gonna get down that hill?" It was a situational thing. Sometimes they were as tough as shit and when they're as tough as shit, you've just got to get on with it.' Peckham, who roomed with Peter on the 1969 trip, said Peter loved the *Hombre* story. From that time on 'How are you gonna get down that hill?' was used 'for anybody who was in trouble'.

The Commonwealth versus USA meeting was held at the LA Coliseum on 18–19 July 1969. Peter finished third in the 200 metres behind Carlos and his US teammate Tom Randolph. But much to his great delight, Peter was a member of the winning 4 × 100 metres relay team – in running order, Lewis, Peter, Lennox Miller and Don Quarrie – that beat the USA team in 39.4 seconds. The relay win remains one of Lewis's fondest athletics memories. He can still visualise Peter charging down the back straight, passing the baton to Lennox Miller, who ran the corner and 'gave it off to a young whippersnapper of a kid called Donald Quarrie. We beat the USA on their own soil. It didn't get any publicity but we loved it. It was one of the few times their national team has ever been beaten. We got a beaut little plate as a trophy'.

Peckham remembered the alternative competition, the 'nude Olympics' held on the same trip.

> After the main competition was over, one hot night at USC, we were all bored out of our minds, so we had a nude race. We dropped our gear and headed off towards this fountain, which was probably about 300 or 400 metres away. Peter and I got to a hedge that surrounded the fountain. I tried to hurdle it, then slipped and skidded through. Peter ran into a post and was a little worse off.

Phil May added that Billy Hooker was involved as well: 'Billy banged his knee up.'

In September 1969, Peter represented Australia in the inaugural Pacific Conference Games in Tokyo, Japan. At the request of the Australian government, and with the approval of the Australian Athletic Union, the team staged a meeting in Port Moresby en route to Tokyo. Peter competed in the long jump. With one of his early jumps he set a Papua and New Guinean record. 'Peter jumped 24 feet 2.5 inches and broke the record all right,' noted May. 'He came back laughing his head off, and saying to me, "I've broken the record!" I said, "Yeah, for about 30 seconds mate."' May duly broke Peter's record with his next jump of 25 feet 0.5 inch. In ensuing years, Peter took great delight in telling all and sundry how he had held the Papua and New Guinean long jump record, albeit for the briefest of times.

Australia dominated the Pacific Conference Games, held on 27 and 28 September, winning fifteen of the 32 events contested between athletes from Japan, New Zealand, Canada, the USA and Australia. Peter finished fourth in the 100 metres race, won the 200 metres and ran with with Lewis, Murray Tolbert and May to win the 4 × 100 metres relay. Peter wasn't renowned for being in such top form so early in the season, so his performances at these Games indicated that a promising home season lay ahead.

May looked back on the relay win as being a 'How are you gonna get down that hill?' situation.

> Normally Lewie would run the first curb, then hand over to me, giving me a full flying run down the back. But on this occasion we couldn't do it that way because Murray Tolbert couldn't handle the change from Lewie. So I had to run the third leg around the curve. I'm 6 foot 5 inches and I'm like a giraffe on rollerskates. I don't run curbs very well. Anyway Murray hands off to me and I run my guts out totally. I sent Peter off early. I thought, 'shit or bust'. I'm going to either over-run him or all of a sudden his afterburners are going to kick in and I'm going to be left behind. I came in shouting at him. He went and I caught him. Normie had to anchor against the USA's Ivory Crockett, the 100 yards world record holder. He caught Crockett on the line. Nailed his butt! That's one of the things I remember Peter for. He could have come second, but he didn't!

Australian coach Ray Weinberg shared a room with Peter, Peckham and Lewis in Tokyo. By his own admission, and as his room-mates were well aware, Peter was an 'unabashed, one-eyed, parochial, true-blue' supporter of the Carlton Australian Rules football team.[3] On his arrival in Tokyo, Peter had laid out a big Carlton flag on the dressing table alongside his bed, so as to show his support for Carlton, who were due to play Richmond in the Victorian Football League grand final later that week. Much to Peter's disappointment, Carlton lost. 'We had a wonderful fellow in the team, Keith Wheeler, who was a Church of England minister,' said Weinberg. 'Peter said, "We've gotta do something about Carlton going down the drain". So Keith conducted a service and we had a wake over the Carlton flag and burnt it.' Peckham took great delight in seeing Peter's flag burn, as he supported Carlton's fiercest rival, Collingwood.[4]

As Weinberg recalled, Peter was a popular team member.

> He would often instigate situations, such as if you'd returned from being in a team overseas, the first thing you had to do was eat a meat pie. That became a tradition. Peter was also an

> instigator of voting on the quality of landing of aircrafts. Each team member would signify their vote by holding up a certain number of fingers, much to the crew's great delight.

Peter enjoyed the camaraderie among the team and was particularly pleased to have hammer-thrower Dick Leffler along on the trip as captain. Leffler was very popular with his teammates. He had always been prepared to stand up to officials for athletes' rights and conditions. He also had the ability to laugh at himself and was known to have an absolute heart of gold.

Peter had been contemplating turning professional for some time as a way of bringing more income into the family. Every Easter for as long as he could remember, he had followed the running of the Stawell Gift, the premier track event in professional ranks in Australia.[5] On his return from Japan, he had a chat with the professional body, as he related: 'They said they'd give me a mark[6] I could win some events from.' The professional body subsequently offered Peter a mark of three metres in a 120 metre race.

> That sounded pretty good. I knew I could beat guys who were running from behind that mark, because I'd beaten them in training. So I got an entry form for Stawell. You could bet on the race, and I thought I'd probably make a lot of money. But then they said I wouldn't get three metres at Stawell. It turned out they'd only give me three metres at Broadford[7], which was only worth $75 at the time. There was no way there'd be a lot of bookmakers there who you could get a lot of money with. So I couldn't afford to turn professional. Plus I was spending a lot of time out of the country. I was getting trips and equipment and when you ran at a certain place in the world [at the Commonwealth versus USA meets in Los Angeles], you were getting very good trophies that they would then buy back from you at reasonable prices. So I was getting a little bit of under-the-table assistance, you might say.

Having eliminated the possibility of turning professional, Peter focused his attention on the start of the 1969–70 athletics season. He finished sixth in the 100 yards and fifth in the 100 metres Victorian championship finals, before winning the Victorian 220 yards final. Peter admitted to sportswriter Jack Dunn, after his one yard victory over Lewis and Eddy, that he had produced something special to retain his 220 yards title. Eddy had been in top form in recent interclub competitions and it was no secret he had his eye on Peter's title. Peter said of the race, 'There has been some feeling between Gary and me, and I felt I could find two or three yards to beat him today'.[8] Dunn described Peter's win in 22.3 seconds as being a fine run 'considering the seven metres headwind' he struck in the home straight. According to Dunn, Peter did not receive any praise from his coach Neville Sillitoe. "'You were shocking on the bend. You will have to do a lot better in the Australian championships next month," Sillitoe told Norman.'[9]

Eddy extracted revenge in the Victorian 200 metres final, beating Peter into second place. Eddy also defeated Peter over 220 yards at Olympic Park, equalling the Australian residential record of 20.7 seconds in the process. Everything was set for a great duel between the arch-enemies in the Australian championships to be staged in Adelaide as the final selection trials for the upcoming Edinburgh Commonwealth Games. Sportswriter Steve Hayward expected the clash to be the highlight of the national championships: 'Norman's powerful finishing runs have swept him to wins in most of his Australian races. But he has had to share the limelight with the rangy Eddy this season.' Hayward predicted an Eddy win.[10]

Prior to the national championships, John Carlos arrived in Melbourne to compete at Olympic Park. Much to the disappointment of Melbourne's athletics supporters and the Athletics International group that brought Carlos to Australia, Sillitoe had supposedly banned Peter, Lewis and Holdsworth from competing. Yet Sillitoe told sports reporter Ron Carter that the sprinters, particularly Norman, were not trying to dodge Carlos and that race organisers were told two weeks earlier that his sprinters would not race against Carlos in the feature 220 yards event. Sillitoe explained:

> The organisers should make it clear that a race between Norman and Carlos had never been planned. I don't want Peter to be criticised for pulling out of a race he should not have been written into. Every year before the national titles, my runners rest for a few days and the meeting is on a rest day. This pattern has proved most successful and the runners agree it should be followed again this week. After all, the trip to the Commonwealth Games in Edinburgh hangs on the outcome of their races in Adelaide.[11]

Carlos told the press that he didn't blame Peter for not running, but added somewhat tongue-in-cheek, 'I don't want to humiliate him'.[12] Peter initially caught up with Carlos at Melbourne's Park Royal Motel and then saw him briefly on the night he raced. 'We didn't get to socialise as he was carted all over the place to press conferences and social outings and I was on other [family] duties.'

Weinberg was president of Athletics International at the time. He was annoyed that Sillitoe wouldn't let his runners compete.

> We needed those fellas to run. Gary Eddy ran, Byron Williams ran, my son Brett ran. But the runners we really wanted – Holdsworth, Lewis and Norman – didn't run. I had to respect their loyalty to Neville, but at the same time I was terribly disappointed and I spoke to Neville at the time and I spoke to the fellas.

Ron Clarke had spent considerable time with Tommie Smith when Smith came to Australia to compete in 1967. Smith stayed at Clarke's house while in Melbourne and Clarke found him to be 'a wonderful personable guy'. By contrast, Clarke said Carlos was 'something else'. Clarke was associated with Athletics International at the time and made all the arrangements for Carlos's visit. Carlos would not consider coming to Australia unless all his expenses were paid and he received US $1000 to compete. Clarke knew payment of such a fee would contravene amateur athletics rules, but he also knew that Carlos would be a huge drawcard in Australia. So he agreed to the payment, but in return, Clarke, then an Adidas representative, sought assurances from Carlos that he would wear Adidas shoes when competing, rather than his normal Puma footwear.

Clarke got quite a shock when he first met Carlos at his motel. Carlos greeted him with a derringer in his hand. 'He's twirling around this gun that he carries with him all the time,' exclaimed Clarke. Clarke immediately warned Carlos that carrying such a firearm was not permitted in Australia and that the police would arrest him if he was seen carrying it. He told Carlos to hide the gun and not bring it out until he was back in the USA. Carlos ignored Clarke's warnings and took the derringer with him everywhere he went in Melbourne. But that was only the start of Clarke's problems: 'Carlos runs the first race in Melbourne, a 200 metres, and he runs it very well in about 20.1. He reckons he's done enough and tells me he's not going to run again. I have him lined up for a 130 metres race at the end of the night. That was the big race that we promoted.' Carlos was unconcerned. He was not running again. Clarke warned Carlos that if he didn't run, he would report him to the US Olympic Committee (USOC) for accepting the $1000 appearance fee. Carlos reluctantly agreed to run but made it quite clear, using strong language, that he would not wear Adidas shoes.

By this time the brand of shoes was the least of Clarke's worries – he told Carlos he didn't give a damn what he ran in, just as long as he ran. Next thing Clarke knew, Carlos was running in the 60 metres event: 'He's in a race he wasn't supposed to compete in. He wears his Puma shoes and he beats Charlie Greene, so he's as happy as Larry!' Delighted at having beaten his countryman, Carlos then decided he'd run in the 130 metres after all. 'He comes out in the 130 in a much better humour, so he wears Puma on one foot and Adidas on the other foot. Just as a bit of a concession to me,' said Clarke, who couldn't wait at the time to see the back of the 'big mouth' Carlos.

While in Melbourne, Carlos took the opportunity to espouse his thoughts on racism to the press. He told reporter Tom Prior:

> You're either a racist country or you're not. America is a racist country. Avery Brundage, the American head of the Olympics set-up, is a super racist. He is out and out 'White Power'. South Africa is a racist country and I must suspect any country which has anything to do with them in sport or anything else. I know Australian sportsmen like Ron Clarke, Ralph Doubell and Peter Norman don't have a racist bone in their bodies. But I'm out here to have a look at Australia, which plays sport with South Africa, and has the reputation of being a racist country, to decide for myself. No one makes up my mind for me but me![13]

Carlos went on to say that he had been irritated by the many Australians he had met on the trip who only wanted to talk about his famous Black Power salute.

> Tommie and I just wanted to let the world know that America had a race problem. The world knew it, but we wanted to underline it and to stir them up into getting on with the job and doing the work they should. All this talk about the American flag gets me. To me it's like an insurance policy. At this stage I'm paying the dues and I'm not getting any protection.[14]

Peter's 200 metres Australian championship win on 22 March 1970 at Adelaide's Olympic sports field, was described by Carter as one of the great runs of Peter's career: 'Norman swept past his opponents as if they were standing still to run away with the 200 metres championship for the fifth year in succession. He won by three yards from Victorian teammates Gary Eddy and Greg Lewis who staged a great duel for second placing.' Eddy clinched second with a desperate lunge at the tape, and then crashed heavily onto the track injuring his hip and shoulder. 'Norman's time of 21 seconds was a great run in the tough, windy conditions, and was three-tenths of a second faster than his winning time in Melbourne last year.'[15]

Peter finished fourth in the 100 metres final won by Queensland's Eric Bigby, and, along with Laurie Fanshaw, Gary Holdsworth and Graham Haskell, he was a member of the Victorian team that won the national 4 × 100 metres relay championship.

Peter informed Carter that he had run in his last Australian championships. He intended to retire immediately after the Edinburgh Commonwealth Games. He wanted to go out while still on top. 'I still have a couple of years of top-class sprinting left, but I've made my decision to quit … knowing that it was my last Australian championship appearance made me go all the harder.' Carter reported that Sillitoe would not try to persuade Peter to change his mind. 'I always like to see athletes go out when they are on top, not when they are has-beens,' Sillitoe said. Peter intended to potter around with the East Melbourne Harriers and run in B- or C-grade sprints next track season. He would leave the A-grade running to young people. He added that he was very keen to become a race starter and had already had a chat with Victoria's chief starter.[16]

Peter found it difficult to concentrate fully on training for the British Commonwealth Games due to begin in mid July. He was concerned about the distinct possibility that he might not be paid by the Victorian Education Department while away in Edinburgh. Other athletes who were teachers – Lewis, Pam Kilborn and (discus and shot-put champion) Jean Roberts – had similar concerns. The Education Department had given Peter and all Victorian teachers on the team six weeks leave on full pay for the 1966 Jamaican Games, and seven weeks leave on full pay for the 1968 Olympics. But seemingly the department's policy had changed since then.

Ruth recalled that these were quite anxious times: 'It all depended on the mood of the government as to whether the leave would be with or without pay.' While it was a great honour to represent their country, athletes such as Peter still had to feed their families. So it was no coincidence that in these circumstances, Peter and others knew they could turn to sportswriters such as Judy Joy Davies to put pressure on the Education Department. Davies had competed in the 1948 Olympics, winning a bronze medal in the 100 metres backstroke; the 1950 British Empire Games in Auckland, New Zealand, where she won three gold medals; and the 1952 Olympics. She then became a highly respected sportswriter for the Melbourne *Sun*. Davies quoted Peter as saying that if he didn't 'get full pay for the four weeks' he'd have to 'seriously consider withdrawing from the Australian team'.[17] The article worked – the Education Department quickly relented and Peter, Lewis, Kilborn and Roberts were paid for the period of the Games.

Money was not the only issue on Peter's mind. He and Ruth had originally talked about her going with him to Edinburgh, but she couldn't go as she had become pregnant soon after his return from Japan and was due to give birth around the time of the opening ceremony.

Heather Norman lived with Peter and Ruth from January through to late April 1970. Heather said Peter was out a lot during this period.

> I remember once or twice he got a bit tetchy with Ruth because he had to repeat something. I thought, 'It's all right for you gallivanting around while Ruth and I sit at home.' But she wasn't greatly upset. I didn't sense there was anything amiss between them at that stage. There weren't arguments. They didn't do that. I don't think Ruth would argue. She would discuss. Peter certainly never argued. He also discussed. Sometimes you understood you weren't going to win the discussion with him.

The week before the Australian team departed for Edinburgh, Peter ran himself back into form with three brilliant time trials at Olympic Park, including a 200 metres run in 20.8 seconds. The *Sun* reported that Peter showed the explosive start and the early speed on the bend that had so far eluded him that winter; speed that would be required to win gold in Edinburgh.

> His early speed appeared in two 10.5 second 100 metre trials last night on the new bitumen rubber track. When in form, Norman relies on the burst of speed when other sprinters are flagging in the straight … He should be able to reduce last night's time by

several yards when he runs against the fast Jamaican sprinters in Edinburgh later this month.[18]

The ninth British Commonwealth Games were to be held in Edinburgh, Scotland, from 16–25 July 1970.[19] Games historian Cleve Dheensaw wrote that it had 'long been the dream of Scottish organisers to bring the Games to their ancient capital', adding that the Games would be 'remembered for many things, including several firsts. It was the first time metric distances and electronic photo finish technology were used at the Games and the first time the Queen attended.'[20] It had been speculated in the British press early in 1970 that many African nations were considering boycotting the Games because of concern over South Africa's rugby tour of Britain and the New Zealand All Blacks tour of South Africa, both of which were scheduled for that year. No such boycott eventuated[21] and 42 countries attended the Games and 1383 athletes took part in competition.

The Australian Games team arrived in Scotland on 9 July 1970 after a flight of more than 30 hours from Sydney. Within half an hour of their arrival in Edinburgh, several members of the team, although tired from the long flight, got rid of the cobwebs by kicking an Australian Rules football around the Games Village. Peter had brought two footballs with him and he was joined in the impromptu kicking session by Lewis, Noel Freeman, Peckham and May, all huge Australian Rules fans.

A few days after arriving in Edinburgh, Peter spoke to Melbourne journalist Barrie Bretland and confirmed that he would definitely retire from major athletics at the end of the Games: 'Edinburgh is the end of the road for me. After this I will have had enough. It would be nice to go out of sport with a gold in Edinburgh. That would be the perfect end to it all for me.' Peter told Bretland that he didn't expect to run for Victoria in future interstate meetings, but would continue running at interclub meetings.[22]

As anticipated, Sandra Louise Norman was born on the opening day of the British Commonwealth Games, 16 July 1970, at the Williamstown Hospital. The *Sun* featured a photo of seventeen-hour-old Sandra with Ruth on the front page under the caption 'Peter's golden girl'. Peter had asked the newspaper to contact him when the baby arrived, so news was passed to him, together with a copy of the photo, at the Games Village. Peter told Bretland that he was 'tickled pink' at the news. 'I am a little disappointed I can't be with my wife at such a special time,' Peter said, 'but it's great to know the baby has arrived and everything is okay. This takes a load off my mind. Now I'll be able to concentrate on winning a medal to take home to the new baby.' Ruth was quoted as saying that Peter would be 'so happy' when he found out because he had been stating for months that they would have another girl.

Sandra was born two days before her parents' sixth wedding anniversary, a fact not lost on Ruth. She told the *Sun* that she and Peter had only spent two anniversaries together in six years of marriage: 'He was running in Kingston, Jamaica, in 1966, in the States in 1967 and 1969 and now he is in Edinburgh.'[23]

Peter began his medal chase well by winning his heat of the 200 metres. He finished second in his quarter-final, before running third in the second semi-final. He was struggling and finished a disappointing fifth (20.86 seconds) on 22 July 1970 in the final won by Jamaican Don Quarrie (20.5 seconds) from Trinidad's Ed Roberts (who'd finished fourth in the 200 metres in Mexico) and Kenya's Charles Asati. Peter was last with 100 metres to go and his expected withering finish was nowhere to be seen.[24] Quarrie also won gold in the 100 metres.

Before the Games, Peter had been favoured to win the event. After the final, he couldn't offer any explanation to the press for his failure except 'old age' – 'I just didn't have anything left in the legs. When I came round the curve I consciously lifted, but my knees would not work.' All the conditions of the race had been right, 'It was just bad running. My time was all right, but not good enough for this competition.'[25]

Peter described the race as the most disappointing of his career. 'What a hell of a way to go out of athletics,' he said to Carter.

> I bombed out completely. I'm too old. My legs just packed up and I could not get going. I had everything going for me. I had the right lane – what excuses can I make? A lot of people will say I should have retired after the Mexico City Olympics. The writing was on the wall. But I don't agree. I think I've run better since Mexico in the last two years than ever before.[26]

Davies described Peter as the most dissatisfied man in the Games Village after his failure to run a place in the final. She noted that Peter was now thinking twice about retiring. 'I was expecting to probably win the gold medal and then retire to become a family man. But yesterday's race has finished all that. Now I'm beginning to feel that I'll run again. I want another international trip to prove myself.' Peter added that athletes needed help from Australian athletics officials: 'Australian teams should not be sent overseas in our winter time without any concentrated training or any chance of international competition.' He described how a pre-Games training camp had helped Australian swimmers achieve success in Edinburgh. (The swimming team won eighteen gold medals.) 'It was the making of their team. Without the special training, there is no doubt that they would not have won so many gold medals here. This is what the athletics team should have before going overseas in our winter to Olympic or Commonwealth Games.'[27]

Peter still had one more race in which to redeem himself in Edinburgh. Along with Lewis, May and Eddy, Peter was a member of the Australian team due to run in the first heat of the 4 × 100 metres relay. Unfortunately, Peter did not get to run due to a mix up with the baton between May and Eddy. The baton was dropped and Peter was left standing on the track as other runners charged past him.

May wasn't originally in the relay team, as he discussed. 'Eric Bigby was. I offered to do some baton changes if they needed me, but the coach said no. Then Bigby pulled a hamstring.' May had already won a silver medal in the long jump and wanted to win gold in the triple jump. But the relay was on at the same time as the triple jump. He broke the Commonwealth record with his first jump, then had to run around to the relay change to run the relay.

> I had had no experience with Gary with baton changing. You need to spend time together. Gary and I stuffed it up. I was shattered, but I had to go back to the triple jump. Mick McGrath had beaten my previous jump by a couple of centimetres. So I had to win it over again.

May did not blame Eddy or himself for the baton mix up. 'I blame the coaches. They should have seen this eventuality. It was awful because Normie was stuck on the last leg.'

Eddy could still visualise Peter standing on the track looking shattered that he didn't get to run.

> It brought him to tears. I felt pretty bad about that but I didn't

> think it was my fault. Phil says it wasn't his fault either. It ended up being Peter's last international race and mine as well. Peter wasn't in the best form of his life. Neither of us got a medal in our individual events, but we weren't in that bad a shape for a relay. We probably would have done really well.

In later years, Peter often spoke about the relay event at Olympic and Commonwealth Games reunion dinners. He would always describe the race – his last chance to win a Commonwealth Games gold medal – as 'his greatest tragedy' in athletics. Triple Olympian and chief executive officer of the Australian Commonwealth Games Association Perry Crosswhite recalled Peter saying that he had 'never felt so alone' waiting at the anchor leg point as everybody went by.

While extremely disappointed with his own performance in the 200 metres, Peter was delighted when Melbourne's Raelene Boyle won the 200 metres gold later that same day to add to her win in the 100 metres. As Carter noted, when Boyle won a gold medal 'everyone felt happy. That's the sort of girl she is'.[28] Raelene won a third gold medal when she, Kilborn,[29] Jenny Lamy and Marion Hoffman combined to win the 4 × 100 metres relay.

Peckham was captain of the athletics team in Edinburgh. He felt that he and Peter, his vice-captain, became closer than ever before in Edinburgh. He recalled the incident that really cemented their friendship.

> Graeme Briggs was the athletics manager and he had allowed Ron Clarke to leave the village to stay with his wife. Arthur Tunstall, the commandant and general manager, decried Graeme for allowing this to happen and said that he was a mess as a manager. The athletics team was really dirty on the release of the story to the press. As far as the general team manager decrying the athletics team manager, who was one of the best we ever had, it just wasn't on. Peter and Graeme Briggs were friendly, so Peter was a strong advocate for supporting Briggsy. He was really on my case to do something about it.

Peckham duly approached Tunstall.

> I told him it just wasn't acceptable and we wanted a retraction, which he agreed to but it never happened. On the day of the high

> jump qualifying rounds, Ivan Lund, the team's administrative officer, chastised me and pointed out that I shouldn't have taken our case forward. But Peter certainly showed me that he had the strength of his convictions.

Peter helped Briggs out quite a lot in Edinburgh and, in doing so, he discovered where the key to the 'grog' cupboard was kept. Gardiner recalled:

> One night Peter came down with Jenny Lamy. He had the key. He said, 'Nobody is in the office so I'm gonna whip down and see what I can find. Come with us.' I said I'd go with them but I wouldn't go into the grog cupboard because I didn't want to get Bert [Gardiner's father and national selector] into trouble. I said I'd keep cockatoo[30] out the front. Jenny and he went off and found a bottle of something or other, came back and gave me a little bottle of something or other for my pains.

May, who roomed with Peter in Edinburgh, believed that Peter returned to his 'normal self' as an athlete in Edinburgh.

> Peter wasn't a natural athlete or an athlete of great, enormous talent. He was a journeyman athlete, who had enormous guts. Pete got there because of guts and hard work and circumstances. There was nothing he ever did without hard work. He never quit. He was always incredibly optimistic. He'd had his shining moment in Mexico. What is better than to have your shining moment there?

May loved his mate 'Normie' and described him as a very giving person. He liked Peter's jokes, his humour and his sayings – his favourite being 'You win a few, you lose a few, and you fight for their drawers'. He also enjoyed going in to 'battle' with Peter on the track or figuring out how they were 'gonna get down that hill'. But May contended that, compared to earlier trips, Peter was really down in spirits in Edinburgh. He put that down at the time to Peter being unhappy with his home life.

> Peter was one of the few married guys in the team. Most were single and enjoying whatever opportunities came up [with female athletes]. We were hard-driving, hard-arsed young men of considerable quality, of great physical capacity and saw the

world as the opportunity to embellish the global gene pool by our active participation in this project. One of our lines was 'Would this face ever lie to a woman?' So Peter probably thought 'They're doing it. Why don't I?' Peter wasn't a heavy player, but he did participate.

NOTES

1 *Australasian Amateur Athletics* magazine, March 1969.

2 Residential records could only be beaten by residents of the particular state or country. This was an important achievement for Peter as he was not a great runner over 100 metres.

3 'It's fun and games for brilliant Blues', *Herald Sun*, 29 August 1994.

4 Peter would have the last laugh when Carlton defeated Collingwood in the 1970 grand final.

5 Stawell is a town 235 kilometres north-west of Melbourne. The Stawell Gift, first held in 1878, is held every Easter. It is run on grass over 120 metres. It is one of the world's most prestigious footraces and, as such, attracts local and international athletes eager to win the race's large prize money.

6 A 'mark' is another word for a 'start'. In professional running, the top runners are handicapped by giving the slower runners a start, or mark – the distance being determined by previous running form.

7 The Broadford Gift is run every December in the small town of Broadford about 88 kilometres north of Melbourne.

8 'Norman is too good', *The Sun*, 23 February 1970.

9 'Norman is too good', *The Sun*, 23 February 1970.

10 'Norman–Eddy 200 metre clash', *The Herald*, 20 March 1970.

11 'Norman not to start', *The Age*, 16 March 1970.

12 *The Sun*, 16 March 1970.

13 'Must they always call us boy?', *The Sun*, 16 March 1970.

14 'Must they always call us boy?', *The Sun*, 16 March 1970.

15 'Norman's brilliant title win', *The Age,* 23 March 1970.

16 'Champion sprinters are getting out while they're still riding high', *The Age*, 24 March 1970.

17 'Games shock, if they dock our pay we may not go', *The Sun*, 18 June 1970.

18 'Norman in form', *The Sun*, 4 July 1970.

19 Edinburgh would also host the 1986 Games.

20 Cleve Dheensaw, *The Commonwealth Games – The First 60 Years, 1930–1990*, ABC Books, Sydney, 1994, p. 97.

21 Dheensaw, *The Commonwealth Games – The First 60 Years, 1930–1990*, p. 105.

22 'Norman will retire', *The Herald*, 15 July 1970.

23 'Peter's golden girl', *The Sun*, 17 July 1970.

24 In later years, Peter admitted that had he treated the Games with the respect that they were due, he might have done better: 'I doubt that I would've beaten Don Quarrie, but I would have given a better account of myself had I taken it a little more seriously.'

25 *The Sun*, 23 July 1970.

26 *The Age*, 23 July 1970.

27 'Peter may run on', *The Sun*, 24 July 1970.

28 'Raelene wins, Norman fails', *The Age*, 23 July 1970.

29 Kilborn also won gold in the hurdles, as did Petra Rivers in the javelin. Geoff Smith won the decathlon. Peckham successfully defended the high jump gold medal he won in Jamaica four years before. In doing so, he became the first man in Commonwealth Games history to clear seven feet (2.1 metres). In the 30 kilometre walk, Peter's footy-kicking mate Freeman won gold, and silver was taken by Bob Gardiner, Peter's former Collingwood Harriers teammate. May overcame the disappointment of the relay to win the triple jump event with a leap of 16.72 metres. Tony Manning won the 3000 metres steeplechase after teammate and race favourite Kerry O'Brien fell at the water jump with one lap to go.

30 To 'keep cockatoo' means to keep watch.

13

THE BEST MAN WALKS OUT ON A MARRIAGE

Peter was known to get moody when he didn't run well and he certainly hadn't run well at the Edinburgh Games. The competition had been a total disaster for him. He knew it and Ruth knew it. But this was nothing compared to the events that would soon unfold in their lives; events that would see their marriage disintegrate.

Ruth remembered Peter as being a different person after the 1970 Games. He hadn't achieved what he hoped to at the Games and he wondered how much more time he had left in athletics. His body was wearing out after some ten years of hard training, preparing for the normal athletics season, plus the Commonwealth Games, the Olympics and all the other big events held out of season. Through 1970 and 1971, Peter often pleaded with Ruth to tell him to give athletics up. 'He just couldn't come to the decision that it was time to move on. I'd say, "I can't do that. You have to decide what you want to do with your future". I could never have made that decision for him because if I had, it probably would have come back and bitten me on the bottom.'

Mexico had been a turning point for Peter. While he enjoyed the resulting notoriety and fame, it came at a price for Ruth. Peter was virtually automatically selected for Australian athletics teams competing overseas after Mexico. So he was away from home for months at a time through 1969 and into 1970 when he went to Edinburgh. When he was home, he was training six nights a week.

Ruth had plenty to keep her occupied during Peter's absences. She was working five days a week and had two children to look after. But she found it very hard being separated from Peter for such long periods – it was a constant struggle to stay relevant to each other. 'In fact we were growing apart!'

To the outside world, however, Peter and Ruth appeared to be happily married. Soon after his return from Edinburgh, Peter served as best man for his long-time rival and close mate Gary Holdsworth when he married Glenda Dennis on Sunday 23 August 1970 at the Coburg Methodist Church. While Peter and Ruth led busy lives, they enjoyed socialising with the couple whenever the opportunity arose. Peter had great respect for Gary as an opponent and as a person. In Peter's opinion Gary was the hardest man in the world to beat twice in a row over the same distance: 'He was equally as hard to beat over 100 as 200.' Peter described him as a gentleman and counted being best man at their wedding 'as an absolute privilege and honour'.[1] Gary felt just as strongly about Peter. He chose Peter to be his best man, ahead of his own brother, because 'he was the best man I knew'.

On 2 January 1971, the two couples travelled together by car to New South Wales to attend teammate Greg Lewis's wedding to Australian high jumper Carolyn Wright. As they drove, Peter and Gary often burst into song. More often that not it was yet another rip-roaring version of 'C'est Moi' ('Tis I)'. This song meant almost as much to them as being out on the track busting their guts to beat each other. The wedding was a wonderful occasion, but little did the three couples know that while one marriage was just beginning, another was on the verge of ending.

John McAdam had met Peter in 1969 when John joined Williamstown Technical School as a maths and science teacher. He and Peter soon became great mates. John considers that the 1970s were the awakening of a new period of questioning in Peter's life. Peter was discovering the world. He'd been to Mexico, the States, Edinburgh and other places and found a different life outside Melbourne, Australia – a world he probably never thought existed. 'All this was just like "Wow!" for Peter. Then he meets this hot young New Zealander teaching at Williamstown, so Peter thinks why not say hi to her and chat her up a bit?'

Peter related his first meeting with Jan:

> I was teaching at Williamstown Tech and I and a bunch of kids were throwing a baseball backwards and forwards. I threw the ball to a kid just as a senior teacher came out a door with this new teacher he was showing around. The kid had his glove up in front of his face as he'd been taught to do, but he turned his head and his glove sideways and I beaned him and dropped him like a rock. By this time I'd seen what he was looking at, the new teacher's very short miniskirt. I thought it was worth a good look too. I took him inside and wiped a bit of blood off the side of his head. That was my first look at Jan.

Janet Rae McQueen was born in Christchurch, New Zealand, on 12 January 1949. She taught in New Zealand for three years until she had paid back her bond to the government and then was free to leave. She came to Australia towards the end of 1970 and, as the Australian school year had ended, she got a temporary job as a comptometrist with a shipping firm. In early January 1971, Jan visited the Victorian Education Department seeking a teaching position in Melbourne. Up until that point she'd been a primary teacher. 'But they were desperate for maths teachers,' recalled Jan, 'so I became a secondary school maths teacher at [the all-boys] Williamstown Tech. I met Peter on the first day as I was being shown around the school.'

Jan is reluctant to discuss the early days of her friendship with Peter 'in deference' to Ruth. 'He was friendly, but I find it awkward to talk about that, especially when he was still married to Ruth at that stage.' Jan readily admitted, however, that she soon realised it was handy having Peter at the school because the students were scared of him.

> He was very tough and would give them six of the best. He told me that the kids at the school he was at before Williamstown, walked all over him to begin with, which is hard to imagine. He said he was determined he was going to be mean and tough when he went to his next school. And he was. He was quite mean!

It wasn't long before Peter was smitten with the attractive and outgoing 22 year old. While not aware of the arrival of the new teacher at the school, Ruth, who was now pregnant again, was growing very concerned over Peter's struggle to settle back into life as a family man. Even though he had been home from Edinburgh for over six months, it was becoming obvious to Ruth that Peter was extremely restless and very much drifting away from her and their two daughters. He was beginning to spend a lot of time away from the family home. She didn't understand why. If he couldn't cope with two children, how was he going to deal with the arrival of a third?

Ruth's faith was very important to her, as it had been for Peter, so she couldn't understand why Peter was now rapidly drifting away from the Salvation Army and Salvationist values. Salvationists weren't supposed to drink alcohol, but Ruth suspected that Peter was drinking after school with some of his teaching mates, particularly after he called an early halt to athletics six weeks into the 1970–71 season. Another thought kept nagging at Ruth – perhaps Peter was having an affair. That would explain his absences. Ruth initially had no proof, but she knew there were single and carefree women around, who would find her fit, athletic, handsome and now well-known husband an attractive proposition.

Looking back, Ruth came to believe that there may have been other affairs besides the one with Jan.

> I knew Jan was on the scene in 1971. I didn't meet her, but I sensed that she was about. Then the kids from the Williamstown School started ringing me and saying 'Mr Norman is going out with Miss McQueen'. Who's Miss McQueen? That's when I first definitely knew. It was scary stuff. It was also pretty tough knowing this was going on. I still loved him!

An affair was so totally unexpected. Ruth could not fathom Peter – surely he knew that she was devoted to him and had been since they first met just before her sixteenth birthday. He was her first and only boyfriend and, in exchanging wedding vows in 1964, Ruth believed that they had committed their lives to each other.

Ruth gave Peter total and unconditional support in his athletics career and professional career, encouraging him to become a teacher so he would have more time to train. She happily worked five days a week throughout their marriage as Peter was not always being paid by his employers when he went away on athletics trips. She had also helped out in the shop on Saturday mornings during his days as a butcher.

Ruth was aware that her husband was now public property and this meant that she had to sacrifice her privacy and her time. Being in the public spotlight was not easy for her, but she travelled with him to speaking engagements on weekends and on weeknights as his sporting fame grew after the Olympics. Peter enjoyed these engagements so Ruth felt the expense was worth it. Ruth was also devoted to Peter's family and they had in fact been closer to her than her own family.

Peter was unaware that Ruth knew about his affair. He decided to make another comeback to athletics in early August 1971, pulling out all stops to gain selection for the 1972 Munich Olympics. Peter told sportswriter Judy Joy Davies that he felt unfulfilled and owed it to himself to try for another chance to wear the 'green and gold' for Australia. His comeback bid meant he was back in training six days a week, spending even more time away from the family home.

Janita and Sandra welcomed a baby brother when Gary Jay Norman was born on 16 September 1971. Gary, named after Gary Holdsworth, was born in the family car while Peter was driving Ruth to the Williamstown Hospital. They were within 300 metres of their destination when Gary decided to make his appearance. A Melbourne newspaper took great delight in reporting that Peter was left flat-footed by the speedy arrival of Gary.

> Baby Gary really beat the starter's gun … All was quiet in the Norman household at Newport yesterday at 4 am. Children Janita, 4 and Sandra, 1 year were sleeping when their mother Ruth decided it was time to go to hospital. Norman failed to realise the urgency of the situation until he tried to get Ruth into the car. 'I don't think I will make it in time,' said Ruth.[2]

Laurie Norman's wife Jill, who was pregnant with their second child Matthew, was staying with Peter and Ruth at the time of Gary's birth. Jill said:

> The affair was on at that time. Ruth knew. Peter would come home from work and play cards with us. Peter was a very funny man. We'd be laughing and carrying on and Ruth would put a hand on him, as you do when you are laughing. He'd say, 'Don't touch my body!' So it was already over then. He was taking more things away every day. She would say he took his records today, and another day he took such and such. It was quite embarrassing to be there.

Ruth described how Peter wasn't around much of the time. 'He'd go away for a week or ten days at a time and I'd never know where he was. He would make all these silly excuses. He'd take a bag of clothes and take the car and sneak away.' Ruth hoped that Gary's birth would turn things around but Peter continued to disappear for days on end. During one of his absences, unbeknown to Ruth, Peter and Jan McQueen flew to Perth in Western Australia to attend the wedding of his mate Phil May on 20 December 1971. 'I knew Peter and Jan were an item at the time,' said Phil, 'so I invited them. They stayed with another athletics mate of mine.'

The birth of her third child should have been a joyous occasion for Ruth but she had to turn to the Norman family for help during this time.

> Friends and family stood by me. I never lost my faith in my God and the people who supported me. But I was in my late twenties with three young children under five, so it was a real struggle with Peter being around less and less. Money was almost nonexistent. Several times George Norman and one of our Salvationist friends went all around Williamstown looking for him, but never found him. For George it was really one of the saddest times of his life.

George and Thelma Norman were devastated to learn that Peter and Ruth's marriage was in serious trouble. Ruth had been accepted into the family virtually from the moment they first met her. Thelma said, 'Peter knew we'd accepted her. She's always been like a daughter to us. And the girls [Heather and Elaine] have always accepted her as their sister. In-law doesn't come into it.'

When Peter told Gary Holdsworth one night at an athletics meeting that he'd met a girl that 'he was madly in love with', Gary didn't take Peter seriously and thought he was just having a brief fling. He had no idea that Peter would leave Ruth and the children, knowing Peter as a committed Christian and as a family man who loved his children. But as the affair progressed, Gary began to realise that Peter's relationship with Jan meant more to Peter than he'd first thought.

Gary knew Peter as an outwardly religious person at this time and woe betide anyone who didn't respect Peter for his religious beliefs. Peter could be very prickly, particularly if you called him a 'Salvo'. Gary had witnessed Peter's reaction when others had called him this: 'If you said something to him with a religious connotation that Peter didn't like, look out.' However, Gary remembered that Peter was always ready to be in things that might not be in strict accordance with Salvationist practices and values: 'Although he had his religion, there was that little spark all the time.'

Glenda Holdsworth initially also thought Peter's affair was just a fling.

> Ruth was pregnant. She had been pregnant for a lot of their married life. I thought he'll get over this and he'll come back and we'll all be happy again, but it didn't happen that way. Jan was the love of his life I'd say. Ruth was the love of his young life.

She described Peter as being a very charming man with a quick wit. She believed that Peter craved another life, a social life, a life he didn't have as an athlete. 'He saw Jan as being so different to Ruth. Jan was so vibrant and she was glamorous. Ruth wasn't glamorous. She was as Salvation Army as you can imagine. No make-up, the whole thing. But she was a lovely person.'

When Ruth learnt that the Holdsworths already knew about the affair, she was upset. Glenda vividly remembered Ruth saying to her, 'You knew! Why didn't you tell me?' Gary and Glenda were still struggling to accept the fact themselves at the time, let alone tell Ruth. Surely it was up to Peter to tell Ruth.

Unlike Gary, Greg was not shocked when he heard about Peter. He was aware how athletes were viewed in some circles, especially when they were on 'the top of the tree' in Australian sprinting like Peter was. 'It was a big deal in those days. You'd be getting public recognition as an athlete and wherever we went, girls would like to be with you, because you were in reasonable shape. You lived the party life and all that sort of stuff!'

Greg felt that Peter had married too soon and had too many commitments.

> I remember he got himself one of the first Honda sports cars to try and break out of it. I thought at the time it was completely inappropriate. It was hardly a family car! But that was Peter. He just wasn't settled with Ruth. It seems to me there was a diverging of the ways, which is what boys and girls do when you haven't got any common ground. In order to reconcile and find some common ground, they spent a weekend in a motel, no kids,

> just to iron out their differences. Once that didn't work, I knew it was all over.

Ruth felt that with Peter's notoriety after Mexico, and having come from a very humble background, he could not stay the same person she'd known and loved since 1960.

> I see a lot of similarity between [cricketer] Shane Warne and Peter. They live in the public eye all the time. Having that notoriety and being out there as everyone else's person, I felt Peter changed greatly. The constant pressure of notoriety and fame came at a price to both of us. In the end, I confronted him and asked him what was going on. Then I actually asked him to leave because I was so hurt. We did some counselling, but if one person doesn't want to be in a relationship, it just doesn't work.

Over the years Peter was reluctant to discuss the marriage break-up. On one occasion he said:

> I guess we grew apart in a lot of ways. I'd stopped going to the Army. Ruth's mum and dad were still very keen on the Salvation Army at that stage, as was Ruth. I just didn't see things that way any more. That was probably the biggest part of the breakdown. One of the reasons I moved away from the Army was because I was supporting a little girl in India. Our family's support was of a monetary nature. It got to a point where the money didn't seem quite enough and at the same time I needed a new Salvation Army uniform which was going to cost quite a few dollars. I felt that could be better put towards another cause, rather than me wearing a uniform to tell people what I believed in.[3] You can show people what you believe in by the way you treat the world and treat other people. It's not something that has to be shown by wearing a uniform. I'm probably a little anti-church in a lot of ways, but I still respect the work the Salvos do. I don't think they are the same movement that they were in those days, but I would definitely support them in any way I could.

Laurie felt that the Salvation Army was a factor in his brother's marriage break-up.

> The Salvation Army was very restrictive. Girls couldn't wear make-up on any day. You couldn't dance, drink, smoke or go to a shop or watch television on Sundays. Ruth was Salvation Army and she abided by Salvation Army principles. Peter was probably what you'd call a Christian and abided by Peter's rules and that's why he did what he did. Peter accepted the strictness of the Salvation Army when he wanted to. When he didn't, he didn't. I don't think it affected him a lot. He played it as he wanted to.

Laurie's wife Jill had seen changes in Peter after his overseas trips and felt that Ruth wasn't worldly enough to fit into Peter's new life: 'Worldly in the non-church things. He was worldly. She wasn't. That was the beginning of the end. So when Jan came on the scene, very flashy, attractive, outgoing, chatty, partying and working with him at the same school, it was just inevitable.'

Laurie continued to keep in touch with Peter following the break-up. As far as he was concerned, what happened was between Peter and Ruth, not anyone else. Laurie knew that he certainly couldn't change things, but wanted to make sure that his brother was okay. Laurie didn't feel sorry for Ruth because he knew she was being looked after by his family. He certainly didn't feel sorry for Peter either: 'It was his decision. He had to live with it, not me!' Laurie never detected any animosity between Peter and Ruth in ensuing years. 'Ruth is not the type of person, nor was Peter, to be nasty to anyone. It was one of those life experiences that they'd been through and it didn't work out. Neither held a grudge against the other.'

Heather Norman was surprised, but not shocked about the break-up of her brother's marriage.

> I didn't expect it, but I can't remember being shocked. Things don't shock me very easily. But if that's the way he felt, I thought it's best out! Ruth had lots to do with working, looking after the children and just being a mum and a wife. Peter by that time was doing a lot of speaking to various groups. I can't say what his motivations were. Ruth was not glamorous. Some of the women that he would meet at functions were, and they were adoring as well. And I think probably with that combination, they just grew apart. Their lives moved in different directions.

Heather recalled that Ruth at one stage tried to 'pep up' her appearance for the public events to become what she thought Peter was looking for. But deep down Ruth was still just a young mother and not the glamorous wife of an Olympic silver medallist who loved the flashy life. Heather said this wasn't Ruth's style at all.

> She was an extremely efficient and very loving girl within the Salvation Army context that she was bought up in. The Salvation Army is a somewhat restrictive religion. No make-up, no this, no that. It changed later on but certainly you weren't supposed to wear make-up when in uniform. Cleanliness was seen as next to godliness. You certainly didn't put on the trims or greatly adorn yourself.

Peter and Ruth had previously sold their home in North Road, Newport, with the intention of building a new house on a block of land in Purnell Street, Altona, which they had purchased not long after they married.[4] They had rented a house in Yarra Street, Williamstown, to which, as Ruth recalled, Peter was 'coming and going'. Janita started school at the nearby Williamstown North Primary School.

Shortly after their separation in early 1972, Ruth moved to Thornbury with her young family to be nearer to George and Thelma, who were very loyal and supportive.

> I didn't have a car because Peter had the car, so I rented a unit first of all, before buying a house in Separation Street, Northcote. I would walk with the children down to the Normans. I made a commitment not long after we'd gone our separate ways that I would never move away [emotionally] from the Norman family because they were my family, my children's grandparents and aunties and uncle.

> Even though it wasn't their fault, George and Thelma made a commitment to look after me and the children. I think George felt responsible for caring for us.

Later, when Ruth resumed working, she would return home to find that George would have been to her house and brought in the washing and folded it all for her. Before Ruth moved near them, two to three times a week Thelma would catch a number of buses from her Northcote home to

Williamstown, a trip that would have taken up to two hours each way, to see Ruth, 'just to be with her; just so she would know that she wasn't on her own'.

George and Thelma never questioned Ruth about what happened between her and Peter, nor ever passed judgment on them. Years later, Thelma has said she still didn't know why Peter left Ruth, other than the fact that 'he got caught up with Jan at the time'. However, neither of them turned away from their son through all the turmoil. 'He was living in different places,' said Thelma, 'but I'd go and see him wherever he was and I told him to always keep in touch with his father and I.' They always wanted to know where Peter was and how he was, but it was an emotional struggle. They loved their son but they also loved Ruth.

Thelma emphatically said they supported Ruth out of love and not guilt about what had happened. They were the constants in Ruth's life at a time of suffering and Ruth has said she believes that it was their support and loyalty that 'probably got me through it all'.

Ruth had no idea how Peter felt about his parents being so supportive of her.

> I guess it was difficult seeing his dad stepping in and looking after us and providing for us where it was needed. But there was never any money from Peter. Uncle Herb Norman said I needed to do something to get some payment. I said I didn't want anything. I was fine. But I wasn't really.

Herb Norman didn't condone what his nephew did to Ruth, having always had a lot of time for her. He believed that Peter had to pay his way, but 'unfortunately Peter didn't provide funds to support them'. He advised Ruth to go to Williamstown Court to apply for maintenance. 'I think it was $10 a week for each child,' recalled Ruth. 'I remember the judge asking if I wanted money. I said I didn't want money for myself. Then Uncle Herb insisted on taking me to the Commonwealth Employment Service.' Ruth's case was assessed as meritorious. She was classed as a widow and began to receive a widow's pension. Peter had always loved and respected his uncle, so he and Herb never had cross words about Herb supporting Ruth. Their relationship would always remain close.

Ruth received strong support from the Thornbury Salvation Army congregation after the marriage break-up, but much to her regret she was not permitted to continue to wear her Salvation Army uniform as a single parent. Officially she had to step down, but she could still worship.

Ruth stated emphatically that she did not make the decision to pursue a divorce.

> It was totally his decision. I felt that maybe it would have all blown over in time. I would never have left Peter. I would have stuck through thick and thin. But he said to me at one stage that he didn't love me anymore, nor did he love the children. That was really the finality, hearing that. Maybe he just said that so that I could get on with my life.

To this point, Ruth still clung to the faint hope that Peter might come back to her and their children. But after hearing this, she knew that it would never happen and it was time to move on with her life, just as Peter was moving on with his life with Jan. To this day, however, Ruth believes that Peter really did still love and care for her and the children in 'whatever way he could'.

Ruth recalled how she subsequently instituted divorce proceedings.

> In those days you had to have cause for a divorce and the cause was adultery. He wanted the divorce, but I had to prove the adultery, before completing the paperwork. I had to have people witness that there was another 'situation' and I had to have evidence of that 'situation'. I remember once going to Brunswick because I had to know that he was there with someone. It was awful stuff. At that time, a divorce took two years from when you lodged the documents, which I did in 1973.

Thelma accompanied Ruth to the Williamstown Court for the divorce hearing on 4 February 1975. Thelma and Peter exchanged hugs outside the court. Peter, who was accompanied by Jan, understood why his mother was there to support Ruth. Peter sought and was granted access to the children, but never took it up. According to Thelma, Peter had seen too many of his pupils affected by the bitterness that can occur when children are handed back and forth between parents. Peter told his sister-in-law Jill that he felt, rightly or wrongly, that the children needed to form a strong relationship with Ruth and whoever else might come into her life.

Peter made a choice not to see his three children. Janita was nearly five at the time of the separation and Ruth said it was particularly hard for her to understand why her daddy was no longer living with them.

> Peter really adored her and she just loved him dearly. I felt Peter should have gotten together with Janita and given her his side of the story. Sandra and Gary didn't know him at all. Gary was only two weeks old when Peter left and Sandra was only fourteen months old. So he was never much of a part of their lives.

From 1971 to 1976, Ruth lived on her own with the three children. She returned to work in 1974 when Gary was three. She enrolled her children at Williamstown Grammar School in 1975, when Gary was only three-and-a-half years old. Ruth bought a car and would travel from Northcote to Williamstown Grammar, then out to Altona North to work. The trip was about an hour's drive, depending on the traffic. After work, she would collect the children and return home. Ruth did this five days a week for two years.

Ruth said, 'When Peter and I went our separate ways, I lost most of my friends because our friends were athletics friends, apart from the family network and where we worked.' But Glenda and Gary were supportive when Ruth most needed help. They had looked after Janita for a brief period after the separation. 'We were just trying to help,' said Glenda. 'We took Janita because she was a little girl who needed to have somebody at that time.' The Holdsworths knew that Ruth had enough on her plate looking after Gary, who was straight out of hospital, and Sandy, who was only fourteen months old. Janita loved Glenda brushing her hair every day, taking her to the ballet and, most importantly, buying her first-ever pair of jeans. Gary recalled how when they were looking after Janita, she would sometimes 'thump' him: 'I was copping what Peter should have been getting.'

Glenda believed that Peter cut off some friendships, including theirs, after the separation because he thought 'We wouldn't think of him in the same way. I believe we were put in that group when we took Janita. I feel he thought we sided with Ruth. But we weren't playing sides. We were just trying to help, but we never got the chance to talk about it with Peter.' John McAdam agreed: 'Peter just started a new life and shut everyone out. It was like his past life didn't happen.'

Around the same time as the break-up, Gary moved out of athletics and joined a surf-lifesaving club, where he sprinted competitively on surf beaches instead of athletics tracks, so he didn't see Peter as often.

> We were very happy to see each other and always had good times, but it was not on a regular basis. And whereas at one time we could talk about anything, when we saw each other it was 'G'day mate, how are you?', but it was all very superficial. To a certain extent, Peter was embarrassed with us over the break-up, especially with Glenda. At one stage Glenda got upset about it and he said to her, 'I didn't really mean to hurt you'. He didn't have to be embarrassed, but he was. It sounds incredible that we could be so involved with each other in our younger days and then all of a sudden we don't go out of our way to talk to each other. Very rarely did we ring each other up post this period, and we never ever got together with Jan and Peter.

Gary doesn't blame Jan for this: 'Peter made his choice.' Glenda agreed: 'You can't blame Jan. He would never have talked about us. She wouldn't know the depth of our relationship.'

Ruth promised herself that she'd never say anything negative to her children about what happened.

> I never said anything against Peter. I made a commitment to myself that I'd never talk to them about Peter in any derogatory way. What happened, happened! There wasn't any abuse or arguments or anything like that. We just grew apart and he moved on to another relationship. That's how I see it. But I never stopped loving him. I always spoke to them when the time was right about how wonderful a man he was.

Over the years, Peter often asked Thelma about his children, as she recalled.

> He was always interested in their progress. Sometimes I would be looking after Gary in my shop opposite where Ruth was living when Peter came to see me. Gary would be playing with his little cars. He would have been about three. Peter would stand looking at him. You'd see the look on his face. What he was missing! That was his little boy. The next time Peter came, he had a box with his own collection of Matchbox cars for Gary.

Adelaide-based Rhonda and Robin Kidney were very surprised and bitterly disappointed about their friend's marriage break-up. The Kidneys had noticed Peter changing after Mexico and subsequent overseas trips. Rhonda described how Peter wasn't as open with them as he had previously been: 'There were things that he didn't want us to know as close friends. He never said that, but I sensed it. Before that everything was open and above board and we could talk about anything. Then he became a little sensitive. That's when Jan was coming on the scene.' Peter took Jan to meet the Kidneys on one visit to Adelaide (before their marriage), but it was an uncomfortably short visit, much to Rhonda's disappointment. Robin and Rhonda did not see Peter for quite some years after that. They felt they were cast aside as having been part of Peter's former life.

Peter's sister Elaine recalled that she and others in the family didn't see Peter for a long period either when he first met Jan. 'He'd see Mum but I certainly didn't see him. He made a complete break. It was a really weird time.' Peter and Ruth's break-up really affected Elaine. By this time Elaine and Ruth were very close and Elaine looked on Ruth as another sister. She was very worried for a time about Ruth as she thought that Ruth had sunk into 'quite a deep depression', but strong support from the Norman family ultimately pulled her out.

Elaine had always pictured Peter and Ruth as the perfect couple and their split came just as Elaine and Michael Ambler were planning their wedding (in October 1972). Elaine found it hard to be planning her joyous occasion in the midst of Ruth's heartache. To compound things, Michael and Peter got on well, so Michael also missed seeing Peter as often as he had previously. Elaine said Michael thought Peter was 'the best thing since sliced bread'. The two used to rib each other about Australian Rules football. Michael was, and still is, a staunch Collingwood supporter and Peter supported the arch-enemy, Carlton. Michael also looked up to Peter because of his silver medal win and is proud, to this day, of Peter's athletic achievements.

Elaine has always thought divorce doesn't just hurt the two people immediately involved: 'It certainly hurts other people as well.' She remembered her father being down on himself over the marriage break-up: 'He was saying "What have I done wrong?" Their generation didn't get divorced. He was very protective of Ruth and the kids. She was a daughter to him.'

For a long time Elaine believed that Peter didn't love his kids and was callous for walking out on them.

> I was very annoyed and thought he was a bastard because he'd left my nieces and nephew. They weren't his kids. They were mine! It was an awful time for everyone. But Heather put me straight about that. She often had him in her arms crying over not seeing his children. I now realise that it would have been hard on him too.

Elaine concedes now that he did what he did with the best intentions for the children's wellbeing and for Ruth's too. He was letting Ruth get on with her life. 'But at the time I sometimes felt he was growing into someone I didn't like, as opposed to someone I loved a whole lot.'

Heather vividly remembered the times when Peter cried in her arms.

> He got on with his life and he accepted responsibility for what happened. It had been his decision to leave. He never ever put Ruth down. He never ever said things like he couldn't live with her anymore. But he certainly missed the children.

Peter talked to her about having students who were all mixed up because their parents had split up. The father would take them to the movies or buy them presents, but was not living with them. Peter realised that his students were unsettled by this, so he was determined that he wasn't going to do that to his children. He wasn't part of their daily lives, so he had to leave them to get on with them. Heather knew what a gut-wrenching decision it was for Peter to make. About this, Peter said, 'There were reasons for not seeing them. Part of it was that I felt it was traumatic for both them and for me, probably selfishly.'

The dark shadow over Ruth's life lifted when she met Don Membrey in August 1976 through some friends. Don was also divorced and had children from his previous marriage, who lived with their mother. Don still had contact with his children, although the contact wasn't without its problems. Ruth and Don moved to Echuca in May 1977. Ruth said:

> Don and I made the decision very early in the piece to retain the children's names as Norman. We felt they needed their own identity as Normans. That was okay with the Norman family and Don was quite comfortable with that too. When Don came into our lives, he just wanted to care for us, love us, and support and provide for us. That was really strange. I had never had that

> before. He was an amazing man. He just said, 'I'll marry you', and he did. He said, 'I'll build you a new home', and he did!

It was one thing for Peter to walk out on Ruth, but did he fully comprehend at the time what it would be like to never see Janita, Sandra and Gary again. Only time would tell if he could ever be truly happy knowing that he had paid such a heavy price for his new love. What a gamble to take. And what a price to pay!

NOTES

1 Peter said, in 2004, 'While we don't see each other very often now, I still consider Gary among my very dear friends.'

2 'Too fast for dad', unsourced press clipping, 17 September 1971.

3 Ruth recalled the girl's name was Joy and that she lived in Madras, now known as Chennai. She did not, however, recall Peter being unhappy over the cost of a new uniform.

4 Peter and Ruth never built their house on the land in Altona and it was sold during the divorce settlement.

14

YOU COULDN'T JUDGE AN EGG-AND-SPOON RACE!

'It was the comeback athletic story that might develop into one of the most dramatic in Australian records,' reported Jack Dunn on Monday 21 February 1972.

> There was Peter Norman, 29, leaping feet into the air in the middle of Olympic Park yesterday afternoon. And shouting three little words, 'I am back. I am back,' in the most exuberant display of his great career ... The glee could have been that of a sixteen-year-old athlete tasting success before a big crowd for the first time. But here was a champion, who had won a silver medal at the Olympics, bubbling over with excitement. Norman, who retired from athletics last year, won the 200 metres at the VAAA [Victorian Amateur Athletic Association] titles yesterday in 21.1 seconds, and immediately became a Munich Olympic prospect.[1]

Peter got off to his usual slow start so he was in the middle of the field after 100 metres. But from the home bend he out-sprinted his opposition to win by almost two metres from Laurie D'Arcy, with Gary Eddy about a metre back coming third. It didn't bother Peter that his time was 0.2 seconds outside the Olympic standard. His main objective had been to win. Peter told Dunn that he was scared stiff when he got to the starting blocks that he was going to be a flop. 'I had doubts racing through my mind while waiting for the gun. Then my start was the worst of the series. Everybody jumped away and seemed miles ahead before I got going. But by the bend I was a lot happier.'

Peter's blistering burst from the home bend electrified the crowd, which began cheering and clapping when he hit the front. Dunn reported that Peter hadn't realised the ease with which he beat off the state's outstanding 200 metres athletes.

> When I told him he had won by almost three yards, he said, 'You must be joking! I didn't think I was that far in front. That tape was my only thought. I had to hit it before anybody else.' But Norman admitted he was not extended fully. 'I had a little bit up my sleeve at the finish. It might have come out if I'd been chasing somebody.'

Dunn predicted that Peter would win the 200 metres title at the Australian championships in Perth four weeks hence, adding that he could be Australia's top prospect of a gold medal in the 200 metres at Munich. Neville Sillitoe was unmoved after the performance, however. 'He has proved now he is back in the top rung of sprinters. But we will concentrate on further improvement now.'[2]

Peter had started the 1971–72 interclub season in his usual quiet manner. In the five weeks of competition before the Christmas break, his best time for the 200 metres had been 21.4 seconds. But by February 1972, Peter was beginning to hit top form. He turned in a great sprinting effort at Olympic Park on 5 February when he dashed over 100 metres in 10.2 seconds to equal the Australian record. Unfortunately, his name did not go into the record books because prevailing wind had given the athletes too much assistance. The following Saturday he equalled his Australian 200 metres record of 20.5 seconds at an Olympic Park interclub meeting. But the run was not recognised as a joint record, again due to too much wind assistance.

On 19 February 1972, Peter virtually wrote his name on the Victorian 200 metres winner's medallion when he won the first of six heats run to decide the finalists for the Victorian championship on the following Saturday. Peter told veteran sports reporter Merv Williams that although he had been running a long time, he was finding it easier now. He thought the secret of his good form was his vast experience, which enabled him to relax and not worry as much as he had done previously.[3]

Yet he was about to feature in one of the most controversial finishes seen in amateur sports in Australia. 'You could not judge an egg-and-spoon race. This is yours. I don't want it.' With these words, Peter threw his silver medal into the lap of a senior race judge. At 4.30 pm on Sunday 27 February 1972 at Melbourne's Olympic Park, Peter raced in the Victorian 100 metres championship. Greg Lewis was judged the winner ahead of Peter and Barry Minehan in 10.2 seconds. The ten-second dash unfurled an hour of drama rarely seen in the sensitive environment of amateur athletics in Australia.

> Norman refused to step on to the second place section of the victory dais beside Lewis, reported Jack Dunn, because he 'would not stand on a place won by somebody else'. Lewis was hooted for a long time by spectators when he took the winner's place at the top of the dais.[4]

The official announcement of the 100 metres placings and time brought a further sustained outburst of hooting from the spectators.

> At the tape Norman, running in number one lane, took the nonchalant attitude of looking across from his right shoulder to see if he had won. 'When I looked over my shoulder I saw Barry Minehan was closest to me. I knew I had won and I'm certain I beat Lewis,' Norman said. But Lewis and Minehan were just as certain first placing was theirs.
>
> Lewis said, 'My father named me GD Lewis. That was for Guts and Determination. That is how I won today. I got up in the last stride to win, but now we have three blokes who will never be satisfied about this championship. I'm upset by the hooting. It's hard enough to win a title without having to tolerate a demonstration over placings. I did not decide the place-getters. I ran to win and I thought I did. I have never been so upset in a race in my life.'[5]

Peter refused to mount the dais for the presentation, so arena manager John Draper, chairman of the VAAA executive, called Lewis, Peter and Minehan into the equipment room in the Olympic Park stand and told them 'he wanted them back on the dais for the special presentation of the Hec

Hogan Trophy, which goes to the 100 metres State champion'. The drama appeared over when the athletes shook hands, walked up the race to the dais and all shook hands again as placings were announced. But at this moment Peter, second-place medal in hand, walked over to chief judge Jack Nixon and threw the medal at him, uttering the words that would come back to haunt him in due course. While spectators, competitors, athletes on the field and over the fence, and coaches argued over the placings, one person was unmoved by the chaos. Track referee Eddie Moore told Dunn the decision of the judges was unanimous.[6]

The next day Peter spent 30 minutes watching replays of the race at the HSV7 television station. He was more convinced than ever that he had won the race. 'I said on Sunday I had beaten Lewis, now I know I won it comfortably. I studied the finish four or five times very closely. It showed clearly that Laurie D'Arcy and Greg threw a long way from the tape. Greg threw three or four yards out when I was still running through.' Peter insisted that he didn't dip until the line and that he was there first. 'I am satisfied after seeing the film that the judges missed lane one where I was running. There was enough margin for the judges to dissent because everybody went over the line close together, but I know for certain I was the winner. As far as I'm concerned that is as far as it will go.'[7]

Thirty-two years later, Peter was still adamant that he had won the race.

> There was no electronic timing back then. The first-place judge was sitting in the front of the stand. That put him as close as he could be. I won by a bit over a metre, looking back over my shoulder. What officials didn't know was because I realised that this could happen, I'd told some of the press guys, 'Don't miss lane one because ten metres from the line, I'm not going to be there. On the line I'm gonna win it.' So the press had it covered with 'magic eye' cameras and sports photographers. They also videoed it. So when the papers came out, photos of the finish showed clearly that I'd won. Big headlines. The association rang me and said, 'You've got to appeal'. I said, 'No I don't! I appealed on Sunday and it was thrown out.' 'Yeah but we've got new evidence. We would like you to appeal again.' I said, 'I won't appeal. I look all right. You look stupid. You get out of it.' I don't think they were pleased about that.

This was no ordinary race for Peter, as he discussed.

> The winner received the Hec Hogan Trophy and he had been my idol. I had a scrapbook on him and it was the first and only time that I was likely to win that race. He was in the field in my first A-grade race in 1958. I was only sixteen and it was two years before his death. Just before the race, he came up to me, patted me on the tail and said, 'Don't wait for me son!' Naturally he won and I will never forget his floppy old white hat and green tracksuit with holes in it. That's why that race meant a hell of a lot to me.[8]

Sillitoe was sitting in the grandstand, directly opposite the finishing line. He said Peter ran a wonderful race and won by a clear metre, but he had the bad luck to be in lane one. 'That really hurt Peter. He so much wanted to win it. I've seen this happen quite a lot where the athlete closest to the judge is at a distinct disadvantage.'

Heather Norman was standing with Ruth Norman at the finish line. Even though their marriage was over, Ruth remained supportive of Peter. Heather described how

> We just all jumped up and hugged each other. 'He's got it! He's got the 100 metres.' It was so important to him. We were just stunned when they announced the result. Ruth said they can't do that to him. He was so disappointed and pretty angry. It was robbery! That championship was probably his final chance. He knew he probably wasn't going to be running too much longer.

Every Saturday, East Melbourne Harriers (EMH) competitor Maurie Drew would see Peter, Holdsworth and Lewis running in interclub competitions.

> They competed consistently and regularly and loved it and bragged about winning. The highlight of Peter's life was probably beating Gary Holdsworth the first time. Bugger Mexico! The low light was being given second in the 1972 Victorian titles. There was no way Peter lost it. I was there, virtually opposite the finishing line. Peter was pissed off!

Olympic coach Ray Weinberg had film footage of the race finish. He had no doubt Peter won the race quite clearly. 'I was there when Peter told the judges to watch the inside lane.' Weinberg's footage clearly showed Peter won by some 22 centimetres. 'It was a margin that the judges should have picked up.'

Lewis continued to be adamant he'd won: 'I won because I've got the medal.' Lewis never ran well in Victorian titles. It was too early in the season for him. But he needed to win to make the Victorian team and have his fare paid to Perth for the nationals.

> I wasn't running all that brilliantly at the time. I knew it was tight, so I made a lot of noise as I walked back to the first-place judge. All the newspaper photos showed Peter clearly in front two metres past the line. An amateur photographer gave me a photo and said, 'Forget all this bullshit. You won the race'. His photo shows my lunge at the line. It was a complete lunge. If I had taken another stride, it would have been on my knees. I collapsed on the line because that's what I needed to do. The photo shows quite clearly that Peter's got one more stride to go and I've gotta lunge and that's it.

Lewis said Peter didn't want to take the silver medal on the victory stand, but he did because he didn't want to show disrespect to his competitors.

> He'd kick 'em, beat 'em within the scope of the rules, but he wouldn't give them disrespect. Ron Carter, the ace stirrer with *The Age* asked me if I condemned Peter for throwing the silver medal in the judge's lap. I loved it! It had no impact on Peter and I. We were always totally full of respect. Peter would no more have expected me to give that title up than fly to the moon.
>
> Peter was a brilliant competitor. He was the toughest son of a bitch. He was less animated perhaps than me, but he would take my aggression, mould it and give it back with interest. Holdsworth, Norman and I were the greatest of friends after we finished because we were the greatest of rivals in those days. I have enormous respect for those two guys. When Peter was on his day and he knew he was on his day, he exuded this arrogance, which was absolutely fantastic. You wouldn't try to puncture it. As long as he was taking it out on someone else, I couldn't give a rat's![9]

> Every now and again there'd be just one little sweep past me before the start of the 200 and it was 'Don't wait for me mate'. He had some terrific little sayings like that. Another was, 'I just hope the line doesn't come up before I can get there first'. He'd say that sort of thing to get in your head. There was no quarter given or taken, even in interclub. You were in for a race regardless. You'd hear him coming. Once he got off that bend and he had that balance and rhythm going, you knew full well that was it. It would make you try and run faster which you can't do in the last 80 metres. All you can do is to be effective. But Peter would always try to get you to run fast because that way you tie up and he'd pass you quicker.

Lewis remembered that, even if Peter wasn't running well, you knew full well, race after race, he'd get better. 'After Christmas he'd come good. It was disconcerting the way it would come. You could read most of the other blokes' form, but when Peter came out of the woods, he came out of the woods. He might just whip out a 20.6 after struggling all season running 21.8s. It was as if he'd turned the tap on.'

The two combatants met again over 100 metres at Olympic Park on 4 March 1972. This time there was no mix-up. Lewis beat Peter by half a metre. The VAAA was taking no chances and altered the positioning of their judges with the number-one-place judge on top of a raised stand and not at ground level. This time Peter was in lane five with Lewis in lane three. The race was never in doubt with Lewis leading from the gun and holding off a strong finish by Peter to win in 10.6 seconds against Peter's 10.7 seconds.[10]

In the 1972 national championships held at Perry Lakes stadium, Perth, on 22–26 March, male and female championships were combined for the first time. The championships were the final event in a series staged that season to decide the final composition of the Australian athletics team for the 1972 Munich Olympics, as Peter related.

> You had to run in Sydney, Brisbane, Melbourne, Adelaide, then Perth. You accumulated points all the way round. I won in Sydney, Brisbane, and Melbourne and that left only two to go. So there was no-one that could beat me. I hurt my knee at the Brisbane meeting but still ran in Melbourne because I knew

> that I needed at least one more win to guarantee my trip. Then in Perth, I ran fourth in the 100. In the 100 I ran the heat, semi-final and final, then ran in the 4 × 100 metre relay. The following day I ran the heat, semi-final and final of the 200. By the time I got to that final with six runs under my belt, the knee had blown up out of all proportion and I finished third. But I still had accrued enough points to qualify for selection.

The 200 metres championship was won by Lewis (21.5 seconds) ahead of Eddy (also 21.5) and Peter (21.6). Sports reporter Ron Carter described Peter's run as a shocker. Peter didn't disagree. 'I am history. I'm out of the team. All I had to do was to win, even in a slow time, and I think I would have been off to Munich. I knew I was in trouble when I straightened up for the finish and I struggled over the last 100 metres. I felt a lot older than 30 today.'[11]

Carter was aware that Peter had carried a knee injury for the previous two weeks and could not run the bend of the 200 metres. Peter had tried to keep the injury a secret and did not want to talk about it after the race. He didn't want to use it an excuse for his performance, nor did he want the Olympic selectors made aware of the injury. Nevertheless, Carter told selector Graeme Briggs as he thought he should know. Carter's view was that Peter should go to Munich: 'If the selectors do the right thing, Norman should still be on the plane to Munich. He has run 20.5 seconds this season and is a good competitor. In Munich he would do well.'[12]

When the Olympic team was announced on Sunday 28 March 1972, Peter's name was missing, much to the surprise of Carter and fellow sports journalist Jim Webster, who noted that Peter had several times run 20.5 for the 200 metres that season – well inside the Olympic qualifying standard of 20.9 seconds. Webster considered this sufficient to get Peter into the Games team.

> But then Norman failed in the Australian championships in Perth … this has cost him the trip. Over there he struggled all the way. But it is highly unlikely the selectors were aware Norman has had an injured left knee. Not until his coach Neville Sillitoe broke the silence would Norman admit there was anything wrong with him and that it was particularly hard for him to run around curves.

Webster would have picked Peter for Munich, as he was a proven Olympic competitor and had shown earlier that season that his speed had not left him. Australia's head coach for the Games, Ken Steward, expressed disappointment that Peter had been left out, saying that, 'On performances in the Nationals, no male sprinter deserved to go, but knowing what Norman can do, it's a great pity he was not picked'.[13]

Melbourne sports journalist Steve Hayward considered Peter particularly unlucky in missing selection, noting that he had only failed in the Perth final that season. 'He was hampered by a leg injury and a cold, but still finished third. If Norman had been judged on his overall performances of the season, including two Australian record runs of 20.5, he should have been in the team.'[14]

Ron Clarke was disappointed that Peter missed selection, writing to Peter on 5 April 1972: 'This is just a quick note to let you know my feelings about your non-inclusion for Munich. Quite frankly, I do not see how they can take some of the distance runners on the basis of their previous performance and leave you out on your Perth effort.'

Peter made no public comment at the time about his non-selection. Instead he maintained his usual upbeat approach with the press. He told the *Sun*'s Judy Joy Davies on 29 March 1972 that he had 'no intention of retiring. I'm training every night and hope to be invited to run in international meetings in California in May'.[15] This was, in fact, a furphy. No such invitations were in the pipeline. Bitterly disappointed at missing selection, Peter immediately pulled the pin on his career.

> I would dearly have loved to have gone to Munich. But when the team was announced on the Sunday, I was cross enough to retire from athletics immediately. On Monday night I went training with West Brunswick amateurs and played [Australian Rules] football the following Saturday and kissed track and field goodbye. I'd run the boundary for them as part of my winter training for the last umpteen years but had never had a chance to play for them, till then.

Peter retired, having won five 200 metres national titles and having come a close second in one 100 metres national championship. He was also a member of six winning Victorian teams in the 4 × 100 metre relay national championships. He won four Victorian 220 yards titles, five Victorian 200 metres titles, one Victorian 100 metres title, and was a member of seven winning EMH 4 × 110 yards/100 metres relay Victorian titles, six winning EMH 4 × 220 yards/200 metres relay Victorian titles and one winning EMH 4 × 440 yards relay Victorian title.

Pole-vaulter Ray Boyd won selection and had looked forward to going to Munich with his mate.

> Peter felt very aggrieved at missing out on Munich. The Hec Hogan race didn't help. He would have upset a few officials by throwing the medal in that guy's lap. Plus he tended to be cocky, very confident, not arrogant, but he could have appeared arrogant to some who didn't know him. You can see how some might not have taken to him. He could have got the selectors offside. They were looking for a way to leave him out and when he didn't win the trials, that was it. There was no court of appeal and they didn't have to justify their actions.

In 2004, Peter expressed the view that previous indiscretions cost him selection for Munich.

> I earned the frowning eyes of the powers-that-be by misbehaving at the state championships when I honestly thought I'd won the state 100 metres title. That, plus the fact that I'd, would you say, misbehaved at my previous Olympics, gave the selectors a good opportunity to leave me home. Even though in that Olympic year I qualified for the 200 metres thirteen times and the 100 metres five times and was ranked number five in the world, they felt quite justified in leaving me home. So in 1972, for the first and only time, Australia was not represented by any male sprinters in Munich. If they had taken any sprinters at all they would have had to have taken me, but they'd rather leave me at home than have me over there.

Was Peter punished by Olympic officials and selectors for his part in what happened on the Olympic dais in Mexico? Did his medal-throwing performance after the Victorian 100 metres championship go against him? The national selectors – Bert Gardiner, Graeme Briggs and Harold Ralph – are no longer alive.[16] Bert's son Bob Gardiner, eight times national walking champion, had competed at the 1964 and 1968 Olympics. He was selected for Munich, but ultimately did not compete due to injury. Bob Gardiner said his father resigned as a selector following the announcement of the Munich team because he felt the Australian Athletics Union and the Australian Olympic Federation had 'mucked around' with his selections.

> Dad was very highly principled. He had very strong beliefs and stuck to them. He kept meticulous records on our athletes. There was always a juggling act with selections. I don't recall any discussion about whether Peter was ostracised because of Mexico, but I can see it may well have happened.

Bob didn't think his father would have punished Peter.

> Discipline was important to him, but he was pretty understanding. He would forgive most things, except really bad behaviour, like people getting drunk and breaking things, which happened occasionally. If people played up, they got left out of teams in those days. You had to toe the line. But I think he would have forgiven Peter.

Paul Jenes replaced Bert Gardiner on the selection committee in 1973. Jenes was a national selector for the next seventeen years. He agrees that Bert Gardiner was very upset about certain things that occurred in 1972, but said Gardiner wouldn't talk about it. Jenes suggested:

> Partly there was interference in the emergencies. In 1964 a very large team was selected to go to Tokyo. A lot of them didn't go well, so the AOF set up a justification committee, which ultimately decided who would end up going. The selectors would put up a proposed team and the justification committee would consider it and make the final decision. That committee was dynamite!

Jenes did not believe that Briggs or Gardiner would have considered Peter not to be a reputable person to have on the team.

> I knew Graeme quite well. Briggsy and Peter were reasonably good mates. He was an athlete, then administrator, then selector. There's no way he would have held something like that against Peter. Bert Gardiner didn't have a mean streak in him. I didn't

> know Harold Ralph that well but I worked with him. I don't think Harold would have either. I don't think it had anything to do with Mexico. This is my educated guess. Perth is a nightmare because it gets the 'Fremantle Doctor'[17] and you cop four metre headwinds. The 200 was very slow. The selectors had a certain number of athletes to pick and because of the strong winds and the sprinters' slow times in Perth, they would have said, 'Oh well', and may have then ranked the sprinters much lower. I know there was a restriction on team size. But whether the sprinters were ranked lower than the other guys I don't know.

Neville Sillitoe was disappointed that Peter wasn't selected. 'Whether he could have medalled in Munich, no one knows. But on his previous record of lifting on the big occasion, I felt they could have given him a chance. But I don't honestly believe that Peter was punished for Mexico.' Sillitoe believed that Greg Lewis should have also gone to Munich: 'He was the 200 metres national titleholder and yet wasn't selected. It was very frustrating.' Lewis was equally frustrated at missing selection. He believed the 'conspiracy theory' had a lot of credibility.

> We're not gonna send Peter because we've had word from Lausanne [IOC headquarters in Switzerland] that we never want to see such a demonstration [as occurred in Mexico] repeated on the Olympic stage again. So the Australian people kowtow. We won't send any sprinters. They're hotheads, so there's another four years wiped out.

Australian Olympic official Judy Patching acknowledged that officials 'mucked up the drill' in the Victorian 100 metres championship race. 'Peter was on the inside lane and they bloody well missed him. Everybody knew that and they got bad publicity and were criticised over that.' But Patching refuted any suggestion of a conspiracy against Peter. He denied emphatically that Peter missed selection because of his reaction to the decision on this race or for his support of Smith and Carlos on the victory dais in Mexico.

Peter's non-selection was not the only shock omission. In what sports reporter Bob Crimeen described as 'one of the biggest athletic shocks for years', 1968 athletics coach Ray Weinberg was overlooked as coach of the Munich Olympic team. Weinberg told Crimeen that he was very disappointed, 'in fact a bit thunderstruck', at missing out on the position: 'After the athletics team's performance in Mexico City, I gave myself a fair show of being appointed again.' Ron Clarke was astonished at the omission of Weinberg.

> Weinberg's credentials are so far above everyone else's that nobody had considered he wouldn't get the job. In my opinion the selectors have in one single swoop done more to upset our Games expectations than anything I can remember. I cannot think of a single senior male athlete who would have entertained the idea of anyone but Ray looking after him.

Mexico Olympics 800 metres champion Ralph Doubell was in total agreement: 'Ray is by far the best-qualified man for the job.'[18]

Soviet Valery Borzov exploded onto the scene in 1972 and won gold in both the 100 and 200 metres in Munich. The irony was not lost on Peter.

> In Mexico I'd attended a genetic research establishment set up in the village. Athletes were invited to answer a series of questions and be photographed with nothing more than a G-string on, standing on a little turntable which rotated while they photographed us on every angle. We didn't see the results, but we got a certificate to say we'd taken part. It was a very detailed study lasting about four hours. They got genetic information about our parents and family. Phil May went through it too. The Russians were thought to be using all sorts of different methods to create or improve their athletes. I don't believe Valery Borzov was a clone, but he was a physical copy of me. Borzov had the same lack of height, same arm and leg carriage, same body lean, and the same pumping piston action of knee lift that I had. Everything about Borzov was as close to me as you could get.

NOTES

1 'It's Norman!', *The Sun*, 21 February 1972.

2 'It's Norman!', *The Sun*, 21 February 1972.

3 'Great 200 run by Norman', *The Sporting Globe*, 19 February 1972.

4 'Silver, but so tarnished', *The Sun*, 28 February 1972.

5 'Silver, but so tarnished', *The Sun*, 28 February 1972.

6 'Silver, but so tarnished', *The Sun*, 28 February 1972.

7 'After film, Norman is sure', *The Sun*, 29 February 1972.

8 'Norman still has a grudge', *The Herald*, *c*. 1974.

9 In its full glory, the expression is to 'give a rat's arse' – or, in polite society, 'I couldn't care less'!

10 'It's Lewis – for sure!', *The Sporting Globe*, 4 March 1972.

11 Peter didn't turn 30 until June that year.

12 'Peter may have lost team place', *The Age*, 27 March 1972.

13 'Silver medallist misses', *Sydney Morning Herald*, 28 March 1972.

14 'Athletes may win seven gold', *The Herald*, 28 March 1972.

15 'Norman to run on', *The Sun*, 30 March 1972.

16 All selectors had died by the time research began on this biography, so it was not possible to interview them about Peter's non-selection.

17 The Fremantle Doctor is the vernacular term for the cooling afternoon sea breeze that hits coastal areas of Western Australia almost daily during summer months. The breeze, which occurs because of the temperature difference between land and sea, is reputed to be one of the world's most consistent winds. It generally hits the coast between noon and 3 pm. The wind is so named in Perth because it appears to come from the nearby coastal city of Fremantle.

18 'Athletes shocked at Games choice', *The Sun*, 21 March 1972.

15
DON'T GET MAD, GET EVEN

With athletics no longer a part of his life, Peter threw his energy into playing Australian Rules football for the West Brunswick amateurs, which he did for three seasons. His teaching mate John McAdam, from Williamstown Technical School, accompanied Peter to most games. Peter never professed to be a top player, but he didn't hesitate to put his body on the line during a game, as John recalled: 'One time at Albert Park he got whacked in the throat. As he was carried off, he was gasping for breath and gurgling. I drove him to Prince Henry's hospital and they found that Peter had ruptured his trachea.'

Peter also did some coaching at West Brunswick, as he recalled:

> We used to spend Saturdays picking up between twelve and eighteen callow youths, loading them, and God knows how, into the back of an all too small Mazda Bongo van, then driving to a football ground somewhere in Melbourne and watching the opposition beat the shit out of them.[1]

Perry Crosswhite represented Australia in basketball at the 1972 Olympics.[2] On his return from Munich, Crosswhite was chosen to be the first recreation officer employed in the Victorian government's Department of Youth, Sport and Recreation. This became the first state department of its kind in Australia. Peter was seconded from the Education Department to the new department in 1973, where he and Crosswhite became colleagues. Both worked on the Matthew Flinders Bicentennial Festival in 1974 and a range of other projects. Peter enjoyed the year he spent working with Crosswhite. 'Perry was over two metres and I felt like his little brother [at just 1.8 metres] when we walked down the street to go to lunch. We got on very well together but eventually we went our separate ways.' Crosswhite and Peter would connect again some years later when Peter's career took a new path.

Jan McQueen said she and Peter 'were madly in love with one another' by this time, but her decision to have a permanent relationship with him was still 'a bit further down the track'. In 1973 Jan went to Europe with two other Williamstown Tech teachers, Liz Connell and Ann Tyson, thinking this would either make or break her relationship with Peter.

> He and I wrote to each other about three or four times a week while I was overseas. Here I was in Europe where I had everything at my feet, but he talked me into coming back. Peter wrote some good letters to get me back. Even though I did correct his spelling on occasions, he was very good at writing.[3]

While Jan was overseas, Peter moved into a house in South Melbourne with John. By now Peter and John had become good drinking mates. Peter described John as

> one of the most brilliant teachers on his day. Not on his day, he could be one of the worst teachers you'd see. He taught maths and science. Some of the experiments he got up to weren't exactly out of the textbook, including the establishment of what was, I think, the first chicken-and-champagne breakfast that was ever held in the science lab in a technical school. The champagne was poured into chemical beakers and the chicken was served in pneumatic troughs. John was renowned for little things like that.

In 1976, Peter and Jan decided to marry in New Zealand in a double wedding with Jan's sister, as Jan related. 'My sister Ali is my closest friend in the whole world. We were thinking of getting married. She and Jim Dahl, an American, were thinking of getting married. So why not have a double wedding?'

The wedding date, 16 October 1976, was significant. It was eight years to the day since Peter had won his silver medal in Mexico. It was a 'biggish' wedding held in Christchurch's stately old homestead Mona Vale, which was resplendent with beautiful gardens and a stream meandering through the property. Thelma and Heather Norman attended the wedding. Heather recalled it was a typical 1970s garden wedding, complete with flowers in the hair: 'It was very pretty.' Jan's bridesmaid was her cousin Kathy Blain and Peter's best man was John. The two couples honeymooned together at a friend's house at Hanmer, which is about 130 kilometres north of Christchurch.

> Hanmer is where all the hot springs are, so we used to sit in the hot springs every night. At some stage, Mum and Dad popped up for a day or two and stayed nearby. Peter used to laugh and say, 'Great, your honeymoon's spent with your mother-in-law, father-in-law and sister-in-law!'

Peter moved with Jan to a house in Minnie Street, Brunswick, where they returned after their honeymoon.

John was very pleased to be asked to be best man, but it wasn't without its problems, as he described.

> I went over to New Zealand with my hair a long way down my back. It was super long! Jan had a problem with that. It was a strong discussion point whether I should get my hair cut. I refused. Peter supported me with that. He said if John wants to wear his hair like that, he can wear his hair like that. End of story!

John had always doubted Peter's real commitment to being a physical education (PE) teacher. He saw teaching as being 'something Peter could do'. John was aware that Peter was a disciplinarian with the students: 'They were scared of him,' recalled John. 'It was a case of "You talk, when I tell you to talk," type of thing.' Jan agreed. It was handy having Peter at the same school because the students were certainly scared of him: 'He was very tough and quite mean and would give them six of the best.'

Williamstown Technical School adopted a different concept of education in the mid 1970s. The school introduced 'open' periods and Peter came up with the idea of slot-car racing classes. He was fully prepared when slot cars became an officially sanctioned PE class, as his own slot-car track was already assembled in the basement of the school's assembly hall. John said Peter won approval for the slot-car classes on the basis that he saw it offering a chance for the students to 'build on this as a catalyst for art, maybe by painting and decorating their cars, for science by calculating the ratio of the wheels and gears so that their car could go faster, for maths by calculating distances etc. But did all this happen? No!' Peter's work at Williamstown 'more or less' consisted of three slot-car classes a day for the whole week.

Peter enjoyed fishing, so he subsequently added fishing to his PE program after obtaining the school's approval to take students out on a boat. Peter didn't own a boat, so he used one that belonged to his old boss Tom Elmi.

> Tom had a rather large motorboat. He told me to treat it like my own. All I had to do was pick up the keys and then make sure that when I'd finished, the boat was safely put away in the boatshed. The next time I'd go down there, the fridge would be full of beer and the briquette bucket would be full of briquettes. The petrol in the boat would be absolutely full. I wasn't allowed to do any of that. I used to do some of his maintenance work for him, like clean the boat down or take it for a service. That's all he expected.

Tom recalled Peter borrowing his boat. 'It was housed at Campbell's Cove. He would take the school kids out fishing for the day. I thought highly of Peter. He was so good with my kids. He was like part of the family for many years after he'd finished working for me in the butcher's shop.'

John remembered that the boatshed became a 'little retreat' for Peter and Jan.

> I was going with Liz Connell at the time. She and I would spend weekends down there with them. Tom Elmi's boatshed had a couple of bunks. We'd take the boat out and we'd fish. We'd barbecue the fish we'd caught, then spend the Saturday night there. We'd go out fishing again on Sunday morning and then drive home.

Peter enjoyed outdoor activities and liked going on school camps at Dromana. John went with Peter twice: 'Peter was like the camp commandant, but he also cooked the breakfasts, lunches and evening meals with the kids. He really enjoyed doing that.'

Trade union participation by Victorian teachers was the norm during the 1970s, and teachers held strikes and demonstrations in the desire to make decent education a right for every student and to protect their rights and conditions. Peter took an active interest in the rights of teachers and union activities, as did Jan, John and fellow teachers at the school. Peter went on strike with his colleagues, and attended the numerous union rallies and marches on Parliament House. 'We marched,' said John, 'but then we would all party afterwards.' Unions would lose their power and unqualified teachers such as Peter would be in trouble – but that was in the future. In the meantime Peter was enjoying partying.

Peter built up a 'terribly strong dependence' on alcohol in the late 1970s and early 1980s, according to John, who drank with him many times over this period. 'We used to drink a lot, but I never started the day off at eight o'clock with a beer, like he did. He'd come around at the weekend in the Bongo van. He'd have picked up some cans and he'd already have started drinking.' Either Peter or one of his friends would throw a party once a week. Peter was always the life of the party, but never the aggressive drunk. Every one loved Peter in the party environment. Peter and John were both fans of the legendary comedians Laurel and Hardy. They would often break into a Laurel and Hardy routine at a party, particularly with a few charges under their belts. Peter would play Hardy. John would be Laurel. No matter what tripped the routine, they'd feed off each other and keep the routine running as long as possible.

When Peter and Jan were living in Minnie Street, Peter and John stayed up drinking at night while Jan was in bed. At the weekend, they would go fishing and drink some more, or they would have a barbecue, which always involved drinking. John always drank beer, whereas Peter mixed his drinks, having spirits, then beer or a mixed drink such as a brandy. John said Peter was drinking when he was teaching. Around 1984, John visited Peter in the basement at Williamstown where he had his slot-car track set up.

> He sent me off to buy a bottle of brandy. I mixed the brandy with some dry ginger and poured it out into a soft-drink bottle, and got rid of the brandy bottle, so no one knew. One of the kids went to pick up the bottle to take a drink thinking it was soft drink. I grabbed it. This was around 2.30 pm. It was certainly before school finished at 3.30 pm. So he was still on Education Department time.

John remembered this started before Peter hurt his Achilles heel. 'The drinking just didn't start when it came out years later that he had a problem with drink and painkillers. It was building up before that.'

John also recalled Jan taking classes at Footscray Institute of Technology two to three nights a week. 'We'd be drinking and many nights Peter and I would crash on the front couch when Jan would be either home or not home. Jan was so pissed off at times with Peter's drinking, but she hung in there.' Peter was also smoking heavily, as was John. 'We always smoked and drank. He probably tried to hide his smoking from Jan.' John remembered Peter smoking at least a pack a day: 'All the time I knew him he smoked.'

One of Peter's favourite sayings was 'don't get mad, get even'. John recalled Peter getting even one particular Melbourne Cup Day. Peter and Jan were by then renting a house in Flemington, just opposite the racecourse. Peter had barricaded part of the street so that friends could attend a barbecue at the house. Someone had the temerity to pinch a parking space left for Peter's friends, 'So to seek revenge on the person, Peter put two nails under each of the four car tyres, so if they reversed out or drove forward, they were going to get at least one nail in each tyre.' Peter's reason, according to John, was: 'They've parked where I've reserved places for my friends, so they're gonna get a flat no matter what they do. And they're gonna get more than one!'

Peter was very interested in three things during the 1960s and 1970s: track and field, teaching and acting.

> In the 1960s and early 1970s, it was all track and field. The reason I stayed in track and field so long was that it was an ego trip. I enjoyed it. It was something I was really good at. The ego trip carried through in a funny sort of way to being a teacher. A teacher has to perform every time he gets up in front of a class. You have to be able to sell the subject you're teaching. Plus you have to maintain control. When I stopped competing, I missed that ego trip, but I still had this ability to perform.

So Peter fell into professional acting. His sisters Heather and Elaine were associated with the Coburg Review amateur theatre company. The company was asked if they could do a melodrama for a theatre restaurant in 1975. Elaine's husband Michael was the company's resident villain. Peter elaborated:

> Elaine was pregnant with their second child and Michael didn't want to be away from home for two nights a week. Heather asked me if I would play the character Texas Dan in the show 'Texas Tickle'. So I had a look at the show. I thought I could probably do it all right. At the time I was about to get married for a second time and was heading over to New Zealand with my best man, my very dear friend John McAdam. I learnt the script while I was away on my honeymoon and was on stage performing within a month of that. When the cast was put up for the following production unfortunately Michael didn't get the part and I did.

Bob Stuart wrote and performed in 'Texas Tickle'. Bob recalled that Peter was only to do this one show as a fill-in part. He expected Michael to come back. But club owner Ken Day was paying for the show and wanted Peter because of his reputation as an athlete. When the opportunity arose, Peter didn't let it slip. When Michael left, Bob received a phone call from Peter's mother: 'She was upset that the family was at loggerheads. There was obviously some concern and she voiced it to me. I explained that it wasn't my doing.' Elaine remembered that Ken Day thought it was a boon to have an ex-Olympian in the show, 'so Michael got the flick!' Cast member Arch Galloway is emphatic that Peter joined the show on talent: 'Peter played the villain much better than Michael. He fitted in really well and took over just as if he'd been there forever.'

'Texas Tickle' was so successful that Day asked Bob to write another one. Before long, the cast of Bob, Peter, Arch, Margot McKay and Julie Enwright was under contract to perform one show a year, starting in March. The show would run on Thursday nights right through until September, at which time it was extended to two shows a week. By the middle of December the cast was performing three shows a week, on Wednesday, Thursday and Friday evenings.

Each production consisted of three half-hour acts, with a fifteen-minute interval. 'We'd start at 8.30 pm and finish between 10.30 and 11 pm,' said Bob. 'The girls and Arch would go on again after that for a half-hour song or dancing bracket. Then we'd walk out into the audience to meet and greet. It was through the meet-and-greet time that we got a lot of bookings. Peter always played the villain in the shows. He liked the limelight and was popular with the audience.'

The productions became so successful that the group formed a company on 9 August 1977. The company, known as Couch Productions, was formed on the basis that equal shares of the revenue from shows would go to the five cast members. Each member had offstage roles to perform as well as those onstage. Arch was the company's accountant and bookkeeper. Bob did all the writing. Julie and Margot looked after costuming, while Peter would help make sets and arrange their painting, as well as look after the sound system.

This was the heyday of the theatre-restaurant. Day owned Churchill's restaurant, one of Melbourne's top theatre venues. Arch recalled:

> We were at Churchill's for about ten years, then approximately eight years at the Highway Inn, and then we had short stints at a couple of other venues. We weren't making enough money to live on, but we were certainly earning enough to make working during the day and working at night more comfortable. In latter years, in December, we'd be doing anything up to five different shows a week, so a different show every night. We had about five shows in our head at the same time.

In time, Couch Productions took their shows to country towns throughout Victoria. These shows were booked through word of mouth from people coming to the Melbourne shows. Initially the cast travelled in two to three vehicles, but they eventually bought a twelve-seater bus so as to be able to travel together and haul their equipment, stage fixtures and props, and costumes. Peter enjoyed driving, so he drove the bus to most country shows. There was a strong camaraderie among the cast and they became firm friends over the 20 or so years that they performed together before the productions ceased in 1994.

Peter loved his time with Couch Productions, especially being on stage as he discussed.

> We performed something like eleven different musical melodramas[4] all over the state. We just had a great time doing it. As the resident villain, I played such notable characters as Count Alacard and Count von Creep. I even played the dastardly landlord Grubby Richard, which suited me down to the ground.

> When we decided to do 'Sinderella', I knew that I was just right for the prince, but unfortunately the costumes were a bit tight. Plus I didn't look good in white stockings and tights! How about the fairy god person then? I didn't look good in a tutu either, so they forced me into the role of the not-so-ugly sister. I accepted not-so-ugly – I refused to be an ugly sister! So I frocked up each night and played the part of Gertrude, the not-so-ugly sister and was just gorgeous. The moustache was a bit of a giveaway though!

Peter had fun writing his biography for the shows' souvenir programs. His biography for 'Passion, Poison 'n Purity' read:

> Peter has worked in front of audiences all over the world and scored runaway successes and notable performances in Los Angeles, New York, Chicago and across the Atlantic in London and Edinburgh. At the height of his success, Peter was selected to perform in front of non-English-speaking audiences in Mexico City … where he was greeted with cries of 'Come on Señor Aussie, come on!! Come on!!'

For a time, Jan worked at Churchill's restaurant on show nights as a waitress. Peter got John a job there too, serving drinks from the bar, setting up props and handling the spotlight. John and Peter had fun preparing John's biography at the time of the 'Passion, Poison 'n' Purity' production, which read, in part: 'John's reputation has preceded him to the Churchill restaurant. In the past sixteen years he has given scores of unforgettable performances in front of royalty … the Duke of Edinburgh, the Prince of Wales, the Empress of India … Even so, he is yet to gain entry to one of these hotels.'

Despite keeping very busy with teaching and theatre commitments, Peter took on another sporting role when he joined the Footscray Football Club as its running coach in 1979. Peter told a reporter at the time that he believed he could improve the players' speed. 'Our program is to increase hip and stomach flexibility, thereby giving players a straighter step. And we want to increase their leg power too.'[5] Ron Simmons, the club's runner and weights coach, and Alec Gardiner, who joined the club as fitness adviser the same season as Peter, both became friends of Peter's.

Alec said Peter's role was to improve the running techniques and speed of the players. 'The bulk of Peter's work was done pre-season. It was a hard job.

It wasn't always seen and appreciated the way we thought it should be, but you didn't let that get to you.' At the time, the emphasis on fitness was nowhere near as strong as it is now. 'We still had to prove ourselves because players and coaches weren't convinced. Peter had a good rapport with the players. He had a tremendous sense of humour, which the players appreciated.' The job was poorly paid. It barely covered the cost of petrol, but Peter enjoyed his five years at the club, before he left at the end of the 1983 season.

Ron managed a nearby fitness centre and was the runner at Footscray for 20 seasons, so he was well-versed in fitness techniques. He enjoyed working with Peter and maintained his contact with him after Peter left the club.

> Peter was a ripper bloke. As running coach, Peter had the players with ropes round their guts pulling tyres and all sorts of stuff like that. Now it's done in a more scientific form, but the results he was getting back then would be equal to what they're getting today.

Ray Boyd was Australia's best pole vaulter for many years. Ray and his wife, Denise, lived with Peter and Jan in Minnie Street for eighteen months, from late 1977 to early 1979. Peter and Ray had been mates since getting to know one another on the 1969 Pacific Conference Games trip when Ray's mother asked Peter to look after Ray on what was the pole vaulter's first overseas trip. 'How could you look after Ray Boyd for God's sake?' exclaimed Peter, 'but I took him under my wing and let him carry my bags on a few occasions!' Peter knew only too well that Ray wasn't known for his gambling skills. 'When we'd get on a plane, everyone would settle down and go to sleep, then word would go around that Boydy was in a card game and everyone would come from everywhere to take his money.'

Peter and Ray would periodically get their athletics medals out to see who had the most. 'At that stage I think I had nineteen,' contended Peter, 'and he had seventeen state and national championships. When he got to nineteen, I'd always trump his nineteen with the silver medal.'[6]

Ray had never forgotten Peter's disappointment at not being awarded first place in the 100 metres race against Greg Lewis back in 1972. How could he forget – it came up during every medal count. Ray recalled Peter receiving an unexpected letter in the mail that drew their medal count to a conclusion. At this time Ray was marginally ahead of Peter.

> Peter really wanted to win in 1972. Hec Hogan was his boyhood

hero. I walked in one night from training and Peter was holding this letter up. It was heavy. Out falls the silver medal from the 1972 Hec Hogan race. The letter said, 'We were going through some boxes at the VAAA offices and came across this medal and we believe it's yours.' So Peter said, 'I think we're even, Boydy!' I said, 'Yeah we are'. I was prepared to accept it was a gold medal too!

Denise remembered how Peter loved acting and cooking, but, in particular, he loved comedies. 'We'd go to bed and Jan would go to bed. But we'd hear Peter laughing downstairs in the early hours of the morning. He'd be leaning against the lounge suite watching a funny movie.' Peter always sat on the floor while he watched a movie.[7]

Ray and Peter enjoyed each other's company. They both had a similar sense of humour. Ray recalled an example.

Somewhere on a trip, something came up about 'Can you call me a cab? Peter said, 'You're a cab!' From then on, if you'd answer the phone and it was Peter calling, he'd start off by saying, 'Can you call me a cab?' He'd always say it with a little bit of an American twang to his voice too. The 'call me a cab' routine went on for 30 years or more.

Denise confirmed that Peter was always upbeat: 'There wasn't any doom and gloom with him. There was always something humorous in a situation. He was always good to be around.'

The two couples remained close after Peter and Jan bought their own home in Williamstown in 1979. Peter and Jan's first daughter, Belinda Rae, was born on Melbourne Cup Day, 4 November 1980, at Williamstown Hospital. Jan relived the experience:

Her birth was the most amazing thing that had ever happened, and Peter was fantastic. Even though he had had children from his previous marriage, he didn't ever say, 'I've already done that', or 'I know what to do'. It was like he was learning as well. He didn't ever make me feel that he'd done it before and that it wasn't as exciting.

There was further joy in the Norman household when a second daughter,

Emma Jayne, was born on Father's Day, 5 September 1982.

Soon after they moved to Williamstown, Peter lost a lot of his club medals in a fire at the house. Heather Norman recounts what happened. 'The medals were in a box in a kitchen cupboard. I think they were down the street shopping on a Saturday morning. The kitchen somehow caught fire.' The kitchen and part of the family's dining room were badly burnt. 'All these medals came out in one molten lump of metal.' Peter's silver medal, however, was not affected.

After the fire, Peter took up carpentry, after, Heather suspected, he had watched the builders repairing their house. Peter pine-lined the laundry, then the bathroom. 'When the girls were small, he built a cubbyhouse for them in the garden. It later served to house various pets. Emma had guinea pigs.' Peter also built decking around their pool and included a Mediterranean-style outdoor eating area. He also added two bungalows. Heather recalled that 'Dad was a master handyman and he thought none of his skills had rubbed off on Peter, until he saw Peter's work. Dad was really proud of him.' She believed that Peter learnt by watching, listening and careful questioning. She had seen Peter quiz her friends on subjects he knew little about, but by agreeing with a statement, he led the person to elaborate. When he left, he would soon read up on the topic and he'd never be caught out not knowing something a second time.

Peter developed quite a talent for building. After completing the larger outdoor projects, he turned his attention to intricate and finely crafted items inside the family home, including a coffee table, a large dining table and several large dining and lounge-room cabinets. 'He initially had no idea what he was doing,' said Jan, 'but he had a Reader's Digest manual. Plus he'd go around and look at what other people were doing on building sites. He'd come back and then have a go here.'

Belinda and Emma brought Peter and Jan a lot of joy. Jan recalled the family going camping at Halls Gap three or four times when the girls were young. Halls Gap, 256 kilometres west of Melbourne, is the tourist hub of Victoria's Grampians National Park. The Grampians are known for spectacular scenery and outdoor recreation, making them a popular holiday destination. 'We stayed in cabins at the Church of Christ camping ground in Halls Gap. We'd go on long walks and sing silly songs as we walked.' Peter was always good for a singalong and could always be counted on to belt out the 'silly songs' with great gusto.

The 1980s would prove to be troubled times, however, for Peter, Jan and the family. As militancy subsided in schools, earlier gains by the union were wound back. As a result, Peter's lack of formal teaching qualifications would be exposed. He would also suffer a horrendous injury that would torment Peter and his family for years to come.

NOTES

1 Peter Norman, email to John McAdam, 26 May 2002.

2 Perry Crosswhite also represented Australia at the 1976 and 1980 Olympics, captaining both teams.

3 Spelling was never one of Peter's strong points!

4 The show titles included 'Texas Tickle – A Western Bang Bang', 'Sinderella', 'Cash on the Knockers', 'Naughty Naughty 007', 'Dial M for Mayhem', 'Once a Bite's Enough', 'Passion, Poison 'n' Purity' and 'The Perils of Percy'.

5 *The Sun*, 23 January 1979.

6 Ray Boyd was twelve times national pole-vault champion. He represented Australia at three Commonwealth Games (winning gold in 1982), two Olympic Games and four Pacific Conference Games. Denise Boyd won four 100 metre national titles, six 200 metre titles and one 400 metre title. She represented Australia at three Commonwealth Games (winning two gold, three silver and three bronze medals), two Olympic Games, two Pacific Conference Games, one World Cup and at one World Championship. Their three children are now achieving success in athletics.

7 Ray said, 'I was talking to his daughter at his funeral and I told her he was always sitting down on the floor, leaning up against the couch. She said, "Yeah he still did that". He'd be giggling away. He used to enjoy his own company.'

16

A SHITHOUSE D-GRADE RELAY RACE

In November 1985, 43-year-old Peter joined former East Melbourne Harriers (EMH) teammate Maurie Drew in a D-grade relay race for the Essendon EMH club.[1] The relay was held mid afternoon in front of approximately 300 people at the club's Aberfeldie Park track. Peter related the story:

> I'm running the third leg. I moved off the mark very easily, took the baton, put my right foot on the ground and, as soon as I picked it up, I knew that I wouldn't be able to put it down again. Something had snapped round the bottom of my ankle. The pain was absolutely incredible. I hopped to a stop and waited until everybody had gone past, then hopped off the side of the track to find that I had blown my Achilles tendon.

Having talked Peter into running in the relay, Drew regretted not warning Peter that they were 'not here to set Olympic records. We're here to enjoy ourselves'. Drew said D-grade was social and for 'old farts' like him and Peter. Peter thought he had a reasonable level of fitness, but according to Maurie he went at it like a bull at a gate.

> That competitive spirit came out and that was his undoing. I gave the baton to Trevor Beecham who gave it to Peter. I heard Peter's

> Achilles snap and rushed to him. Jan also rushed on to the track. Peter knew he was in real trouble. We carried him into the weights room and laid him down on one of the training bags until the ambulance arrived. Jan went with him in the ambulance to the hospital.

Beecham remembered that the team was in front when Peter took off with the baton: 'I thought this is going to be embarrassing. We're going to blitz them. I'd given Peter the baton, so I felt awful.'

Jan recalled little of the day.

> I blot out those memories. I was there with the girls. One minute he was running flat out, the next minute he was hop, hop, hopping. He thought he was actually a lot fitter than he was. He thought he could just get on the track and run, but he'd done no training. He literally hopped on the track and then it happened.

Peter later admitted to his friend Robin Kidney that he was a 'bloody fool' for running and that he should have said he was too old to compete.

Peter said that, because it was late November, the doctor suggested he finish the school year and then have the operation to have the tendon reattached and repaired, so that he'd be ready to teach again by the end of the school holidays. Peter was operated on by an orthopedic surgeon at Prince Henry's Hospital[2] in mid December: 'They put the tendon back together and told me it was a pretty painful procedure and that I'd be suffering a bit, so I tried to put the pain out of my mind.'

Jan remembered that Peter was initially going to stay in hospital over Christmas. 'We'd even booked our Christmas dinner in hospital. The day before Christmas though, they took one look at Peter and said, "You can go home". They sent him home with a gangrenous leg!' Peter sat at home that Christmas as pale as a ghost with his leg encased in plaster.

> He was in agony, lots of agony. When he eventually got to see the doctor after Christmas when he went for a check-up, he said to him, 'How much agony should I be in?', because he didn't know how painful it was meant to be. By this time we were down at Mount Eliza. A friend had lent us her house. Peter had to come back to the city for the check-up. He hopped on a train and went back to the hospital. They took his plaster off and took one look at his leg and he didn't come out.

Peter continued:

> I went back for an outpatient visit and found that gangrene had set in underneath the plaster. They were prepared to take the leg, but a plastic surgeon who had run against me at Melbourne University said, 'We can't take this guy's leg off as he's a physical education teacher, an Olympic sprinter, and his legs are his life. We've got to try and save it.' So he suggested a procedure. He told me that if I could last the procedure I'd probably go mad, but I could still buy shoes in pairs.

Drew recalled Peter saying to him on several occasions that 'he couldn't believe he was perhaps going to lose his leg over a shithouse D-grade relay race'.

The plastic surgeon was Peter Dixon. He had first met Peter when he was training with famed coach Franz Stampfl at Melbourne University. Peter was competing against some of Stampfl's stable, including Gary Eddy and Phil King. Dixon was a fifteen-year-old schoolboy competing in the 440 yards hurdles at the time.

Doctors called in Dixon, one of the visiting plastic surgeons at Prince Henry's Hospital, when they took the plaster down and saw that Peter's wound was not healing. Dixon's recollection of events differed slightly from Peter's.

> I decided to take the procedure on because of my enthusiasm for Peter Norman and my understanding of who he was. The fact that Peter knew me gave him confidence. Peter had had this surgical repair and then the wound broke down over the repair. He was presented to me as a skin defect overlying his ruptured Achilles tendon repair. If the defect wasn't covered, the repair would rupture and there would probably be no way of easily completing the problem of the Achilles rupture.
>
> We talked about the more aggressive or more extensive surgery we had to do because of the time that had passed and because the tendon had shrunk. But I don't think amputation was ever a real consideration. In fully discussing alternatives with him, I would have mentioned that in the highly unlikely event of the infection getting out of control, or if it was truly gangrene, then he may lose the lower part of his leg. I don't know that it was gangrene.

> Gangrene is too harsh a word. With an incision over the Achilles tendon, the tissues down there are at the end of the vascular tree. They have the least nutrition and are more susceptible to wound breakdown and infection. Also the plaster may well have irritated potential for the wound to break down.
>
> The procedure that we did wasn't consistent with having such a serious infection as gangrene because we got onto it fairly early and quite successfully.

Dixon had no doubt that the problem was compounded by the initial delay in carrying out the surgery.

> By then the tendons had retracted and scar tissue had formed in their place. You then had to be more aggressive in finding the tendon ends and trying to mobilise them. So you're doing a more expansive operation in this area of marginal blood supply than you would have done if he had been in and out.

Peter's operation, which took place on 7 January 1986, would have taken approximately two hours. Dixon described the operation:

> We would have done the cleaning up of Peter's wound, and the orthopaedic surgeons would have done either a peroneal tendon graft or pedicle tendon graft across it. Then we did one of the last cross-leg flaps.[3] With a cross-leg flap, you take the tissue from the calf of the good leg, leaving it attached to that same leg and making what is called a pedicle of tissue. You raise that up, turn it and place and suture it over the hole in the injured leg. You then take a skin graft from one of the person's thighs to fill in the area on the healthy leg where you've taken that pedicle of tissue.

Dixon likens the tissue taken from Peter's thigh for the skin graft to a 'deep graze'. This area of skin would be different in texture and often colour to what it was originally. It would also be more prone to sunburn than the normal area.

The operation would have then been almost complete. All that would have remained was for a piece of broomstick to be placed between Peter's legs, and plastered to prevent him moving. His legs would have been positioned so as to ensure, as much as possible, that he could cope with having his legs bound together for a period of three weeks. Dixon said:

> What you're hoping will occur over those three weeks is that you'll get enough blood supply coming in from the leg which had the Achilles repair and that enough blood will flow backwards into that tissue, so that when we divide it away from the good leg, the tissue that had been transferred will remain viable.

It was imperative that Peter awoke smoothly and comfortably after his operation. Had he woken up and tried to move his legs, even though everything was splinted in place, he could have destroyed the operation.

It was also important that the nursing staff position Peter correctly: first, because his legs were going to be strapped together for three weeks and, second, to ensure he was comfortable, especially in the first few days after the operation when he could have been anxious. Dixon can't remember Peter being any more or less anxious than anybody else. Peter then needed to be moved constantly for comfort. After a few days, assuming that everything was progressing normally, it was expected that Peter would be able to use the frame above his bed to lift himself up, move around a little and gradually, over the three weeks, become more mobile.

Dixon got to know Peter well while regularly visiting him, particularly during the first days after the operation. As well as checking on Peter's general disposition, Dixon also needed to ensure that the cross-leg flap remained viable and stayed attached to Peter's legs and wasn't being pulled apart.

Dixon asserted that Peter would have been put on pain relief straight away: 'You would use morphine-based medication for the first two to four days. It would be painful. Plus there is a period of anxiety and shock. There's pretty intensive monitoring to make sure patients don't move or pull their legs apart and strain, and also to make sure they understand exactly what's going on.'

After three weeks in plaster, Peter underwent a second operation of around 40 minutes duration to remove the plaster and broomstick.

A day after the second operation, Peter's dressing was taken down, and the flap examined to make sure it was still viable. 'We would have then started to get him exercising his ankle in bed,' continued Dixon. 'We'd have gotten him up with crutches and started to get him walking and hopping on his good leg. A week later he would have been encouraged to partially weight-bear on his leg.' Physiotherapists would have begun to move his ankle, and gradually, over three to four weeks, get him walking without the aid of crutches. According to Dixon, 'You have to protect the repair and that's why I talk about this graduated return to walking and therapy.'

Peter found lying flat on his back in hospital 'pretty demoralising'.

> I couldn't do anything. But all through that, Jan would bring our two daughters in every day. Emma and Belinda would perform excerpts from 'Annie' while standing up on the windowsill of the hospital room. That was lovely and it kept me going.

Jan said that even though Peter hated hospitals, he was a really good patient and all the nurses liked him.

Heather Norman was attending a summer school in Melbourne, and was staying at the Victoria Hotel in the city centre at the time of Peter's surgery. She walked to Prince Henry's Hospital to see Peter every day for several weeks. 'It was a horrible time for him. He was pretty down.' Heather used to rack her brain to think of something that Peter could do, given he had to remain in the one position. He could only do a certain amount of reading, so she took him some puzzles to complete. Elaine recalled her brother being quite impatient with his daughters during one hospital visit: 'It was, "Jan, take these girls out, now!" He had had enough of them! Having said that though, Peter didn't like hospitals. It was a big thing for him to visit people in hospitals. If you were in hospital and got a visit from Peter, you were damn lucky!'

Peter said that leaving the hospital on 1 March 1986 was the most amazing feeling.

> Jan drove me home with my feet up on pillows. Here I was being driven along, absolutely petrified. Cars were going past so close, because for all this time I'd been looking out of a third-storey window into St Kilda Road. The only thing I could see were all these little miniature cars going past. Now all of a sudden they're these huge big things again! Then to get inside the house in a wheelchair and everything had changed. The indoor plants were much bigger.

Peter was so overwhelmed he broke down: 'I didn't just sob. I bawled my eyes out. I knew that if I had missed seeing the plants grow that much, I had missed seeing the two kids grow too.'[4] Jan recalled that Peter was in a

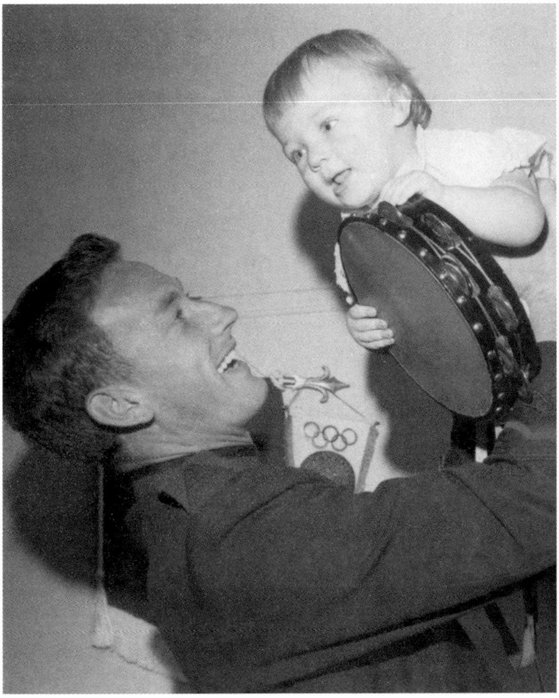

Left: *Peter auditions his daughter Janita (born 1967) as a timbrel player in the Salvation Army band.*

Below left: *Australians John Farrington, Phil May, Peter Norman, Ray Weinberg and Raelene Boyle relax in the Olympic Village in Mexico City, 1968.*

Below right: *Australian track coach Ray Weinberg passes on some advice (run well or else!) to sprinters Dianne Burge and Peter during training in Mexico City.*

A MEDAL OR YOUR LIFE

"A medal or your life" Australian track coach Ray Weinberg seems to be telling Dianne Burge during training in Mexico City. But it's only a starting pistol he is holding as he talks to Mrs. Burge and 200 metres king Peter Norman.

(A.A.P. photo)

shown dividends. Doubell recorded Australia's have topped seven feet. — AAP-AP picture. Smale and Ralph Roberts,

Tipped to become the new golden girl of Australian international athletics is 17-year-old Melbourne student Raelene Boyle in a training session. Raelene was wearing special gold-coloured spikes designed by her father, Mr Mac Boyle, of Coburg, Vic-

Top left and right: *Australia failed to enter a relay team in the 1968 Olympics, but in pre-Games competition relays Peter ran himself into top form as these photos, taken 30 September 1968, show. At top, Peter takes the baton some three metres behind the Soviet runner. At bottom, the Soviet runner crosses the line ahead of Peter by just 30 centimetres.*

Above: *The photo finish shows Tommie Smith winning the 200 metres final in Mexico by just over a metre from Peter, whose powerful finish enabled him to edge centimetres clear of John Carlos.*

Right: *John Carlos, Tommie Smith and Peter begin their long walk across the Olympic stadium for the 200 metres medal presentation. Their lives were about to change forever.*

USA
USA

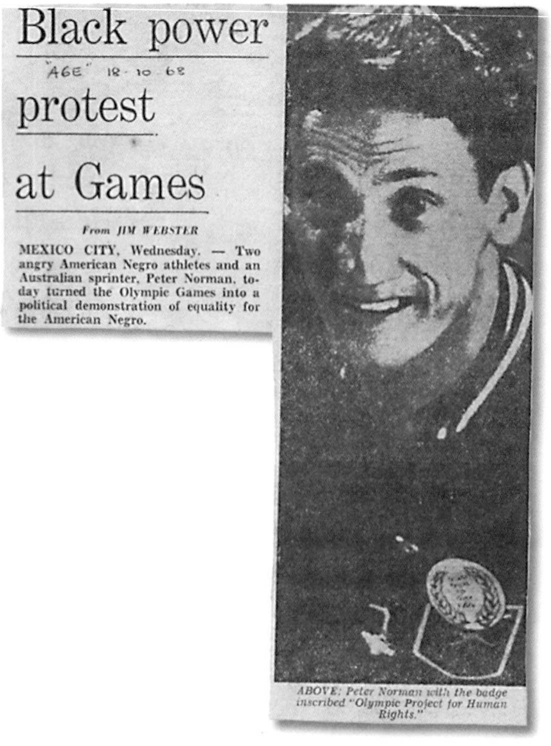

Black power protest at Games

"AGE" 18-10-68

From JIM WEBSTER

MEXICO CITY, Wednesday. — Two angry American Negro athletes and an Australian sprinter, Peter Norman, today turned the Olympic Games into a political demonstration of equality for the American Negro.

ABOVE: Peter Norman with the badge inscribed "Olympic Project for Human Rights."

Previous page and above: *Cameramen record the event that shocked the world. The event has become an iconic image not only of the Olympics but also of the twentieth century.*

Left: *Peter wearing an Olympic Project for Human Rights badge in support of the stance taken by Tommie Smith and John Carlos at the medal presentation ceremony – in his own words, 'I thought this was a good chance to have a white man on their side'. 1966.*

Left: *Peter visiting the author, Damian Johnstone, in his hometown of Heathcote on 15 December 1968. Damian has never forgotten Peter's thoughtfulness.*

Below left: *Peter sets a new Tasmanian 100 yards record at the North Hobart oval during a rare visit to the state in January 1969. on Ruth's 20th birthday, 18 July 1964.*

Below right: *East Melbourne Harriers teammates Greg Lewis, Peter and Gary Holdsworth, pictured after all three recorded 10.4 seconds in the finish of the Victorian 100 metres championship at the Landy Field in Geelong on 7 January 1969. Peter was judged the winner ahead of Greg and Gary.*

OLYMPIAN Peter Norman, who won a silver medal for Australia in the 200 metres at Mexico City, ran the 100yds in 10.5s at North Hobart yesterday, to set a new Tasmanian record. Norman also won the 220yds in 22.1s, 2-10th of a second outside the Australian record. He is seen striding easily to an effortless win in the 100yds.

FASTEST MEN

The fastest men in Australia. These three athletes all recorded 10.4 seconds in the finish of the 100 metres Victorian championship at Landy Field last night. From left, Greg Lewis (placed second), Peter Norman (first), and Gary Holdsworth (third). See results page 24.

Above: *Peter competing by special invitation over 100 metres against Charlie Greene, John Carlos, Ronnie Ray Smith, Bill Gaines and Lionel Urgan in the inaugural Martin Luther King International Freedom Games in Philadelphia, USA, on 18 May 1969.*

Olympic Games appeal gets a $13,000 boost from Government

The Olympic Games fund to send the Aus- ... years ago when the Olympic team went to Mexico

Middle: *Judy Patching, Lawrie Peckham, Peter and Lindsay Thompson (Victorian Minister for Education) launch a fundraising appeal to send the Australian team to the 1972 Munich Olympics. The accompanying newspaper article stated that Lawrie and Peter were 'certain to be in the squad'. Lawrie was selected, but Peter, controversially, was not.*

Right: *Peter was best man when long-time rival and close mate Gary Holdsworth married Glenda Dennis on 23 August 1970. Gary chose Peter for the role, because Peter was 'the best man' he knew. Helen Grisca was bridesmaid.*

Above: *Peter and Ruth pictured with Janita (five), Sandra (20 months) and Gary (six months) in late March 1972. Despite the happy poses, Peter and Ruth's marriage was all but over by this time.*

Left: *Peter had no doubt that he defeated Greg Lewis to win the 1972 Victorian 100 metres championship. The judges did not agree and nor did Greg, who said 'I won because I've got the medal!'*

Above: *Despite missing selection for the 1972 Munich Olympics, Peter was never one to refuse a photo opportunity. Here he poses in an Australian team blazer for the Munich Games – a great pity it wasn't his.*

wheelchair for some weeks after he came home. 'He had a nurse who used to call in and do his dressings, not only on the Achilles, but also on the skin grafts at the top of his leg. That leg always looked unusual after that. You could never get sun on it.'

Dixon continued to see Peter as an outpatient for six months after the operation. Peter was then left to his own resources. Dixon expected that, after six months, Peter would have been walking and weight-bearing.

> We would have normally anticipated over the next twelve to eighteen months that he would have had reasonable mobility, but by his standards, be considerably hampered. After eighteen months or so, I would have expected Peter to walk reasonably well, but the ankle would always be a bit stiff and wouldn't be as flexible as the other one. In cold weather it would be a bit tender. But there would have been a significant disability from what he had been before he had the Achilles rupture.

Peter was now home after his operation, but if he thought he was well on the road to recovery, he was wrong – the battle was only just beginning. He was about to move into the darkest days of his life.

NOTES

1 By this time, EMH had become an incorporated entity with the Essendon Harriers athletic club.

2 Prince Henry's Hospital was decommissioned in 1991 and the building was demolished. Peter took great joy in watching the demolition and taking home a souvenir brick. The hospital didn't hold fond memories for him.

3 This procedure has now been replaced by microvascular surgery, but Peter Dixon contended that the results of the cross-leg flap procedure were 'brilliant' for the time.

4 'Norman's conquest', *The Herald Sun*, 13 August 1993.

17

EIGHT YEARS OF HELL

Peter was in immense pain when he came out of hospital and could not cope without medication. He attempted to return to teaching, but it proved impossible. He told sportswriter Ron Reed that he had started to 'wag' school, which wasn't good for a teacher to be doing. He had to give up his hobbies: tennis, squash and skindiving. This led to deep depression.

> I virtually went nuts. I had a breakdown. I'd take medication to knock out the pain, then have a couple of drinks, and I was a goner. I spent probably three years like a zombie. You become impatient that the medication isn't working fast enough, so you take more. By the time you're convinced it is working, you're so dopey you have no idea what you're doing. So you take even more, and so it goes on.

Peter related how he once took enough medication for three months in a week and had a couple of pretty bad turns: 'I was destroying myself, and I think I came pretty close to finishing the job a couple of times. It wasn't a matter of being suicidal, it was a matter of not being able to control the circumstances. In the worst scenario, I'd be dead by now.'[1]

Peter Dixon would have expected Peter to be able to take up sport again, including squash, after the operation: 'Amputees can play squash! But it all depends on what the person wants to do and how motivated they are to do it. What I see with elite athletes is a great sense of loss. Somebody who has had greatness and has now got to confront everyday life with a disability questions their sense of self-worth.'

Dixon was aware that Peter had become severely depressed.

> There's nothing like looking mortality in the face. Plus Peter knew that he may not be able to walk properly again. And he's a person who has won a silver medal and who already has an intrinsically depressive disposition. Generally sprinters are loners and if I was to write a pen picture of Peter, it would be one of a somewhat isolated, depressive type of person. I formed that opinion during this time. Even though we laughed a lot together, related well together and there was a lot of mutual respect for each other and our understanding of things, I recall his quite intense anxiety around the period that I cared for him. What he said to Ron Reed supports that point of view about his pre-morbid disposition.
>
> We would have only given him morphine or pethidine in hospital, then got him on to some sort of codeine-type product like Panadeine Forte. I would have been surprised if he had gone home on too much opium-type medication. But then you may have the interplay of an underlying personality anxiety application, questioning self-worth. He hasn't worked for a period of time and is a man who is physically disabled. So his self-esteem and his body image have all been blown apart. His pre-morbid disposition amplifies this whole scenario. His environment, his professionalism, his physical disability, his loss of personal self-esteem are going to amplify into what he then described to Ron Reed and the issues became confused.

Peter had known Maurie Drew for many years as a teammate and as a friend. Drew had been there when Peter ruptured his Achilles tendon and it was to him, in his capacity as a pharmacist, that Peter now turned for advice. Peter and Drew discussed taking painkillers versus feeling pain, as Drew related:

> He would ring and say he was hopelessly addicted. He was concerned about wanting to give the pain relief away, but he also had this desperate need to ease the intense pain. The short

> answer always was you can eventually get off the pain relievers. But the only way you're going to get through your life is to get past the pain now. And the only way you're going to get past the pain now is to take pain relievers.

Drew expected that, from what Peter told him, Peter would have been taking eight to ten strong painkillers a day, but should have been taking no more than four. After a while the body tolerates that level of drugs and in order to get pain relief Peter would have felt the need to take more. Drew suggested:

> He would have then thrown Panadeine Forte down his neck like lollies, consistently all day long. He would have been hopelessly constipated and he would have been floating like mad. There would have been times when he was so spaced out he wouldn't know where he was or what he was doing. That's the zombie part. I know he drank. Mixing pain relievers and alcohol is the worst thing you can do.

Drew said that, under normal circumstances, most athletes, including Peter, would not have taken drugs in this way: 'You tend not to do it in later years after you retire, but Peter had this desperate need to ease the pain.'

Jan said that Peter must have been going to various doctors to get access to so much prescription medication. 'I can't absolutely say, but that's the only way that I can see how it could have happened. At one stage I wrote to one doctor pointing out how bad it was. I thought, how come he's still giving him all this medication? What is the doctor thinking?'

Dixon did not know if Peter was 'doctor shopping', but he knew that 'doctor shopping or tricking' was a method of supply and survival used by sports people: 'These people confront doctors with a plausible story about their pain. The doctor prescribes according to what they've been told and then the person goes around the corner and trots the same story out to another doctor. It's very difficult in the early stages to track that sort of behaviour.'

By chance, Heather Norman was listening to a talkback program on the radio one night and heard Peter talking about the effects of his injury. She cried as she listened to her brother speak frankly about his ordeal. Peter had cut himself off from his family after getting out of hospital, so Heather was hearing the details for the first time. She tried to phone Peter after the segment had finished. He either wasn't home or didn't want to come to the phone.

> I spoke to Jan. She was distressed and just about at her wits' end. She said Peter had been drinking a lot. She didn't know what to do about it and needed to tell somebody in the family. She said, 'I just need you to know.' It was good for her to know that somebody knew about it. She was carrying the burden on her own.

Heather told Jan that she needed to make herself and the girls safe, and asked her if she had heard of Al-Anon,[2] an organisation that provided help to people living with an alcoholic, 'because that's what she said he was'. Heather had heard of Al-Anon from one of the families at the school where she taught.

Heather gave the number to Jan and phoned the organisation to get some information for her. Jan was calling Al-Anon at the same time, as Heather recalled.

> Strangely, as I was talking to someone there to check if it was the right number, the woman had to take another call and from what I heard her saying, I guessed it was Jan. I went to the first meeting with Jan quite a while after Peter suffered the injury. She found some interesting points, but a lot of it didn't apply to her. She was right once she had been the first time. She didn't need me to go along with her again. She was then comfortable enough to go on her own if she needed to.

Jan told Heather at that time that she would leave Peter if things didn't improve, especially as Belinda and Emma were a little older by then. 'Some years later we talked. I asked how things were going. Jan said, "Well from talking to friends and people around, it's as good as it gets. Half of them are living in the same sort of thing." She was just going to stick it out. I think they just lived in the same house!'

Heather broached the subject of medication with Peter on one occasion when Peter showed Heather his asthma supplies. Heather was surprised at the quantity of his medications: 'I said, "That's a bit much isn't it?" He said, "You never know when you need them." I don't know the type of painkillers he was on, but he said he was on them all the time. But he didn't tell me it wasn't water, he was taking with them.'

Thelma Norman remembered Jan ringing her on one occasion. 'Jan said Peter had thrown a lamp at her, cutting her head. I asked if she wanted me to come down. She said, "No. It'll be all right." I said put Peter on.' Thelma spoke to Peter on the phone but couldn't get much sense out of him. 'Peter was drinking heavily and things were less than pleasant. We didn't really communicate very much at the time.'

Elaine always endeavoured to see Peter when he visited their mother, who by now lived across the road from Elaine and her family. 'I'd see him when he'd visit Mum. It would be a bit weird. Peter was always fairly quick-witted, but on these visits he wasn't particularly coherent all the time.' Elaine recalled that Peter didn't look well. He'd be puffy in the face and he smoked a lot. 'He could be snappy and short with you. When I was a kid Peter could be sarcastic and cutting with his comments, but during this time, the cutting side was more obvious. But we didn't have a lot to do with each other at that time. He hid from the family.'

Neville Sillitoe had seen Peter rupture his Achilles tendon and he observed the changes in Peter after the operation. He felt that Peter's personality had changed from being bubbly to more sedate. Sillitoe didn't see Peter regularly, but they talked on the phone from time to time. Peter didn't whinge and moan to Sillitoe or say he was depressed, but he was severely frustrated that he couldn't do what he wanted to do: 'He'd say to me, "It's driving me mad".'

Bob Stuart didn't feel that the Couch Productions theatre shows were unduly affected by Peter's injury and post-operation trauma. 'He had times when he was down and depressed, but it never really affected his performance. In fact, I believe the shows kept Peter going.' Arch Galloway remembered Peter doing shows after rupturing his Achilles tendon even though he could hardly walk.

> He should have had the operation straight away. He wouldn't have been worried that somebody else would have taken his place. But it would have been a big job for an understudy to learn it at that short notice because we were doing five different shows at once at that time. He would have missed a lot of money though by not doing the shows.

Arch didn't see the 'zombie' side of Peter.

> He was never depressed with us. He enjoyed it too much. It was an escape. We knew he drank and took painkillers. Towards the end we were talking about giving it away, partly because Peter couldn't remember his lines any more. Peter was stubborn and would never admit it was time to give it away. It was very hard for us to tell him that the shows were going down because he couldn't remember his lines. What saved us from having to do that was me getting sick.

Arch had a heart attack on stage at Williamstown's customs house during a performance of the cowboy show 'Western Bang Bang'. Peter immediately called an ambulance and travelled with Arch to Williamstown Hospital, both still in their cowboy gear. Medical staff couldn't stabilise Arch, so he was transferred to the nearby Western General Hospital. 'Being dressed up in cowboy outfits, they decided we were gay. I'm dying and they wouldn't touch me because they weren't sure whether I was gay or had HIV!' Arch duly walked out of the hospital after pulling out all the tubes. 'Peter got me into Royal Melbourne Hospital. From there on everything was fine.'

Arch had bypass surgery and went back to the shows after a few months' recovery. He subsequently got sick again and had a second operation. This coincided with Peter forgetting his lines. Arch said he was giving it away: 'That saved us from having to tell Peter.'

Arch contended that the alcohol and prescription drugs caused Peter to forget his lines. Despite this, Peter enjoyed doing the shows and, Arch believed, that without them Peter would have been a mess: 'Plus he needed to keep himself together to be able to perform. Had he not had that and been sitting home alone with nothing to do, it would have got into his head. The shows probably kept him going for a long time.' Jan agreed that Peter's theatre work kept him sane: 'He loved it. He was a born show-off and could not think of anything better than getting up on stage where everyone was listening to him and where he could sing. He loved to sing.'

Peter's leg was still troubling him as late as 1990 when he was an athletics commentator with television station Channel 9 at the Auckland Commonwealth Games. Peter regarded it as a privilege being on the commentary team, and he particularly enjoyed working with his great mate Phil May, who was also on the team. The feeling was mutual, as May described: 'We just had good times and good fun. We had the odd beer in the evening. Peter loved it and was very good.' But Peter paid a price for making the trip. He was in constant pain and found it difficult to move around freely while in New Zealand. He wasn't well when he got home and it took some time for him to recover from the ordeal.

By 1992 Peter was in discussion with Melbourne's television station Channel 7, which planned to fly him to the USA in 1993 to meet up with Tommie Smith and John Carlos to record an interview for a program the station was compiling to mark the upcoming 25th anniversary of the 200 metres race in Mexico. Peter related the story:

> I hadn't seen the race for nearly 25 years. I had seen stills, but had no footage of it. I was talking to this guy at Channel 7. He said, 'You must get a real buzz every time you see the video.' I said, 'I probably would, but I haven't seen it.' He said, 'I was looking at it the day before yesterday. I'll send you a copy.' At that time I was off work with the serious leg injury. I was at a pretty low ebb. This package arrived. I knew what it was. I went to the fridge, got myself a beer and sat down, but I couldn't turn the TV on. When I finally did, it was amazing because the tape contained the first and second rounds, semi-final and final, all in black-and-white. I had a good cry for about half an hour, just playing the final backwards and forwards. In my mind, I could still remember every step of the race and what went on before the race. It wasn't until I'd seen the tape that I realised how accurately I'd remembered all of it.[3]

In July 1992 Peter was due in court to fight Prince Henry's Hospital for compensation for suffering permanent disability, allegedly caused by the hospital's initial negligence in treating his Achilles injury. Coincidentally the case was scheduled to begin on the same day as the running of the first round of the 200 metres at the Barcelona Olympics. The significance was not lost on Peter: 'I don't know whether it's an omen or not, but it's rather ironical.'[4] The case was settled out of court, as Jan recalled.

> Peter sued the hospital for negligence and got back a fairly minimal amount that virtually covered his medical expenses and I think we might have paid the house off. It was the most nerve-

> racking thing he had to go through. The lawyers said if you go to court it could mean you'll end up with nothing. So you had to agree to take what they were offering.

Dixon agreed that the injury hampered Peter's life.

> He was severely disabled. That's why it is not surprising that it ended up in litigation. But I'm always sad when such things come to litigation. The orthopedic surgery at Prince Henry's wasn't third-world country – it was excellent. And being the person that he was, the junior doctor wouldn't have done that procedure.

Dixon said you don't expect such procedures to break down – one out of a hundred might have a wound problem caused by a combination of factors that would affect the wound's ability to heal.

> I recognise why it came about because of the extensive surgery involved. But you'll never get a patient to understand the complexity of what had occurred, and the combination of factors, some of which he contributed to by delaying the operation, to cause the wound breakdown that caused the problem.

Peter's years of smoking before and after the operation didn't help his cause. Dixon asserted:

> If you have a cigarette in the postoperative healing period, it causes the vessels to go into spasm and diminishes the amount of blood getting through. So you've got poisons, a lower oxygen-carrying capacity of the blood, and then you add spasm of nicotine to a wound that's already struggling to survive from that big a dissection!

Peter had tried several times over the years to give up smoking, but never fully succeeded. Bouts of stress, such as he had been under, always triggered a return to smoking. 'He really tried to give up,' said Jan. 'You would think he'd given it up and then he'd be smoking again and that's what I knew. Maybe he was smoking all that time anyway and I just didn't know.'

After eight years on painkillers, Peter finally stopped taking them in mid 1993. He had been desperately unwell and heavily dependent on medication during the three 'zombie-like' years from 1986 to 1988, and then moderately dependent for the next five years until he decided to get off the painkillers.

Drew contended that, during the 'moderately dependent' – or the 'God, I better have some pain cover in case' – stage, Peter's pain would have dropped to a minimal level. At some point in this stage, Drew suspected that someone would have had a 'bloody good talk' to Peter and told him that he was popping pills day and night unnecessarily – his leg had healed and he was walking again. But Peter would have been worrying about the pain coming back. Drew continued:

> Peter would have spent the last two to three years weaning himself down to a level where he could probably feel comfortable saying, 'Bugger it! I'll try and go without.' He was probably dependent unnecessarily towards the end. That's the addicts' 'I can't give it up in case the pain comes back'. When you've been through extreme pain, the last thing you want is for it to come back again. That final step is mental, not physical.
>
> Once off the pain relievers, he started to turn his life around. His body never repaired to the stage where he was going to race again or be able to jump at a basketball hoop. But at least he was walking again. As trivial as that sounds, it was important for someone who'd been through what he had.

Peter told Ron Reed in August 1993 that even though the pain had still not totally disappeared, he didn't dare take any more pain relievers. He knew he had no choice but to learn to combat the pain. Peter was very candid with Reed, telling him that he was amazed that Jan had stuck by him, given what she, and Belinda and Emma (who were twelve and ten at this time), had gone through. Peter admitted he was tormented by what the ordeal might have done to their daughters.

> Being young girls, they were certainly affected by it. Imagine seeing their dad in that condition when other dads could keep it all together. Other dads had a job, other dads could go for a ride on a bike, other dads could go to Little Athletics and jog laps with them. They never came to me about it, but they certainly spoke to their mother about it. Jan was very patient, but it is a wonder that she didn't throw me out. The marriage was very

> close to breaking up, and, if that had happened, it would have been the end. Eventually she became very forceful about what I had to do. Now I have picked up the ball again and am trying to make the most of what I do have. It is my last chance. You only get one shot.[5]

By now Jan was a member of the Altona athletics club, having joined the club around the time Peter suffered his injury. Jan didn't compete, rather she ran for exercise. Peter's exercise was restricted to walking and Jan accompanied him from time to time. Peter would walk for up to an hour at a time around Williamstown streets, but his exercise came at a price. Invariably after such a walk, a sleepless night followed.

Jan is understandably reluctant to discuss the ordeal in detail, describing it as a terrible time. 'I prefer to shut out some of those memories of him drinking and being quite scary sometimes.' She later agreed with Peter's comments of the time to Reed about the state of their marriage. Her response was immediate: 'Oh God, yes! I felt our marriage was in jeopardy. When I look back, it was a wonder I didn't throw him out. But I just toughed it out! I put up walls to keep me safe. Something like that. And you rely on your friends.'

Jan added that she can see why it happened. 'How frustrating for him to lose his amazing talent to being a semi-cripple! Once the wound started healing, he could still walk, but he just couldn't run and do a lot of other things.' But Jan had to dig deep at times.

> At that stage the kids were still small, so I was only working two days a week. But we couldn't survive on that money. Peter wasn't earning money, so I needed to work more. I went down to the school and pleaded to get a full-time job so that we had enough money. Thankfully they gave me the full-time job.

As for Peter's comment that she became forceful about what he had to do, Jan suggested, 'I suppose any wife would do that – give ultimatums and things.' She frankly admitted that her marriage to Peter never fully recovered from the traumatic years that followed Peter's injury: 'Once you put up walls to protect yourself, it's very hard to take them down!'

As Reed noted at the time, Peter, 'to his everlasting credit', firmly rejected the option of wallowing in self-pity. He could not see why he deserved a better hand than what life had dealt him.

> It could have happened to any other D-grade runner. But it didn't; it happened to me. Perhaps I had more to lose than some people, but I've just about got over that part of it. Now it's more anger with myself for being so stupid in the first place.[6]

Peter attempted to return to teaching at one stage during these eight years, but by then Victorian teachers had to be fully qualified. As Peter didn't have formal teaching qualifications, the Education Department was reluctant to allow him to return. The teachers' union, although knowing it was on very shaky grounds, sought and obtained a temporary reprieve. Peter was reinstated and took up a PE position at a Melton school.

But as Drew recalled, Peter was placed on what he described as 'bullshit light duties'.

> Peter was, beyond belief, frustrated at that. He said light duties meant you monitored kids on the playground and picked up papers. He said it drove him mad. He felt almost worthless. He couldn't teach what he used to teach. I remember him specifying basketball. He couldn't show the kids how to throw a basketball, because he simply couldn't stand the pressure on his legs. He said to me on more than one occasion it drove him absolutely bloody mad not to be able to show the kids how to do things physically, because his body wouldn't allow it.

Arch, who had worked with Peter in live theatre for 20 years, was a close friend and Peter had confided in him a number of times over the years that he was never really happy teaching.

> Peter didn't enjoy teaching. Teachers had to keep doing courses to keep up with trends and changes in education. He never did that and fell behind to the point where he just couldn't teach any more. His trouble started when he wasn't really qualified to do much else – or at least he didn't think he was.

Peter's return to teaching was short-lived. He was 'invalided out' of the Education Department on medical grounds in 1993. Jan said Peter then went on a pension and was 'required to go off to counsellors because of what he had been through'. Peter then did some butchering at the

Tuckerbag supermarket in Williamstown, but as Jan recalled, 'That was pretty horrible. He'd be up at the crack of dawn, going off and standing on cold concrete floors with a gammy leg all day. Then I think he was a butcher at Melton.' Arch remembered Peter telling him that he wasn't happy doing that either.

One of Peter's old sprint rivals, Bob Lay, came back into Peter's life at this time and provided support when Peter really needed it. Bob remembered that Peter was 'pretty down and had lots of problems' when he engaged him to be the master of ceremonies (MC) at some fundraising functions for the Victorian Olympic Council: 'He did a fantastic job lecturing and facilitating at our Olympic academies for kids up to the age of eighteen.' Bob also got Peter involved in some evening athletics events and in a special 24-hour relay event. Bob gave Peter '$4000 or $5000' to help him promote some of these events.

> He appreciated that and we became good mates because of that. I ignored his drinking and his drug-taking and just tried to keep him happy. We just hit it off. He was friendly and there was no bullshit about him. I knew that every time I asked Peter to help, he'd be the first to put his hand up and say yes. He never ever said it, but I think he really did appreciate my support during a difficult time.

When Dixon and Peter accidentally ran into each other in the late 1990s, Dixon found Peter in a reflective mood. They immediately greeted each other with great warmth and were genuinely pleased to have the opportunity to spend time with each other.

> We talked for quite a while. Things were on the up and up for Peter. He had a sense of purpose again. That meeting defined how I found Peter. He told me about where life had taken him. He was prepared to give of himself and to be honest that he hadn't spent his whole life in the sun, that he had a flawed personality and life, which added to the colour of it all. He talked at a very personal level about personal issues, which not many men can do.

Dixon was very positive about his overall experience with Peter. He initially performed the operation on Peter because of their earlier athletics association, but felt that their relationship 'ultimately went far beyond the doctor–patient relationship. It was based on mutual respect. I cared for him as a friend'.

Peter, by his own admission, had been a 'bloody fool' for attempting a comeback to athletics. His fall from grace had already begun with his drinking escapades as a teacher, although he had never been caught in the act by school authorities. But his fall escalated at a truly dramatic pace after the 'shithouse D-grade relay race'. After eight years of hell, Peter had hit rock bottom. His teaching career was over and his marriage was teetering on the edge. There was only one way for Peter to go, but he had one hell of a climb ahead of him.

NOTES

1 'Norman's conquest', *The Herald Sun*, 13 August 1993.

2 Al-Anon is a community resource providing support to those affected by someone else's drinking. Its primary purpose is to help families and friends of alcoholics. It is not part of Alcoholics Anonymous, although it cooperates with this organisation.

3 ABC, television segment, 1992.

4 ABC, television segment, 1992.

5 'Norman's conquest', *The Herald Sun*, 13 August 1993.

6 'Norman's conquest', *The Herald Sun*, 13 August 1993.

18

I KNEW IT WOULD BE YOU!

Sandy Norman, Peter's daughter from his first marriage, said that the 1968 photo of Peter on the Olympic dais was how she knew her father during the early part of her life. The photo was very important to her. Sandy and her brother Gary were interested in sport so they would often watch sports events on television, particularly when the Commonwealth or Olympic Games were on. Sandy said, 'The Olympics were pretty important to me. My dad was one of those people who had achieved. The meaning of what he'd done at the medal ceremony was over my head at the time though.' None of her friends or classmates at school ever connected Sandy's surname with the famous Olympian in *that* photo unless she told them, 'then because Dad wasn't around, it was a case of "Oh yeah, sure!"'

Just before the 1984 Olympics, sportswriter Jack Dunn wrote an article[1] that led Sandy to wonder if Peter wanted to know them. 'There was a photo of Dad in a Roman-centurion-type hat and one of his daughters, Belinda, running down their driveway. The article was all about his family and I thought, "What about us?"' So Sandy wrote to Dunn not long after her fourteenth birthday. Sandy had no idea if the veteran writer would reply, but one thing was in Sandy's favour – Dunn had always had a soft spot for Peter, and vice versa.

In a heartfelt letter to Sandy, Dunn explained that he knew Peter had other children but didn't mention his first family in the article because

Peter hadn't volunteered any details during their interview. Sandy later met Dunn. He remembered she had written to him and he recalled his discussions with Peter. Sandy said how 'I didn't pursue it any further at the time, but I still wanted to meet Dad and to know if he wanted to know us and me.'

Sandy described how her closeness to Peter's extended family meant that her family was not like the 'normal divorced family'.

> Our closest grandparents and aunts and uncles are Dad's family. We lived literally around the corner from Nana and Papa Norman until we moved to Echuca in May 1977 when I was nearly seven. We've always been invited to Norman family functions since. It's been good for us to be part of the Norman family and obviously we are still grandkids and nieces and a nephew.

Located on the banks of the Murray River in northern Victoria, and known for its beautiful historic port and its fleet of paddle-steamers, Echuca is some three hours drive from Melbourne. Despite the distance involved, Sandy's mother Ruth always took her children to as many Norman family functions as possible.

Sandy never questioned her mother or other family members about the break-up of her parents' marriage: 'No-one ever talked about it. But I'd always notice that the adults in the family, that is Nana and Papa and our aunts and uncles, either didn't talk about Dad or they'd stop talking about him when we were around. That was even when we were still in Melbourne.'

Sandy, Janita and Gary often spent a couple of weeks of their school holidays in Melbourne at Nana and Papa Norman's. Anyone entering Thelma's home could never doubt how important her family was to her – family photos from Thelma's childhood to the present day are proudly displayed. Sandy always enjoyed looking at the photos and would sneak looks at her father and Jan and their two daughters to see what they looked like. Sandy was pleased they weren't athletics photos: 'It was just Dad!'

Sandy recalled seeing her father on three occasions as a young child. The first was when Sandy was at primary school at Williamstown Grammar. She remembered a man putting something around her neck as she sat near the fountain in the frontyard of the school. It occurred to Sandy that this was her father and it was the silver medal he had put around her neck. 'He knew we went to that school. He'd been to the school to give a talk, but not to my grade. He didn't say, "I'm your Dad". He just asked how I was.' The second occasion was when Sandy was around eight and the third when she was about ten or eleven.

> [Aunty] Elaine had to swap a car over with Dad while we were all down at Nana's on holidays. Elaine met him at Albert Park. I wanted to get out of the car and see him, but we all had to stay in Elaine's car. I couldn't see what the big deal was. The third occasion was at Nana and Papa's, and Dad was picking up Willie, his labrador. He had a chat to Gary and me because we were out the back playing table tennis. He always seemed all right when we saw him, but why wasn't there more? I would have liked more.

For a time Sandy and Gary were of the same mindset: 'We wanted to meet Dad. Slowly Gary didn't, and Janita didn't want to talk about him much.'

By 1988 Sandy had completed her school education. She was studying first-year nursing[2] in the Melbourne bayside suburb of Frankston, where her grandparents lived. The Olympics were being held in Seoul in September 1988 and, being an Olympic year, Sandy's attention again turned to her father. With the encouragement of her new boyfriend, Chris Kadri, Sandy wrote to Peter early in 1989 suggesting it would be good to meet him.

> I purposely wrote my address on the back of the envelope so that if Jan got the letter and didn't want it to happen, that would be fine. And if Dad didn't want to open it, that would be fine, too. I did that because I didn't want to shock them too much.
>
> I told Elaine and she sat with me while I told Nana. With tears in her eyes, Nana said, 'I knew it would be you!' She said that two or three times. She was pretty pleased and relieved.

Peter rang Sandy and arranged to meet her outside Melbourne's Spencer Street railway station. He was waiting for Sandy when she arrived. 'He was friendly. There were hugs and all that sort of thing. He even bought me a little shaggy soft toy. It's holding a little thing that said "I love you".[3] That was really nice.' Peter had made Sandy feel very special.

Sandy and Peter went to a bar in the city for lunch and had a long chat.

For Sandy the lunch was just like it should be. She didn't ask Peter any in-depth questions but instead saw it as a 'get to know you' meeting and a wonderful opportunity to spend time with her father after being denied the opportunity for most of her life. Chris hadn't thought it appropriate that he should be at that first meeting, but he fully supported Sandy in her endeavours to get to know her father and was very pleased that the first meeting went so well.

Heather Norman drove her niece to see Peter perform in a 'boo and hiss'-style theatre show at the Masonic Hall, Ascot Vale, on 13 May 1989. Sandy had been made aware by Dunn's article that Peter performed in theatre-restaurant shows. She had never been to such a show before, but she was soon hissing and booing along with everyone else. She recalled her father being very much at ease with the audience and she was impressed with his ability to play to the crowd. Sandy wasn't overly nervous on the night. She gave a lot of thought to the event, preparing herself in advance so that when the big night came, she was composed and relaxed and able to enjoy it.

Sandy and Heather stayed the night at Peter and Jan's Williamstown home after the show. 'Mum and Don said if that's what I wanted to do, that was okay with them,' said Sandy. 'Jan was very welcoming. And Belinda and Emma thought it was just like having another big girl around.' Heather was very pleased to be part of the night. 'Peter came out to see us before the show and we talked. He was fairly calm. He was very pleased to see Sandy and made her feel special. Like Peter, Sandy keeps her emotions in check, but she was beaming. Everything was right!'

In 1990, Sandy introduced Chris to Peter and Jan, and the young couple stayed the night at Williamstown, as Chris recalled. 'Peter, Jan and the kids were really nice. Jan was very accommodating and basically said any time we wanted to catch up, we were more than welcome.' It meant a lot to Sandy to have her father meet Chris and vice versa, and also to have Jan support her quest to get to know her father better. Sandy felt comfortable talking to their girls, but was somewhat perplexed when Belinda and Emma asked her why she called their father 'dad'. Sandy immediately looked at Jan and asked if she wanted her to explain. Jan readily said yes.

> I drew them a picture of Jan and Mum and Dad. I said, 'We've got the same dad and that makes us half-sisters and that means

> I call him Dad too.' They were only young [nine and seven respectively]. They said, 'Okay', then took it away and processed it. I think Jan was glad it wasn't her trying to explain that.

Sandy was due to turn 21 in July 1991. It was important to her that she invite Peter to her party to be held in Echuca. But it was equally important to Sandy that her mother did not feel uncomfortable or have people watching her reactions. So she arranged that she and Ruth would meet Peter at his home about a month before the party.

> Mum and Dad had a chat. Mum was stressed and nervous and that was understandable. I really appreciated her doing that and I was glad that Mum and Don were okay with Dad coming. I don't know whether Dad was comfortable coming, but he came. Jan didn't come. I think Nana was the one feeling it most, seeing how it all went, and seeing her family come back together again.

Peter later attended Sandy and Chris's engagement party held in Ruth and Don's backyard in Echuca in January 1994. Sandy then considered it 'extremely important' that Peter, Jan, Belinda and Emma attend when she and Chris married in Echuca in 1996. Much to Sandy's great delight, they all came for the special day. Don and Ruth walked Sandy down the aisle and Peter was the MC – a role he was 'pretty chuffed' to perform. Years later, Peter described his son-in-law Chris as 'a beautiful guy'. 'Chris was family from the first time I met him, which was a long time before he and Sandra got married.'

Chris and Sandy Kadri went overseas in September 1998 and lived in London for two-and-a-half years, after visiting Chris's family in Tanzania. Sandy endeavoured to keep in contact with Peter while in London, but much to her disappointment, she didn't hear from him by email or letter, nor did he phone. 'He wasn't good at writing back. I emailed him quite a few times and I remember calling him on his birthday once or twice, but that never impressed him. Mum always said that he hated getting older.' Sandy was pretty sure Peter was happy to hear from her – but not necessarily that she had remembered his birthday. Sandy took a couple of shots at Peter when she returned to Australia but Peter 'just gave that cheeky smile and glinted those blue eyes, like that's all I was getting from him.'

Laura Mae Kadri was born to Sandy and Chris on 22 May 2002. Peter was in Echuca giving a motivational talk in October 2002 and, much to Sandy's disgust, didn't contact her. Laura was already five months old and Peter had not yet met her. Sandy let Peter know in no uncertain fashion what she thought of him when they caught up later that year. Peter's excuse was that his schedule was tight at the time of his visit, but Sandy told him he could have telephoned.

> He'd been up a couple of times and hadn't contacted me. I accepted that he didn't write or ring when we were overseas, but when he comes up to Echuca and doesn't contact us and then tells us that he couldn't find us in the phone book. Well we are the only Kadri in the phone book, so come on! You've gotta have a better reason than that.

Contact with Peter was always spasmodic and mostly at Sandy's initiation. 'But I think he was pleased that I made the effort. It meant there weren't any more issues. Laura and our second daughter, Maya Victoria, who was born on 26 October 2004, gave him a lot of pleasure. I could see it in his face.'

Sandy said that she's glad she re-established contact with Peter: 'It's been very worthwhile for me. And Dad obviously wanted it too because he said yes to meeting me.' Sandy enjoyed her father's sense of humour and seeing him have a good laugh, but she regretted she didn't get to know her father in more depth: 'The distance made it difficult, but I got the impression that if I'd been closer, he would have done anything for us. He was very grateful to Don for stepping in and helping raise us.' Sandy believes her father loved all the family and that he did a pretty good job with 'the [life] map that was set out for him'. She looks back on first meeting Peter at Williamstown Grammar and their first real get-together in 1989 as being 'pretty big' memories: 'They were pretty good, as was watching Dad play with Laura, and at Christmas mucking around by the pool, and dressing up as Santa.'

Janita was nearly five when her father left the family home for the final time. She has some vivid memories of Peter from her childhood. She recalled Peter calling her 'Jimpy' and taking her to the aquarium, just around the corner from her grandparents, to buy tropical fish. Janita said that just the smell of fish tanks takes her right back to when she was tiny. At one stage Peter kept a yabby[4] in one of the tanks. He would get the yabby out and put it on the floor to terrify his daughter. Janita remembered playing with Peter's model cars. Some of them were 'old antique-type things', which may have come from his childhood. Some were new and exotic like Ferraris and Porsches. Janita used to play on the racetrack that Peter had set up at Williamstown Technical School.

Peter liked to cook and Janita recollects eating Peter's spaghetti bolognaise and having coffee that he'd made using the family's coffee percolator. 'It's interesting now because food is a very important part of my life. I love to cook for my friends. It's like, "Please come over so I've got somebody to cook for."' Janita remembered Peter taking her with him when he trained at Royal Park, near the Melbourne Zoo. This hadn't escaped the attention of sportswriter Judy Joy Davies, who wrote in 1971 a feature article describing Peter's energetic four-year-old 'blonde moppet' as his new training partner.[5] Several cute photos of Janita in racing stance accompanied the article. Peter would also take Janita to Princes Park to see Carlton, his favourite Australian Rules football team, play. Like Peter, Janita has been a lifelong Carlton fan. The legendary footballer Alex ('Jezza') Jesaulenko was Janita's hero when she was tiny – little wonder as 'Jezza' was a big favourite of Peter's.

Janita recalled Peter being a practical joker and teasing her. The family had a television with a remote control. Peter would stir Janita by changing the channel with the remote and pretending it was magic. He would also get Janita to complete jigsaw puzzles and time her with a stopwatch.

> That has probably, in some ways, given me the skills to do my building designs because I often refer to them as jigsaw puzzles and I can do them very quickly.[6] He was competitive and probably instilled that in me. I set exceptionally high standards for myself and constantly challenge myself to do better. I think I was a fairly full-on child. I suppose being the first grandchild and child, you're always, dare I say, that bit special because you are the first and you get lots of attention and there is a lot of expectation. I think that makes you a bit more perceptive because you are dealing with adults and you're in an adult world.

Janita did not recall ever talking to her mother about what happened between her and Peter. 'Nobody really talked about it because everybody in the [Norman] family wanted to protect us. The family has been such an important part of our lives. Even with Peter stepping out of the picture, the family was unflinching. It didn't change for me one bit.' Janita considered Peter to have been an incredibly talented athlete, and she had great respect for his stance on the dais in Mexico, but athletics was not something she was passionate about.

When Sandy first contacted Peter, Janita had no interest in rekindling a relationship with him. She didn't want anything to do with Sandy's reunion plans; it was a case of 'that's fine for you, Sandy, but you can definitely count me out!'

Janita had been old enough to remember the separation and how she had felt as a young child losing her father. Peter's departure had left a great void in her life. She had loved him dearly and the intervening years had done nothing to curb her ill-feeling towards him for walking out on her and her family. She had been hurt badly and was still angry and bitter towards Peter. 'I didn't want any part of it at that time. I didn't want to know a great deal about anything. I had the walls up at the time.' When she met Peter at a family get-together, she was 'cool' towards him. She felt that because Peter was the adult and the father, he should have taken the first steps towards reconciliation: 'I put all the responsibility on him. I thought if he wants to make amends or reconcile or do whatever, it's his responsibility.' Janita always felt quite conspicuous at family events because it was expected that all should be chummy and friendly.

> No-one really said anything, but I felt a lot of pressure to do the right thing, whereas I probably would have liked to have gone up and hit him. But I just smiled and said, 'How are you?', that sort of thing. So I played it pretty cool. I'm good at that – terrified underneath, but very calm on the outside.

Janita didn't invite Peter to her wedding in 1992. She just didn't want him there because of her own feelings and also because of her loyalty to Don: 'I know that Don wouldn't have been put out had Peter come, but my wedding day was for my close family. Besides, wherever Peter goes, he commands attention.'

Janita's first child, Brittany Alexandra, was born in Echuca on 8 June 1994. To her great surprise, Peter visited Janita and his first grandchild in hospital. In doing so, Peter had to step out of his comfort zone. He knew only too well that he still wasn't 'flavour of the month' with his oldest child, and he detested hospitals and avoided them whenever possible. But to his ultimate benefit, he went ahead with the visit. Janita was shocked that Peter made the effort, but his visit pleased her: 'I felt good about that. It softened my feelings towards him.'

Around 1995, Peter invited Janita, Shane (her then husband) and Brittany to his home for dinner.

> Jan and Belinda and Emma were there too. This was the first time I'd really met them and been able to spend some time with them. To see Peter in that family environment, without the rest of the family looking on, was a good experience. The girls were lovely and took to Brittany. Jan was very welcoming as well. I think the girls adored Peter.

Janita gave birth to a son, Liam Connor, on 25 July 1996. Peter and Ruth now had a grandson. As a young person, Peter had always enjoyed Christmas parties with the extended family, so he decided to resurrect the family tradition. For three years in the early 2000s, the Norman family gathered at Peter and Jan's home to celebrate Christmas together. Janita took her family.

> They were good days. I think he loved having everybody there, but he always seemed a bit distant. Not just from me and Gary, but I think from everybody. Maybe there were all sorts of things going on underneath for him to deal with in having everybody there. Perhaps he had to be a little bit on his guard.

Peter enjoyed playing Father Christmas and giving out presents to his grandchildren. He'd always enjoyed wearing costumes in his theatre work and this was no different. Being Father Christmas gave him the chance to disappear in the costume instead of being on show as Peter Norman the son, the father, the husband, the uncle. Even though he enjoyed the limelight, this was different. It was private time. Chris believed that these Christmas functions were Peter's favourite time: 'He didn't have to be conscious of what other people thought. You could see the enjoyment he got out of it. He got to see how they'd developed from one year to the next or since the last time he'd seen them. And the grandkids adored him.'

Heather also felt that the Christmas parties were very special for him. She was thrilled to see him with all his children and grandchildren at the parties. 'It was lovely to watch him with the boys in the pool. He had always been terrific with kids, but you could see that Liam was his own. That was very special. I loved it. There was definitely a sense of he was where he should be, family-wise.'

Janita saw Peter once or twice a year in the later years of his life. Her attitude towards Peter certainly softened during that time: 'Having gone through a marriage split myself, you learn that things aren't always as you want them to be.' Janita believed her experience made it easier for her to understand how difficult a marriage break-up could be. The experience made her a more understanding person. She also acknowledged that she could relate to the depression that Peter suffered following his Achilles injury.

> I've been through that sort of stuff myself. I've had a bit of depression. I haven't relied on painkillers and I don't have a problem with alcohol as such, but I could certainly see how somebody's life could take that path. That in itself has perhaps made me more understanding.

Janita no longer felt any anger or resentment towards Peter. While she regretted that she didn't talk to him about the family break-up, she was pleased that contact between Peter and her family had been re-established, affording her the opportunity to spend 'a bit more time' with him: 'I'd love to be able to say I was getting to know him more, but I probably didn't really get to know him that well because a lot of the times we met were more encounters.'

Janita liked Peter. She thought they probably could have been wicked and caused some mischief together, as they had a similar sense of humour. 'A close friend of mine dealt with Peter quite a bit through the Tri-State Games. She said, "You are so much like your dad." Because she knows me so well, she is probably the one person I think who would be qualified to make that comment.'

> Peter was always in Brittany and Liam's lives – a very small part of their lives, but it was all positive for them. Peter was really lovely around them. He was probably more comfortable with the children than he was with me. He had a real affinity with kids. He had a very gentle way of dealing with people. He was incredibly intelligent and he was a deep thinker. I think there was

> a lot going on in his head. I don't know that he was particularly good in close relationships. I'm sure he was a kind person and had a lot of time for people. He was a real people person and I think it must be incredibly difficult to be up close and personal and be a public person.
>
> Peter being in the Olympics and on the dais has always been part of my life. It always pops up. People know he's my father. The kids can experience Peter in a different way. They haven't had all the negative and the hurt that I've experienced. So their relationship is a little more simplified. They can just enjoy having him as their grandfather and experience having a famous person in the family, quite unadulterated by all the other crap, which is lovely for them. I haven't actively encouraged a hands-on relationship between the kids and Peter, but any time he has been involved with them, it's always been positive and I never ever put any dark clouds over the way they perceive their grandfather.

Janita kept two beautiful little ponchos that Peter brought her back from Mexico[7] and a number of postcards that Peter sent the family while away at the Olympics. She wore with pride the friendship ring that Peter gave Ruth when they first began going out together: 'I really like it and it's engraved inside.'

Because he was only a few months old when his parents' marriage broke down, Gary considered that it had no real bearing on his life at the time. He never asked questions when he was young about why and how it happened. His philosophy was that whatever happened, happened! 'There was never anything said. Mum was never bitter about it. She never showed bitterness about it towards us kids. Life went on. That's to Mum's credit.'

Gary recalled watching the Olympics as a child, but later in life, although he was a keen triathlete, he no longer followed the Olympics too closely. Gary was in his teens and in secondary school before a few close friends got to know that Peter was his father. 'Whenever there were any reports in the paper, it was always Peter and Jan and the two girls. There was never any mention of a first wife or family.'

Gary first met Peter in 1989 when he was in Melbourne at trade school studying turf management.[8]

> As he was my Dad, there was a bit of excitement, a bit of anticipation about how it would go. We got along all right, but there was no 'When you come down to trade school next time, let's catch up'. One phone call back then could have made all the difference.

Gary did not hesitate for a second about whether he would have seen Peter if he had called: 'Without a doubt! I would have liked that.' Around the age of seventeen, Gary had been keen on catching up on lost time with his father, but as he got older he realised that establishing a relationship was probably always going to be difficult. 'Our stepfather Don was so fantastic in our upbringing and Mum as well, so there wasn't a real need to reach out. I was pretty comfortable where I was, with the upbringing I had.' Gary wondered if Peter perhaps felt the time had passed and that there was never going to be any catch-up. Gary believed that he and Peter could have quite easily put past events aside and started afresh, and he was certainly prepared to do so: 'We could have gone on from then, but as time went on, I got less and less thinking I could like it.'

Peter had every reason to feel proud of his son, who was very likeable and had done well academically and was undertaking additional studies in his chosen field. In common with Peter, he was also keen on sport, particularly Australian Rules football, although they supported different teams.[9] Both could have enjoyed some friendly banter on that subject. There was no doubting they were father and son – they were like two peas in a pod. However, Peter chose not to follow up with Gary for whatever reason – perhaps guilt, or that Peter was trying to get his own life back after years of alcohol and prescription drug abuse, or because he was still just getting to know his daughter Sandy, or because Gary reminded Peter so much of himself.

Gary and his wife Lara went to one of Peter's family Christmas parties when they returned to Echuca after several years of living in Perth. Gary felt strange being in Peter's house. He wondered how life had been for his father – had he had a good life? 'As his kid, you want to know that he's lived all right and is feeling okay.' But the opportunity to ask those questions didn't present itself on the day. Not only were there a lot of people present, but also Gary felt that he was on show in front of relatives and particularly his Nana. Gary did, however, enjoy helping his cousin

Matt Norman, Laurie and Jill's child, throw Peter in the swimming pool.

Gary also never broached the subject with Peter as to why he left the family. 'It was never mentioned because we were always on show the few times we got together. I probably would have liked to have asked a lot of questions. It would not have been easy to ask, but now that I've got kids, I guess the big question would have been, "How could you leave three kids and a wife?"' Lara added, 'If Gaz hadn't asked, I would have. I certainly wouldn't have asked in any judgmental way because I don't know what their circumstances were back then. But it would have been interesting to hear his perspective on how and why it all turned out the way it did.' Gary would have had an ear very close to such a conversation.

In 2002 Peter became associated with the staging of the Tri-State Games, a week-long sporting event held every November, attracting some 250 athletes with significant disabilities from disability organisations throughout Victoria, New South Wales and South Australia. In 2003 and 2004 the event was staged in Echuca and nearby Moama.

In 2004 Peter relished his role as a sports MC and announcer. 'I'm partially here because of state government involvement, but this is also part of my holidays.' Peter was in his element, as evidenced by existing film footage of Peter interacting with competitors. He described the event:

> The competitors are just beautiful. They compete in track and field, boxing, tenpin bowling, indoor cricket and T-ball. A number of competitors have got a lot to put up with, but they work very hard and are very keen. It's a big week for them and for me, too. I love it. The competitors love medals. A number don't have a great concept of competition, but you see them cross the line in last position and they raise their fists in the victory triumph and then high-five all the other competitors. To be in the event means as much to them as being in an Olympic final!

Even though Ruth had only lived in Echuca since 1977, there were people in the community who knew she had been married to Peter at one time. 'Each time there was a Commonwealth Games or the Olympics, that photo would appear in the paper. People would talk to me and that would all come up again. It never went away.' Ruth didn't see much of Peter the first year he was at the Games in Echuca, but she and her husband Don did a lot of volunteer work at the Games the second year. Ruth had a twofold purpose: to do a community service and also to spend time with Peter to see how he was. She spent a lot of time with him during the 2004 event and one night she and Don invited Peter to dinner with all of the family.

Gary recalled the family dinner with Peter:

> It would have been tough for him to walk into a house with Mum's husband Don and the kids and grandchildren. But he was quite chuffed about sitting around and seeing five grandkids: Brittany, Liam, Laura, Maya and our daughter Hannah. At that stage, our daughter Georgia wasn't born.[10] You could see he was proud of them. My sisters are decent girls, and that would have meant something to him.

Gary described Peter as always seeming quite jovial, pleasant and nice whenever they met. However, there wasn't a lot of reciprocal conversation – it was virtually all one way: 'We would ask him a question and we'd get a good answer, but he didn't indulge by asking us any questions. There wasn't even a "How is the business going?" or stuff like that.' Gary believed his Nana probably kept Peter up to date with family news. Gary always made Peter feel welcome whenever he met him: 'I know the girls were the same.'

Lara had the impression that Peter felt awkward when Ruth's husband Don was around: 'Whenever they caught up, Don was always there. I imagine Peter would have felt like he was stepping on people's toes.' Gary wished he had invited Peter to their home so that they could have caught up on their own. Lara thought this would have been a good idea: 'They could have sat out in the backyard, had a beer together and been more themselves with one another, rather than having other relatives looking at them. Gaz loves to have a drink and talk about footy and sport, whereas Ruth is not like that.'

Lara suggested that whenever she saw Gary and Peter together, Gary wasn't himself so Peter never got to know the true Gary. She believed that Peter may have had a preconceived idea about Gary through Ruth: 'He most likely didn't know that Gaz could be the joker that he is. It would have been nice to have been able to get to know that side of Peter; that is, the one-liners, smart comments and quick wit, because I think he and Gary would have related.' Gary agreed:

> Peter Norman has been known to be a joker and a bit of a smart-arse. I'm a bit of a smart-arse at times, which is quite funny because there's been no real contact. It's a bit bizarre to think you've got some of the same characteristics and you haven't been brought up by that person. I guess that's genetics. A lot of that may stem from George Norman as well because we spent a lot of time with him and Nana as kids. That's got to rub off.

In 2004, Peter described Janita, Sandy and Gary as being 'absolutely terrific kids'.

> Ruth and her husband Don can rightfully be very proud of the way those kids have been brought up. They are beautiful kids and they've got some beautiful kids, too. I can see some things of me in Gary, but he is his own person, as are Janita and Sandra. They are a credit to Ruth and Don and a credit to themselves and to each other. They are very close and I can't say that I am proud of them because that makes it sound as if I've had some major part in what they are. I can say that I am proud to know them. I think they're wonderful.

He added, 'It's nice to be loved. I love Ruth, but it's not the kind that a marriage can thrive on. It's more of a family kind of love. Mum and Dad have always been very fond of Ruth. They gave her great support too.'

Peter said about this part of his life that every decision has got a positive and a negative.

> You never really find out whether you've made the right decision or not, because you never know what would have happened if you'd decided the other way. It could have been better, it could have been worse. As far as relationships are concerned, I don't think so. I still love Ruth as a member of the family. I still love Jan as my wife. Love her very dearly. Love the kids and, although it probably makes me feel very old to see those gorgeous grandchildren running around, yeah, I love them, too. They're hard to ignore.

Ruth kept many mementoes from her life with Peter that she continued to treasure, including a beautiful dinner set he brought her back from his

1969 trip to Japan, and some things from his 1968 Olympic trip. Ruth reflected on her life with Peter as being part of God's plan for her. She considered it a real privilege to have been part of his life, to have three of his children and to see them virtually every day: 'I see parts of him through them, so I have a daily reminder of Peter Norman in my life.' She regretted that Peter never allowed himself to see, at close quarters, their three children grow up, marry and have children of their own or to follow their careers and really get to know the beautiful adults they had become, to see their kindness, thoughtfulness and the support and love they have for each other. Ruth said, 'God has been good to us and brought us many blessings.'

In 2004 Peter reflected on what Sandy had done years earlier: 'Sandra was instrumental in putting me back in touch with the family and saying everything was okay. It was pretty strong of her to do that.' There had been no guarantee of success when the young teenager set out 20 years earlier in the lone pursuit of meeting her father with no idea how he would respond. The thought that he might have rejected her may have crossed her mind, but if it did, it did not deter her. Her goal was to 'meet Dad and to find out if he wanted to know us and me' but she did more than that in fact – she brought Peter back into the family fold. The extended Norman family benefited from the determination, persistence and love shown by Sandy, or as one sportswriter referred to her at birth 'Peter's golden girl'.

NOTES

1 'Power and glory at Mexico City', *The Sun*, 18 July 1984.

2 Sandy is still working in the nursing profession today.

3 Sandy described how her two daughters fight over the toy. She said to them, 'No, that's Mummy's special toy from Papa.'

4 A 'yabby' is an Australian freshwater crayfish.

5 'Janita is comeback assistant', *The Sun*, 5 August 1971.

6 Today, Janita is a partner in a very successful Echuca-based building design consultancy, which focuses primarily on residential buildings: houses and townhouses.

7 Sandy's two daughters wore them to Peter's funeral in 2006.

8 Today Gary runs the Murray Goulburn Tree Service in Echuca. Gary is an arborist and his company plants, prunes and removes trees.

9 Gary barracked for his grandfather's (Peter's father) football team, Collingwood, while Peter supported his mother's team, the dreaded enemy Carlton.

10 Hannah and Georgia Norman were born on 14 September 2003 and 17 February 2006 respectively.

19

THERE'S A JOB GOING AT SPORT AND REC

Peter and Greg Lewis had been mates since their running days. After they retired from competition, their contact was somewhat infrequent, but they knew they could always count on each other if they were ever in trouble. Peter visited Greg in hospital during the late 1980s when he was having a gallbladder operation. As it was near Christmas, Peter went dressed as Santa Claus. 'Peter came into my room carrying a sack on his back, and saying "Ho Ho Ho, I bought the young kiddies some flowers", and he takes out these stinking bloody cauliflowers and leaves them on the table near my bed. I couldn't get to them as my guts were crook, but he loved it.'

By 1994 Greg was president of Athletics Victoria and Peter the vice-president. At an annual general meeting on 26 July 1995, Greg proposed a number of changes in an attempt to kick-start the sport in Victoria – attendances were down and the sport was dying. The number of registered athletes in the state had fallen from 8000 to 4000 since the amalgamation of the men's and women's athletics bodies in 1982. A vote of 'no confidence' in Greg was put to the meeting. Peter addressed the meeting at which, according to Greg, nobody had anything good to say.

> Peter wasn't backwards in saying what he felt. He said, 'Here's a president who has got some refreshing ideas and all you can say is, it costs too much.' I thought good on ya! We were always

> brothers in combat, but here he was getting up in politics. It was a priceless moment.

Even though Greg had only been president for a year, he was voted out of office. This prompted a walkout of the other six board members, including Peter, 1992 Olympic long-jump finalist David Culbert and Victorian Olympic Council executive director Bob Lay, who considered Greg's removal to be a vote of no confidence in the entire board. Greg claimed that conservative forces in state athletics were afraid to step forward into the modern era of professional sport. He described it as like 'dealing with a blancmange. You push in one direction and bits fall off in another'.

The row dismayed Athletics Australia general manager Neil King, who told the press, 'There are good, solid people involved here, but unfortunately change is not comfortable for many of them. It has to change. Our sport is not attractive to kids at club level, and Greg Lewis and his board were addressing that.'[1]

Greg and Peter had enjoyed working together on the board but were pleased to walk away from it in the finish. Greg said, 'Peter and I got very close that year. He threw his support behind me 101 per cent.'

Bob Lay didn't forget Peter's work with Athletics Victoria and he contacted Peter when he saw an opportunity for which he thought Peter would be ideally suited.

> I said to him, 'There's a job going at Sport and Rec. You should apply for it. With what you've done, you'd be a bloody good chance for it.' So he applied with me pushing him. I gave him a good reference. He got the job and I feel very humble that I helped get him into that. He'd never have applied if I hadn't.

Peter joined the events area of Sport and Recreation Victoria in 1997. He was no stranger to the organisation, having previously worked there on secondment in the early 1970s for about eighteen months. He had done some consultancy work for the organisation after that, including some professional development work on goal-setting in the late 1980s.

General Manager Brian Mott said Peter had two major tasks.

> One was contract management and development of events. His longest involvement was with the Rip Curl Pro, which is one of the world's leading surfing events. Peter's second major role in

the early years was to organise international teams to come to Victoria to establish pre–Sydney Olympic training bases.

Peter was responsible for over 2500 overseas athletes coming to Victoria for training, including some 1500 athletes two to three weeks before the 2000 Sydney Olympics. 'Peter's personal stamp on that was sensational,' added Brian. 'Victoria saw a lot of economic benefit. Different studies showed that he generated $10 to $20 million worth of economic impact from that work. He was supported by a lot of other people, but he did a terrific job.'

Peter enjoyed working for and with Brian: 'He has been so helpful in making sure that I stay on the straight and narrow as far as getting the job done. He's a good guy to work with because he is one of the boys. He knows most of the answers and if he doesn't know, he'll back you to find them out.'

Pam Ryan had known Peter since the 1962 Perth British Empire and Commonwealth Games, but she got to see a different side of Peter at this time. Pam and her husband managed two sets of apartments, ideally situated in South Yarra near all of Melbourne's major sporting venues.

> I worked with Peter quite a lot. The British Olympic cycling team stayed with us for three weeks prior to going to Sydney for the Olympics. Peter used to call in and we'd have a coffee and talk about how they were getting on, what he was doing, and if he had any other work for us. Peter loved doing that. He still had the same sense of humour, the same bouncing around. He was so full of life.

Peter continued to organise training bases after the 2000 Olympics. He had established such strong relationships with a number of countries that, regardless of where the Olympics or world championships were being held, they chose to continue training in Victoria. Peter was very successful in finding suitable training venues, not only in Melbourne but also in provincial Victoria, including in Bendigo and Ballarat. He was a strong advocate of the 2004 Commonwealth Youth Games held in Bendigo. Peter was also heavily involved in preparations for the 2006 Melbourne Commonwealth Games, including the athletics events held at the Melbourne Cricket Ground (MCG).[2] Peter had two official functions at the Commonwealth Games: he supported the teams that chose to train in Victoria and made sure their arrangements were in place, and he also chaired a lot of the functions or was a meet-and-greet person.

Peter loved mixing with athletes and officials once again. He threw himself into his work and was prepared to sacrifice much of his free time to ensure that nothing was missed. 'The thing that stands out,' said Brian, 'is the number of times he'd go out to the airport to pick officials up. The first group might come in at 1 am, and then somebody had to go back at 4 am. Peter would always say he'd go. That typified Peter. He'd take responsibility.' Peter's dedication earned him the affectionate nickname of 'Car 54' from his work colleagues – the nickname being taken from the early 1960s television police sitcom, 'Car 54, Where Are You?'

Brian recalled Peter's compassion, relating how Peter once asked him if he could take a few weeks recreation leave to work on the Tri-State Games.

> I suggested he take a week's leave and do a week on behalf of the Department. Because obviously some of what he was doing was fundamental to what the department was trying to do; that is, strengthen up community organisations. He got involved in the after-event activities and assisted in making them much more enjoyable for the athletes. He organised barbecues, and a little bit of theatre.
>
> Because he'd had struggles in his life, he'd relate to and support anybody who was giving it a go. It wasn't just in the area of disability. When I was cleaning out his locker [after Peter's death], I found some interesting stuff about different people who were down and out and who he'd supported. If Peter saw somebody who was down and depressed, or if he knew somebody had been having a tough time at home, he would ask how things were going or he'd buy a cake or put a bottle of wine on their desk. He was a very caring person. He was not rich, and each time he put his hand in his pocket, it was a sacrifice.

Peter got involved on the Table Tennis Australia Board, despite the potential conflict of interest in being a public servant and part of a sporting organisation at the same time. But according to Brian, Peter felt it was an organisation worthy of change and he 'worked his butt off' to try and achieve that. Ron Carlton, a former javelin thrower who had narrowly missed selection for the Mexico Olympics, was the chief executive officer of Table Tennis Australia. 'Ron asked me to join the board of management,' said Peter, 'to help lift the profile of table tennis. I accepted the role and spent five years on the board.' It was no coincidence that the Australian table tennis open was a highly successful international-standard event for those five years.

Jan said Peter's job at Sport and Recreation was the making of him. He would have done the job for nothing: he was in his element, involved in sport again, working with people, making speeches, everything he was good at. He was well-connected and knew everybody. 'His feelings of self-worth definitely increased. To him it wasn't really a job, so he didn't mind putting in long hours. I was happy he was doing it because he loved it.'

Peter's father, George Norman, passed away aged 82 on 19 October 2000, after several years of poor health. The loss of the family patriarch hit Thelma, Peter, Laurie, Heather, Elaine and the extended Norman family very hard. George was accorded a large funeral – he had touched so many lives with his warm, fun-loving and generous nature, and his loyalty and compassion. Peter paid tribute to his father in a moving eulogy. Thelma initially asked Herb Norman to scatter his older brother's ashes at the Chelsea cemetery. Herb said he would have been honoured to have done so, but he thought Peter, being the oldest child, ought to do it: 'That's what happened. Peter appreciated that.'

In mid May 2002, the Couch Productions team returned to the boards for one final show. Peter related the story.

> A little old lady who saw quite a few of our shows rang and asked if we would perform for her 50th wedding anniversary. Well, the upshot was that we all got together for three rehearsals and put on our first show in some ten years. We did 'Sinderella' and it was a real hit, despite the ageing cast and very tight costumes. All the wit, humour and superb acting of Bob; Archie worrying if the set was actually level and if there was enough reverb when he sang; Margo, mother of six, still lovely as 'Sinderella'; Julie still bitching about all and sundry; and, of course, the beautiful, graceful Gertrude the not-so-ugly sister. Ah yes, it was all still there. Somehow I think that was the last, last show that will

happen for Couch Productions, although the $$$ were very nice for having a good time.[3]

In June 2002, Peter turned sixty. Around the time of his birthday, Peter was surfing on the internet and found the 'School Friends' website.

> I plugged into that and was looking for a cousin who had gone to Preston Girls' School. I came across this name Helen Pletzer Whelan. I thought there could only be one Helen Pletzer. Helen was one of my girlfriends at the Thornbury Salvos, the kind who you'd have a milkshake with or go down and play the pinball machine with after the youth club on Friday night. Bad things like that!

Peter subsequently contacted Helen. She said, 'I spoke with him just after he turned sixty. He tracked me down from the School Friends website. It was a case of, "So what have you been doing for the last 40 years?" We had quite a chat and we said we'd catch up for coffee, but sadly we never did!'

By this time, Peter and Surfing Victoria's executive director, Max Wells, were warm friends. Peter had really embraced surfing. He enjoyed the free-spirited approach to the Rip Curl Pro, held every Easter, which is the world's longest-running professional surfing event. Max stated that Peter was a major contributor in brokering the partnership between Surfing Victoria and the Rip Curl organisation: 'As contract manager, Peter brought commonsense to the table. He became incredibly fond of Rip Curl and took great pride in being part of the event. In turn, the Rip Curl Pro board of management thought very highly of Peter.' Even though Peter had never surfed before, he tried it in the 2004 Rip Curl celebrity event and nearly drowned in the process after suffering an asthma attack midway. Although shaken by the experience, it didn't dampen his enthusiasm for the event. Max felt that he and Peter got on extremely well, partly because they were both 'broken-down old physical education teachers', but also because they had great respect for each other. 'Peter was intensely loyal. He was upfront and told you the way he saw it. There wasn't much bullshit about him.'

Peter continued to keep up with Bob. They enjoyed each other's company and would often get together for a coffee and a good chat. Bob had concerns about Peter's health.

> Peter was overweight, and still smoked. He also had a drinking problem. When I took Peter away, say to Bendigo or Ballarat to

meetings, I was always careful. I don't drink a lot and I always tried to make sure we kept his drinking low, particularly if he was driving. He never overdid it with me.

Peter's drinking eventually landed him in trouble. According to a newspaper report in September 2004, Peter's 'sporting relevance didn't resonate with cheers in a courtroom as a magistrate expressed concern for the potential danger Norman posed as a multiple drink driver'.[4] Peter pleaded guilty to a fourth offence of exceeding the Victorian blood alcohol limit of .05, having committed two offences in the previous ten years. He also pleaded guilty to a charge of unlicensed driving.

> The Sunshine Magistrates Court was told that Norman was stopped for a random breath test in Williamstown on 24 June 2004. He later recorded a blood alcohol level of .073 per cent. When asked why he was driving, Norman replied, 'I'm 62 years of age and the job I have requires that I drive.' Defence counsel Tony Burns told magistrate Belinda Wallington that Norman 'apologises to the community and the police. It is an understatement to say Mr Norman is embarrassed to be here.'
>
> As Mr Burns referred to the 'enduring image' of the Mexico medal ceremony, Ms Wallington interrupted. 'I'm more concerned with the risk he poses to the community on the road and what he has done about it. There are lots of people who have drinking problems who had contributed to the community … what the community wants is people addressing their alcohol problems.' Peter was found suitable for a twelve month community based order. Ms Wallington ordered him to be assessed and, if necessary, treated for alcohol abuse. He was fined $500 and disqualified from driving for fourteen months.[5]

Peter admitted that he was 'pretty stupid', especially as he had previously been 'busted' for similar charges.

> I stopped off at a hotel that I was doing business with. The new owner was more hospitable than I would have anticipated. This hotel is probably three kilometres from my house and I didn't feel I was affected, so I drove home. Half a kilometre from

> home I got pulled over, random tested and as the officer said, I was probably one beer over the limit, but now there is a zero tolerance on over the limit.

Peter was annoyed at his own stupidity in placing himself in this situation and letting people down.

> My family and to a very large extent Tommie Smith and John Carlos, because they were shown in the paper in a colour shot [on the dais] standing with me, a convicted drunk driver. There we were as the threesome. The photo of me outside the court was fair game, but to use that photo as a recognisable way of presenting me wasn't quite fair to Tommie or John. But it's a lesson that was pretty hard to take and I'm very sorry for being such a stupid fellow and its not going to happen again.

Belinda Norman said that by losing his licence, her father became healthier. It afforded him the opportunity to ride his bike, which Belinda said he enjoyed doing.

Peter shared a very close bond with Belinda and Emma and constantly talked about them to friends and work colleagues. Even after they moved away from home, Emma said her father would visit them often. 'We'd have a beer together and play pool. It was like having a friend over. He'd bring us roasts in containers. We'd get so many food deliveries from home.' It was the same when Belinda and Emma visited their parents. 'He'd be stacking bags up with stuff when we were about to leave,' said Belinda.

Peter was very supportive of Belinda and Emma. He encouraged them to do their own thing. Emma recalled that even when they got into trouble while they were growing up, their father was quite lenient on them. 'He was never very hard on us. We grew up thinking he could do everything, and he would have told us that as well.' As he had done with his sisters, Heather and Elaine, years earlier, Peter constantly advised his daughters on a range of topics, particularly their outfits and accessories: 'We'd ask his advice on everything, like outfits,' commented Belinda. 'He'd say, for example, "You need some longer earrings."' Peter could always be relied on to rescue the girls and their friends if they had locked their keys in their car. Emma recalled one instance at the local beach. 'Dad picked up a few tools, like wire, and came down. He said, "You can time me if you want."

So we did. Twenty-eight seconds later he was into that car. This was just one of a number of times he did it.' Peter had numerous other talents that the girls marvelled at, including his ability to crack combination locks, fix jewellery, replace batteries in watches, perform magic tricks at their parties and play Santa in his 'fabulous' Santa suit. Belinda and Emma also enjoyed seeing and hearing the great pleasure their father gained from musicals. Belinda said, 'We knew all the words to "Les Mis" and "Phantom of the Opera" from every road trip we took with him.'

By this time Peter was in a relationship with a financial adviser from country Victoria. In 1997 Peter met Sandy Miller when he spoke at a financial advisers' conference at Sorrento. Sandy, born in California in 1965, had visited Australia briefly in 1982, and settled permanently two years later. A friendship developed between Peter and Sandy, initially by phone, but then Peter began visiting Sandy in her home town of Shepparton (approximately 200 kilometres north-east of Melbourne). In 1999 Peter told Sandy that he had feelings for her, but according to Sandy, he thought it best to maintain the status quo at that time.

> Peter struggled with his emotions towards me. At that stage he hadn't reconciled the fact that he was going to give up completely on Jan. He felt that he wasn't able to offer me a full-time relationship, and he didn't believe he could give me enough because of the distance between us. But as our friendship grew deeper and deeper, we got more intimate on a personal level, not sexually, but personally. We just fell more in love with each other until it was finally unavoidable. By 2001 we felt our feelings for one another were too strong to ignore.

Peter told Sandy that his Achilles injury had changed his whole life.

> He mentioned that his relationship with Jan was never the same after the injury. I think the pain he went through with the Achilles was so debilitating at some point that he had to focus elsewhere. He told me that he'd had a couple of other relationships before he met me, but he said they weren't fulfilling. He started to lose self-confidence. He felt he'd failed in his relationship with Jan. He told me that they pretty well much cohabitated, but had separate rooms. She took her own holidays and he took his. There wasn't much togetherness at

> all. He cooked for himself and she cooked separately.
>
> Peter's family found out when my then estranged husband Craig wrote a letter to Jan around November 2003. Craig and I had separated six months earlier. Emma called me and told me to leave Peter alone.

Jan described how she was 'just devastated' when she received the letter from Craig Miller. She didn't know what Peter's thoughts on the subject were: 'He denied it until it was obvious that he couldn't deny it any more. I guess he led me to believe that it wasn't going on any longer, but I didn't know if it was or if it wasn't.'

Miller's letter did not stop the relationship. 'We realised that whatever time we had was more important,' said Sandy, 'but there was a limit as to how much he felt he could give to me of himself. He didn't want to wreck his close relationship with his daughters. He spoke about them pretty well much every time we spoke. He said they relied on him for everything.'

Sandy's daughter initially believed that Peter had caused her parents' marriage break-up, but Sandy quickly assured her the marriage was 'well and truly over' by then. Sandy's son understood her situation: 'He told me that if Peter made me happy, he'd totally support it. Peter generally tried to keep our relationship private, but he had no problem coming up to Shepparton and going out with my friends.' Peter and Sandy also got together when Peter was in Echuca for the Tri-State Games. 'Peter was just another little kid at the Games. The kids were trying their hardest, and he was so proud of them and so full of praise for what they were achieving.' Sandy admitted that she was the reason why Peter didn't always call in on his family in Echuca: 'Any amount of time we had together was just so precious and we were both very protective of it.'

Peter's strength of character and his softness of heart appealed to Sandy.

> By softness of heart, I mean he was a genuine caring soul in the sense of being non-judgmental to just about everybody. You had to hurt him a few times before he'd give up. And he'd help anybody who needed help. He was very giving in the way he related to other people. He was very affectionate towards me. We were so open, so able to talk about anything. He told me that he'd woken up again with me. He was living again, not just

> existing. I probably contributed to his happiness by allowing him to be completely himself and to explore deep emotions, to be totally and unconditionally loved for who he was and as he was. Peter needed to be loved and needed to know that he was loved. He had such an enormous capacity to give.

Sandy and Peter endeavoured to do something different, something new, every time they were together.

> He used to stretch me out of my comfort zone. One of my favourite memories was when we were down in Torquay at Easter for the 2003 Rip Curl Pro, we went up in a Tiger Moth. He liked theatre, so I went to the theatre with him in Melbourne and he'd go to concerts with me, both in Shepparton and Melbourne. One of his favourites was 'Chicago'. In the middle stages of our relationship, I was probably in Melbourne at least every five weeks. He'd come up to Shepparton every few months.

When Sandy visited Melbourne for training courses, Peter would stay with her at the Rialto hotel. By coincidence, one night she saw Peter and Jan at the theatre in Melbourne. Sandy was sitting with friends three rows from Peter and Jan. Peter and Sandy managed to meet discreetly while having a cigarette in the foyer.

In 2005, Peter encouraged Sandy to find someone else. He broke off the relationship, fearing that he would lose the love of Belinda and Emma if he continued to see her. Sandy later met her partner John. John met Peter twice, initially with some jealousy on John's part. That soon disappeared as John realised that Peter was pleased that Sandy had met someone who would look after her. Sandy and Peter last spoke to each other by phone in mid 2006: 'Peter told me that I'd given him so much and he was grateful for what we'd shared.'

Peter was back in his element working with Sport and Recreation Victoria. Arch Galloway was delighted to see his theatre mate happy: 'The last few years he was in his glory. It was where he should have been right from the beginning. He had a purpose in life again.' Peter had always enjoyed the fame his silver medal had given him, but even he would be astonished by the recognition that lay ahead. His time of glory had well and truly come.

NOTES

1 'Walkout sparks crisis', *The Herald Sun*, 28 July 1995.

2 Peter's silver medal is on loan to the National Sports Museum housed at the Melbourne Cricket Ground. At one time Peter kept it in a brick-sized box that held open the front door of his home. In 1999 Peter told a reporter from the *Australian*, 'Who'd ever think to look there if someone came around to knock it off.'

3 Peter Norman, email message to John McAdam, 26 May 2002.

4 'Track legend falters in driver's seat', *The Age*, 18 September 2004.

5 'Track legend falters in driver's seat', *The Age*, 18 September 2004.

20

YOU NEVER TIRE OF BEING GREAT

The torch relay is the Olympic movement's call to bring together the world's finest athletes to celebrate the Olympic Games. The torch is indelibly linked to past and future Olympics – passing the torch from one carrier to the next is a symbolic re-enactment of the ancient tradition of handing down fire from generation to generation.

> In 2000, as the Olympic flame travelled first through Greece, then through Oceania and finally around Australia, athletes across the world were beginning to make their way to Sydney for training and to celebrate the Games of the XXVII Olympiad. Sydney's Olympic torch reflected the values which the organisers regarded as key elements of the Sydney 2000 Games – the egalitarian spirit of Australia, the commitment to Olympism and the motivation of innovation.[1]

The Olympic torch relay officially began its journey on Australian soil in the Northern Territory's Uluru–Kata Tjuta National Park on 8 June 2000, when Nova Peris-Kneebone – the first Australian Aboriginal person to win a gold medal at an Olympic Games (as a member of Australia's women's hockey team in 1996) – accepted the flame. On Day 53 (Sunday 30 July) of its journey, Peter Norman carried the Olympic torch across Melbourne's

Westgate bridge. Peter was permitted to take ten people on to the bridge to see him run.

> I had family [including Jan, Belinda and Emma] and a couple of friends, which made it just that little bit more intimate. I'd already gone through the crowds on both sides of Williamstown Road, seeing a lot of old friends and kids I taught at school who were there with their kids. It was just the biggest buzz.[2]

Peter was very proud to have his father George present on the bridge. Although in poor health, George's beaming smile showed his pride in his son and his achievements.

In Judy Patching's opinion, Peter epitomised the Olympic spirit. Patching admired Peter's honesty, integrity and willingness to help raise funds, to talk to schools and to participate on sports committees.

> Peter went far beyond the bounds of duty or responsibility. He'd been an Olympian and wanted to help other people become Olympians. Peter portrayed to me all the attributes you'd find in a great sportsman. If you wanted someone to sell your product, which was Olympism, one of the first guys I'd pick would be Peter. He had a wonderful personality. He was always positive. He could be very forthright, but didn't hold a grudge.
>
> Peter was a very gregarious person and he was friendly with everybody. He was kindly. I was going to say humble. He was exuberant and his exuberance probably disguised his humble attitude in lots of things. I put him in a very high category with [Betty] Cuthbert, [Marjorie Jackson] Nelson, John Landy and the like. They were great, but humble people.

The 2000 Olympics opened on 15 September. Peter had hoped to attend a day of athletics during the second week of competition, but thanks to USA Track & Field official Steve Simmons, he saw much more than that. Simmons had never met Peter but had talked to him on the telephone in 1998 when he arranged for Peter to be interviewed for 'Fists of Freedom', a documentary on the 1968 Olympics. Simmons expected that he would meet Peter in Sydney during the Games: 'I assumed the Australian federation would have the Olympic greats, including Peter, assembled in Sydney.' On his arrival in Sydney, however, Simmons learnt from a newspaper article that this assumption was incorrect. Peter didn't have specific plans for Sydney as he hadn't been included in any official events. He and Jan were trying to find cheap flights from Melbourne to Sydney. Simmons got angry with the Australian Athletic Union: 'In my estimation Peter should have been part of anything they were doing, whether it is hosting alumni or foreign dignitaries … you bring the great people out to something like that.'

Simmons immediately telephoned Peter, who told him that he had been invited to one day of track-and-field competition by a Melbourne-based company. On hearing this, Simmons told Peter that he would buy plane tickets for him and Jan to travel to Sydney as guests of the 1968 US Olympic team. He also undertook to arrange accommodation and to meet them at the airport the next day. Peter was overwhelmed by his generosity.

> Steve took Jan and me up to the Olympics when it seemed that we weren't going to get there. Steve was the most generous host you could ever meet and insisted that we stay at his hotel. He not only gave us Games tickets, but we went with a bunch of his friends.

Peter and Jan arrived in Sydney the night a big party was being staged at Planet Hollywood to celebrate legendary sprinter Michael Johnson's thirty-third birthday. In 1996 Michael Johnson had become the first male athlete to win both the 200 and 400 metres at the same Olympics. He created further Olympic history at the 2000 Olympics by becoming the first male to successfully defend his 400 metres title. Simmons had spoken to Johnson earlier and he readily agreed that Simmons should bring Peter and Jan to the party. Peter and Johnson had met previously, as Peter recalled: 'Michael Johnson is a thorough gentleman. I first met him in Sydney in 1995 when he was here to compete in our nationals. I spent an hour or so with him and his brother in the bar of the hotel we were staying in.'

Simmons continued the story.

> Mike Powell, Dan O'Brien, Edwin Moses[3] and some other guys from the US were there when I walked in with Peter. I introduced Peter to Edwin. Edwin Moses is a very quiet, distinguished guy. Ed shook Peter's hand and said it was an honour to meet him. Peter was a little taken aback. The next thing Jan knew she was

> sitting at a table with Michael, Mike Powell, Dan O'Brien and Edwin Moses. Jan leant over to Peter and said, 'I'm not sure we belong here'. I said, 'Oh yes you do!' Edwin Moses leant over to her and said, 'This is one of the greatest honours of my life to have you here. I consider Peter one of my greatest heroes.' It was a seminal moment to see these champions at the one event.[4]

Peter had been inducted into the Sport Australia Hall of Fame on 24 November 1999, considering it a 'big buzz' to be inducted in front of family and friends: 'My two teenage daughters have never seen me compete so I was thrilled to share this recognition with them.'[5] But recognition by US track-and-field greats was something else again.

Jan said that she and Peter had the 'most amazing time' at Johnson's birthday party.

> People like Jesse Owens's granddaughter were coming up to Peter and saying, 'I'm honoured to meet you'. He was already in the Hall of Fame, so things like that happened quite frequently, but that's the first time we were surrounded by these amazing American athletes. Peter was flabbergasted and overcome by it all.

Peter's boss from Sport and Recreation, Brian Mott, recalled Peter being 'almost embarrassed' at the way the Americans treated him.

> It was not only that they took them up there, but the way that they went out of their way to make sure he met the top American athletes and the response of Michael Johnson. He was so proud that Michael would think that much of him. He was just tickled pink by the whole thing.

Judy Patching thought it was a wonderful gesture by the Americans to recognise Peter's contribution so many years later.

> We don't understand in our country that an Olympic medallist is held in such high esteem. Here in Australia we take it for bloody granted. That silver medal of Peter's should have made a huge impact. It might have been blemished by the media writing about all this crap on the dais. That diminished what it really meant.

Raelene Boyle agreed that Peter never got the recognition he deserved for his success in Mexico: 'Pete was a very elite sportsman. Football players are going to be remembered longer, even if they only played one game, than Peter will be for winning a silver medal at the Olympics!' Raelene also thought that Peter deserved international recognition and applause for what he did on the dais in Mexico.

> He didn't get that at the time, but certainly now, internationally, people respect that he had the balls to do that. It's made him quite famous. Sadly it was something that stayed with him all his life and he talked about it constantly. Whenever I saw him, he'd always give me an update on whether Carlos or Smith had called him, particularly Carlos, because he bonded very well with Carlos. He'd also tell me what he'd been up to or if he'd just had a trip to the States to do something with them. Those guys had a pretty unique relationship. At the time we probably all went 'Oh my God, why did you do that?', but in the end I've certainly held him in high esteem and with great respect because of what he did.
>
> There's not many of the more modern-era track-and-field athletes in the Australian sports hall of fame club and Pete certainly is. We would always catch up, have a good laugh and the odd beer and update each other on what we were doing and our families, at different stuff associated with the Hall of Fame and the Victorian Olympic Council dinners.

Raelene described Peter as a great mate and a nice guy with a great personality and a lot to offer.

> But there were issues with Peter. He did look sad for a long time. But then he'd start talking about his running and Carlos and Smith and it would pick him up again. We talked more about the old days of athletics, specifically Mexico and the two guys, and that would lift his spirits. It was something that made his life worthwhile.

One night at a Hall of Fame dinner, Raelene began conversing with Peter and realised he was pretty drunk. She just kept chatting to him as she walked him downstairs and talked him into getting into a taxi and going

Left: *Peter Norman and Jan McQueen marry in New Zealand on 16 October 1976, eight years to the day that Peter won silver in Mexico.*

Middle: *Sandy Norman is delighted to have her father Peter, sister Janita and brother Gary help celebrate her 21st birthday in July 1991. This was the first major step in reuniting Peter with his children from his first marriage.*

Below left: *Peter (far right) as Gertrude the not-so-ugly sister in 'Sinderella'. Peter described himself as looking gorgeous, but adds that 'the moustache was a bit of a giveaway'. Julie Enwright and Margot McKay (as Sinderella) accompany Peter on stage.*

Below right: *Peter on stage as the cunning Count von Creep in the theatre-restaurant spicy melodrama 'Cash on the Knockers'.*

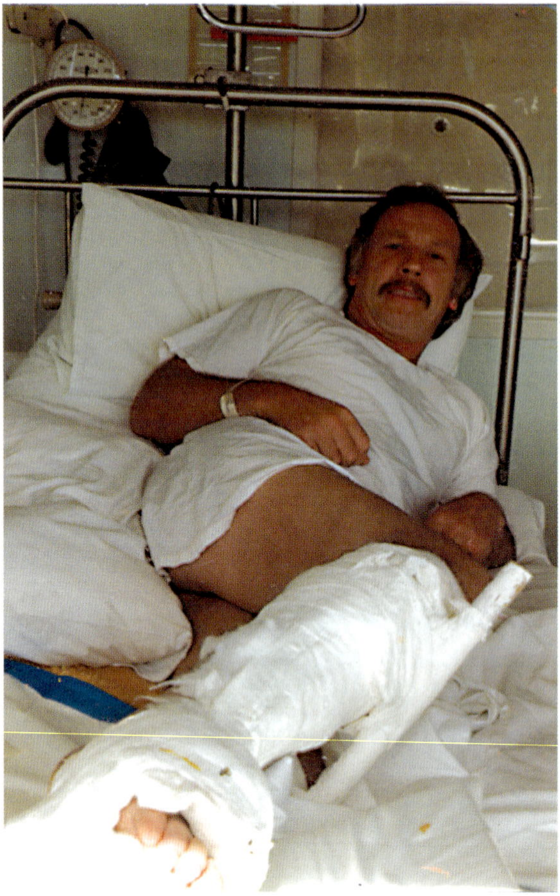

Left: *Peter immediately after his operation – his legs were splinted together for the next three weeks. So began 'eight years of hell'.*

Below left: *The Norman family celebrate Thelma's 70th birthday at the Salvation Army hall in Frankston on 6 July 1991. Back row (left to right): Peter and Jan, Michael and Elaine, Jill and Laurie; front row (left to right): Heather, Thelma and George.*

Below right: *Peter's legs showing the cross-leg flap procedure to repair his ruptured Achilles tendon, circa January 1986.*

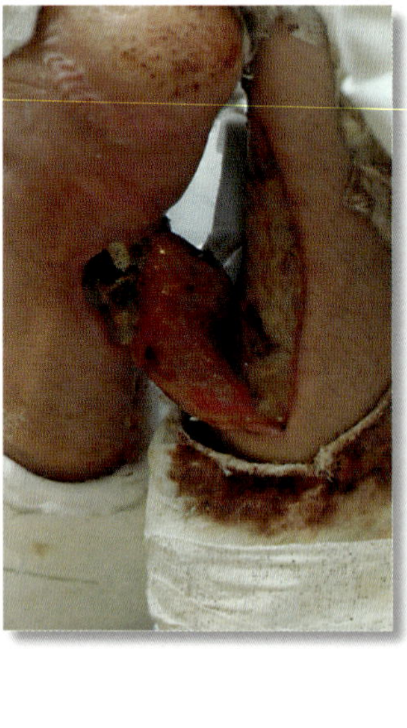

Left: *Peter and Jan and their daughters, Belinda and Emma, in the early 1990s*

Below left: *Peter and Jan at Sandy and Chris Kadri's wedding on 30 March 1996. Pictured left to right are Jan, Peter, Thelma, George, Sandy, Chris, Heather, Michael and Elaine.*

Below right: *Peter and his five children – Belinda, Emma, Sandy, Gary and Janita – pose with Thelma and George at Sandy's wedding.*

Next page: *A proud moment for Peter – his induction into the Sport Australia Hall of Fame on 24 November 1999. Peter considered it a 'big buzz' to be inducted in front of family and friends.*

HALL OF FAME
honours
Peter Norman
as a
MEMBER
for
Excellent Performance
in
Athletics

Left: *Although in poor health, a proud George Norman witnessed his son Peter carry the Olympic Torch across Melbourne's West Gate Bridge on 30 July 2000.*

Middle: *Peter, US Olympic great Michael Johnson, Jan Norman and Australian Olympic swimmer Michael Klim at Michael Johnson's birthday party during the Sydney 2000 Olympics.*

Below: *Peter in front of Melbourne's John Landy – Ron Clarke statue that commemorates the outstanding sportsmanship shown by Landy during the 1956 Australian mile championship. Landy stopped during the race to check on the fallen Clarke, thereby sacrificing his chances of breaking his world mile record. Greg and Gary.*

Left: *Peter is less than amused after having been thrown into the pool at his home by his nephew Matt Norman (left) and his son Gary Norman (right), 26 December 2003.*

Middle: *Peter with his eldest grandchildren Liam and Brittany (Janita's children) at Peter and Jan's Norman family Christmas at their Williamstown home, 26 December 2003. Ruth's husband, Don Membrey, can be seen behind Brittany.*

Below left: *Peter back on dry land on 15 March 2006 after carrying the Queen's baton on board the tall ship Enterprize in the lead-up to the opening of the 2006 Commonwealth Games in Melbourne. Jan and Emma Norman can be seen in the background.*

Below right: *Peter took a strong interest in the career of Australian athlete John Steffensen. A month after Peter presented John with a signed copy of the famous dais photo, John won the 400 metres at the 2006 Commonwealth Games in Melbourne, much to Peter's delight.*

307
1
3
2

Previous page: *John Carlos, Tommie Smith and Peter at California's San José State University on 17 October 2005 following the unveiling of a large statue depicting Tommie and John's protest at the 1968 Olympics.*

Right: *Peter was delighted to spend time with John Carlos, Don Kassing (San José State University president), Tommie Smith and Lee Evans during his October 2005 visit to the USA for the statue unveiling.*

Middle: *Peter's coffin is taken from the Williamstown Town Hall by pallbearers: at left (front to back) Tommie Smith, Colin Stevens, Gary Norman, John Whittington; at right (front to back) John Carlos, Laurie and Matt Norman, and Chris Kadri.*

Below: *Tommie Smith, Gary Norman, John Carlos, Matt and Laurie Norman outside the Williamstown Town Hall after the service, the 'Celebration of Life for Peter Norman', on 9 October 2006.*

home. 'There's probably many people who would have done that to me over the years. And I believe that's what the mateship of what we've been through is about.' Raelene hadn't seen Peter like that very often and she was surprised. 'It really stood out that he was down. But then in life often we get to a certain age and we do get down. I suffer with depression so I can relate to it. You fall off the wagon for a while and dig yourself a hole, but then you pull yourself out of it.'

Raelene doesn't think that the last few years of Peter's life were that happy.

> He hadn't been happy for a while. There was the depression and he was hitting the grog a bit. It was sad. He deserved to be happy. In many ways Pete lived the life of his athletic memory every day. It was there all the time. Jan came into his life after he'd essentially finished running. I think probably this daily memory and attitude or whatever it was, the bit of American slang that came out of his mouth, probably pissed her off more than made her happy.

Raelene's lasting memory of Peter is of him telling her the story of the 200 metres final.

> He'd just about broken everyone else in the field and the last one he couldn't get to was John. He used to have great joy in telling me about the telephone ringing. He had this silly little chuckle and he would chuckle his way through it when he told me. I loved watching the delight not only in his face and his body language but also in his voice when he told that story.

A major highlight of the 2000 Olympics for Peter was Cathy Freeman's performance in winning gold in the 400 metres. He described her achievement as 'nothing short of brilliant' and was full of praise for the strength of concentration and character she showed in the final. He said after her win that he doubted whether anyone else in the world could have carried the burden that Freeman did during that period of her life: 'She was built up by the Australian press as being Australia's only possible track-and-field gold medallist before the heats were even run. The press had everyone believing that Catherine Freeman was going to win the gold medal.'

Peter was particularly delighted that Freeman wasn't criticised for carrying the Aboriginal flag and Australian flag tied together on her lap of honour in Sydney, remembering the controversy that erupted after she defiantly carried both flags on her lap of honour after winning the 400 metres at the 1994 Commonwealth Games in Canada. She had been severely chastised for her actions by the Australian Commonwealth Games team manager, Arthur Tunstall. Peter reacted savagely towards Tunstall at the time, telling reporters that Tunstall was not worthy of representing Australia. Peter was angry that Tunstall had singled out the flag-waving incident when swimmers had not been criticised for taking boomerangs and cuddly toys on to the victory dais. He expressed the view that, 'Obviously Cathy was feeling very proud of her heritage and what she has done for herself … and she was demonstrating that in a happy way. She had every right to carry that flag, and she's got every right to carry it again.'[6]

Peter elaborated on the flag issue after the Sydney Olympics.

> Catherine was born Australian. She was born Aboriginal. So the two flags are synonymous with her. Fair enough the Aboriginal flag hasn't always been part of Aboriginal tradition, but the colours and the design of the flag symbolise Aboriginal tradition and therefore she's got the right to carry two flags. They're both Australian.

During the 2000 Olympics Peter expressed his vehement opposition to the Australian government's treatment of Aboriginal people: 'What we do to our native Australians, our own Indigenous people, is nothing short of horrific.' Commenting on the government's proposed $1.5 billion expenditure on Aboriginal programs for the coming year, Peter stated that 'throwing money at them is not the answer'. In Peter's opinion, the federal government had to initially apologise for the many wrongs inflicted on Indigenous people over many generations by a succession of governments, before beginning to address issues such as their disadvantage in health, education, employment and housing. 'We've got a prime minister who won't say "Sorry",' Peter said of the prime minister at the time, John Howard. 'The problems won't be resolved. But by saying "sorry", I think they could begin to talk. I can't say "Sorry" on behalf of Australia, but the prime minister surely can.'[7]

On the night of Michael Johnson's birthday party in 2000, Steve Simmons conceived the idea that one day he would get Peter to the USA so that Peter could really experience what some Americans, especially American track athletes and black athletes, thought about him. In July 2004, Simmons arranged sponsorship for Peter to visit the USA during the US Olympic track and field trials in Sacramento, California, held to determine the make-up of the US athletics team for the 2004 Athens Olympics. Peter enjoyed his time at what is arguably the world's biggest track meet outside the Olympics and world championships. Over the years, in excess of 50 world records have been set at the trials by such legendary Olympic figures as Michael Johnson, Bobby Morrow, Bob Seagren, Rafer Johnson, Bob Mathias and Florence Griffith Joyner.

In January 2003, Peter began filming and recording a series of interviews with his nephew Matt Norman, who was compiling a film documentary about Peter's silver medal win and his involvement in the dais protest at the 1968 Olympic Games.[8] Additional interviews were recorded while Peter was in Sacramento, including several hours of discussion between Peter, Tommie Smith and John Carlos. Peter also took part in several events associated with a reunion of members of the 1968 US Olympic team where he was thrilled to catch up with the likes of sprinters Wyomia Tyus, Charlie Greene and Larry Questad; long jumpers Willye White and Ralph Boston; rowers Paul Hoffman, who had given Peter his OPHR badge to wear on the dais in Mexico, and Cleve Livingston; and Payton Jordan, coach of the 1968 US athletics team.

Simmons was delighted to see Peter enjoy the trip and the opportunity to mix with US Olympians: 'He enjoyed his Olympic experience once again 36 years later as he should. We have a lot of admiration for Peter in this country. I don't know that Australians understand how much we do.' In discussing why African-American athletes have such an admiration for Peter, Steve said, 'It's linked to the dais. He became a part of what Carlos and Smith were doing and he's forever embedded with these two guys. Peter Norman was not dragged along. He was there because he had a feeling of fairness in him.'[9]

Speaking at a symposium, Peter stated that it was 'a privilege and pleasure' to be in Sacramento with some very dear friends from a long time ago.

> There are very strong family ties in track and field, ties that can only be experienced in two places: in the field of sport and in

> the field of conflict or war. Listen to any guy who's ever been in the forces and been under fire. Listen to them talk about the friends they had in that situation. It's different. Talk to anyone who has ever been in sport at just about any level, it's different and there is an empathy between the guys from 1968 that can't be described.

Peter was incredulous about the reaction he received on the trip. He was amazed at the friendship and recognition given to him by 'these beautiful people'.

> Here you're not a track-and-field runner, you're a track star. As far as track and field is concerned, this is where it all happens. I'm just absolutely stoked to be here. Every time you walk into a room you meet someone new and someone else wants to meet you. It's beautiful. The people here have got a much greater appreciation of track and field. The track-and-field purist knows what it means to be an Olympic silver medallist and a lot of people realise the importance of the victory ceremony with Tommie and John.

George Williams certainly knew the importance of Peter's support on the dais. Williams, an African-American, was at the 1968 Olympics as a spectator and saw the 200 metres final and the victory ceremony. In 2004, Williams was the US Olympic head coach for the men's track-and-field team at the Athens Olympics. Williams described Peter as not only being a great athlete but also a good humanitarian.

> He believed in people. He didn't care what colour a person was. He believed that everyone should be free and have the freedom to do what they liked within the laws … I just wish Peter was an American because we need someone like that, but I'm quite sure Australians would be very proud of him. It's a pleasure for me to know Peter Norman and its pleasure for my people to know Peter Norman.[10]

Bob Lay recalled that Peter described his 2004 US visit as being just sensational: 'He thought it was the highlight of his life.' Jan agreed that Peter's trip meant the world to him, just as Carlos, Smith and Simmons did: 'He's feted in the US in a way that he never expected to be here. Over there he's treated like a hero.'

Peter returned to the USA in October 2005 to be reunited with Smith and Carlos at California's San José State University for the unveiling of a large statue depicting Smith and Carlos on the 1968 Olympic dais, complete with black-gloved fists raised. As alumni of the university, only Smith and Carlos were recognised in the statue but Peter was not upset over not being included. He said before the unveiling, 'Anyone can get their picture taken and be a part of the event. I am honoured to be commemorated in part of the celebration.'

Peter told the large crowd assembled for the unveiling that back in 1968 on 16 October at a big sports stadium in Mexico City two men made a statement that reverberated around the world.

> It was like a pebble being thrown into the middle of a small pond and the reverberations of the ripples that went from the centre of that pond are still travelling. Another pebble [the statue] has gone into the water and another ripple is travelling to the other end of the pond. It is a very big pond. It's the entire world.

Peter's mate from Williamstown Technical School days John McAdam was then living in the USA. John hadn't heard from Peter for a couple of years until Peter called him 'out of the blue' at the time of the statue unveiling. 'Peter told me he was pleased that people could have their photo taken in his place.' Emma Norman agreed: 'He loved watching people line up to stand in his shoes. He said it was the proudest day of his life.'

Much to Peter's delight, the Commonwealth Games were held in Melbourne in March 2006. The Queen's Baton Relay has become a Commonwealth Games tradition since its inception to celebrate the 1958 Games in Cardiff, Wales: 'The baton's journey symbolises the unity and shared ideals of the Commonwealth of Nations, and enables communities beyond the host city to share the Games celebrations.'[11] The 2006 Queen's Baton Relay was the world's longest, most-inclusive relay, travelling to all 71 Commonwealth nations over the period of a year and one day.

On Day 50 (15 March) of the relay, Peter was chosen to carry the Queen's baton on board the tall ship *Enterprize*, which travelled from his home suburb of Williamstown to Melbourne's Docklands precinct, where it was then carried to Waterfront City. From there, the baton was taken via another vessel up the Yarra River to the Melbourne Cricket Ground (the venue for the 1956 Olympics athletics program) for the Games opening ceremony later that same day.

Peter enjoyed his official Sport and Recreation meet-and-greet role during the Games, but his greatest joy was watching the athletics at the MCG. Peter had always taken a keen interest in young athletes and was keeping an eye on Australian 400 metres runner John Steffensen. Before the Games, Peter told sports journalist Ron Reed that Steffensen had a lot to offer athletics.

> He's really going places. He's got things a few of our guys haven't got, a little bit of fire, a little bit of get up and go. And he backs up what he says with actions. A lot of guys are 'gonnas', but so far he's delivered. If he keeps on doing that, who knows, he could get a gold in four weeks.[12]

Born in Perth to South African parents, the dark-skinned Steffensen had greatly admired Peter's actions at the 1968 Olympics, so much so that he bought a T-shirt in the USA featuring the photo on the dais. He started wearing it when he returned to Australia to prepare for the Games. After learning about Steffensen's T-shirt, Peter sought him out at the Victorian state titles held just prior to the Commonwealth Games. He presented Steffensen with a copy of the dais photo signed by all three medallists. Steffensen said,

> It blew my mind to have somebody with such credibility take time out of his life to encourage me, and tell me he believed in what I was doing, and that I could achieve whatever I set my mind on. That gave me that extra bit of confidence for the Games.

Steffensen subsequently won the 400 metres gold medal on 22 March, much to Peter's delight, as Steffensen recalled.

> After I won, I was outside the MCG. I'd just finished some interviews and a drug test. He'd been waiting for me and we had a big hug. He said, 'Well done. You did it!' Then we just talked. Not about the race. He was just really concerned about me.

Peter told Steffensen he had a testing time ahead of him. He stressed that Steffensen should be careful about who he trusted and that he should always be himself. 'After the Games, athletics changed for me. I had notoriety. I was now a [Commonwealth] champion. I expect to be a champion all the time.' Steffensen felt Peter knew what was coming, and didn't want to see him hurt as Peter could see his vulnerability. It had a big impact on Steffensen that Peter took so much time to be with him.

> I'm a big believer in the way these people come in to your life and you have to pay attention to them. To have them say I believe in what you're doing does help you reach your goals. It hurt me a lot what happened to him. He'll definitely be running with me in Beijing!

Peter was always very generous with his time. He had been a past committee member and great supporter of the Williamstown surf lifesaving club. He enjoyed having the family with him when he regularly helped out at the club's swim and social events, his favourite occasion being the Australia Day (26 January) two kilometre swim. Peter would MC the event and his voice would echo across the Williamstown beach along with the sounds of the Beach Boys, their music coming from his vast collection.

He never knocked back an invitation to speak to schools or clubs in metropolitan Melbourne or across the state. 'He would drop everything to go and speak for nothing,' said Jan. 'This was a pretty common occurrence, especially around the Olympics or Commonwealth Games.' Jan said she never considered such events as an invasion of their privacy, but it bothered her sometimes that Peter 'got all this attention over the silver medal' when the Olympic and Commonwealth Games were coming around: 'It just seemed like regurgitating the same thing over and over again. But Peter never tired of it.' Emma hastened to add, 'You never tire of being great!'

Emma and Belinda enjoyed seeing first hand the attention paid to their father during the Commonwealth Games. Emma described how

> We went into the Legend's Lounge [at the MCG] with him. We sat at a table with a few athletes and Dad was in his element. He had an audience. He knew what he was talking about, so they just listened to him. It was fun to see people queuing up to get his autograph. Belinda and I even queued up. I'd been to things all my life but wasn't really old enough to take it in till then.

Perry Crosswhite was the director of the 2006 Commonwealth Games and is now chief executive officer of the Australian Commonwealth Games

Association. Crosswhite had worked with Peter during the formative days of Sport and Recreation, then worked closely with him on the 2004 Commonwealth Youth Games and subsequently the Commonwealth Games. Peter enjoyed his association with Crosswhite and respected his abilities: 'Perry is very good to work with. He is very astute, knows his sports and more importantly he's got a very good idea of sports people. He is right up there with the best sporting administrators in Australia today.'

Crosswhite said Peter made a career out of being a silver medallist, 'even up until the end. We all applauded it because he deserved what was ever coming to him. It was a significant event and we might have downplayed it. He never did. But now it's being raised again and he loved being part of it. He made the most out of it and good luck to him.'

During 2004, Peter commented on a range of athletics issues, including his status in Australian sprinting, his coach and drugs in the sport.

> I am the fastest Australian ever over 200 metres, but I'm modest enough to say that I am the third-best sprinter that Australia has ever had behind Hec Hogan and Gary Holdsworth. I come in third for a number of reasons. Hec Hogan won seven national 100 yards sprint titles in a row, plus two 220 yard titles and a bronze medal at the Olympics. Gary Holdsworth won seven national sprint titles over 100 and 200 metres. I could never do that. I got the 200 five times but to have seven spread over 100 and 200 is just fantastic. There are others who have won five in a row or won five, but I discount someone like [Matt] Shervington because of the crap he's running against.'

Peter lamented the fact that no Australian runner had come close to breaking his Australian 200 metres record.

> You never ever own a record. It's up there for grabs, and it's something of an indictment on our sport that the record has lasted for so long. When I ran that record, it was about two-tenths of a second outside the world record; now it's nearly a second outside the world record. So the rest of the world's gone away from us, and we've been marking time for 36 years in that event.[13]

Greg Lewis contended that, although not meaning to belittle anybody, Peter really did revel in the thought that nobody had broken his Australian record.

> That's a terrific achievement, but in the long run you've got to face up to the fact that who cares! There are only a handful of people that really know the magnitude of what you've done. I feel a little bit nonplussed that the sporting community at large doesn't recognise the magnitude of what he achieved.

Greg added that the best thing he could ever have is someone like Peter, who he really respected and admired, saying, 'You were a tough son of a bitch.' – 'That to me was worth 100 gold medals.'

Peter had enormous respect for his long-time coach and friend Neville Sillitoe.

> I bump into Neville frequently and we talk about track and field as it was then, and as it is today, and sprinters as they were then, and the lack of them today. Neville is a beautiful person but he's also very private. It's very hard to understand because he's such a public person in a lot of ways as far as track is concerned. Just about everyone who's been in track in the last umpteen years has either crossed with Neville at some stage or known of him. He is an absolutely devoted coach, mentor and master tactician. He's probably coached at least as many state and national champions in Australia as any other single coach.

Neville also had the highest respect for Peter and his teammates Gary Holdsworth and Greg Lewis. He said that training together was the best thing that ever happened to them and it was one of the main reasons why they performed so well on the track.

> If you said do a 100 and finish off to the best of your ability over the last 50 metres, it was intense. Not one of them wanted to be an inch behind when they hit the line. But once it was over, they were good friends. There was never any animosity. Gary Holdsworth was not what you'd call naturally talented. But to win seven nationals, and to run in the Olympics and the Commonwealth Games, was a great achievement. Greg Lewis had a lot of natural talent and some wonderful achievements. But you'd have to say that Peter's performances were the best.

Peter had passionate views on drugs in sport. 'Dope and the ingestion of steroids and performance-enhancing drugs is a real bitter pill, so to speak. I've only got one thing to say to someone taking performance-enhancing drugs and that is, "You are a cheat!"' Peter believed drug cheats should be drummed out of sport: 'Two-year bans are not worth a crumpet. They should be banned for life and damn the tree-huggers and the do-gooders that say this impinges on their rights. Yes it does, but it also impinges on the rights of a lot of other people.' Peter said people forget that when Ben Johnson was rubbed out at the Seoul Olympics, he wasn't just depriving Carl Lewis the opportunity of standing on the victory dais to accept the gold medal.[14]

> In the first round Johnson ran someone out who would have gone on to the next round. Someone missed out on going through to the semi-final and someone missed the final because Johnson was on juice. Once he was rubbed out, everyone moved up one place and one guy from the semi-final got satisfaction knowing he should have run in the final, but you can't undo that. So drug-takers ruin lives, ambitions and the opportunity to get to the highest level. For mine, that's punishment for life, as in 'don't come back ever again'. I get hot under the collar when we talk about drugs!

The 2005 statue unveiling ceremony proved to be the last physical reunion of the three Mexico 200 metres medallists. Peter considered the bond between the three would exist forever.

> I love those guys and I think they love me a bit too. It's a funny thing with friends who are separated by the tyranny of distance. It's usually a pretty long time gap between seeing either one of them, but usually the conversation just starts up as if we've seen each other often.
>
> Tommie and John are totally different characters but both have an enormous amount of respect for each other. I believe John really admires Tommie, but I feel he wishes he was actually in Tommie's shoes. John has always been the cheeky rabblerouser who gets things done and usually gets them done the hard way because that's the way John works. John was always fairly

> brash and very strong-willed. If he didn't like you, he certainly let you know. Tommie is very strong-willed as well but much more reserved in his approach. He doesn't charge headlong into things and fight the 'town hall', whereas if you upset John, you've lost a friend. I'm very grateful that I count John among my close friends. Heaven forbid that I should ever be an enemy of John Carlos!
>
> The podium launched the three of us to infamy or fame. It was infamy for a long time. Now everyone is a little more comfortable with it. John has made a statement on a couple of occasions where he believes that the three of us were put on this earth to make that statement that day. It's nice to be included as one of them when he says that.

Peter said the image of the two athletes standing on the victory dais with their heads bowed, their arms raised and stockinged feet is now a symbol of African-American unity, respect and many other things that symbolise the way black Americans were treated in the 1960s and 1970s, and the 200 years prior to that.

> It's only been in comparatively recent years that the rest of the world looks up now and sees these two guys as heroes. I felt that they were heroes right from the very start and no one could convince me otherwise. The statement that they made lasts. Everybody remembers what then became known as the 'Black Power salute' and what it meant. But not too many people replay footage of the race riots and the looting and the police brutality, and vehicles being turned over and burnt. What's remembered is these two guys standing in a solemn statement and it will still be remembered for a long, long time.

Peter recognised that things had changed since the 1960s, but not nearly enough. He believed this was a real indictment against society and man's acceptance of man.

> In the 1960s, there were the Martin Luther Kings and the guys who were instrumental in getting the 'Project for Human Rights' movement working, who were hot gospellers for the cause. Now there doesn't seem to be the urgency.

To Peter's way of thinking, the urgency was even greater now because discrimination was still rife.

> Let's not beat around the bush. This isn't just the USA. This is very much to do with Australia and other parts of the world. Human rights have still got a long way to go before they come up to anything that's anywhere near acceptable. That's why they're still relevant today.

NOTES

1 Sydney Organising Committee for the Olympic Games, 'Journey of the Flame: The Olympic Torch Relay', Official Report of the XXVII Olympiad 2001, at <www.gamesinfo.com.au/postgames/en/volume_en.htm>.

2 Interview with Peter Mitchell, 'Follow The Flame' 2000 Olympics segment, Channel 7.

3 Mike Powell won silver medals in the long jump at the 1988 and 1992 Olympics. He won the long jump at the 1991 and 1993 world championships, breaking Bob Beamon's 23-year-old long jump record (set at the 1968 Olympics) in winning the 1991 event. Powell's record of 8.95 metres still stands at the time of writing. Dan O'Brien won the decathlon at the 1991, 1993 and 1995 World Championships and the decathlon gold medal at the 1996 Olympics. Edwin Moses won gold medals at the 1976 and 1984 Olympics in the 400 metres hurdles. He also won this event at the 1983 and 1987 World Championships. Between 1977 and 1987, Moses won 122 consecutive 400 metres hurdles races and set the world record four times. In retirement, Moses has been an innovative reformer in the areas of Olympic eligibility and drug-testing.

4 Steve Simmons, interview footage, *Salute*, 2008.

5 'A big buzz for Peter Norman', *Active State* magazine, Autumn 2000.

6 'Olympian savages Tunstall', *Herald Sun*, 25 August 1994.

7 Peter would have been delighted when newly elected Australian Prime Minister Kevin Rudd formally apologised to Australia's Indigenous people on 13 February 2008 'for the laws and policies of successive parliaments and governments that have inflicted profound grief, suffering and loss on these, our fellow Australians.' Mr Rudd made particular reference to the 'stolen generations' of many thousands of young Indigenous children who were forcibly removed from their families by Australian state and federal authorities. He described the mistreatment of the

'stolen generations' as a 'blemished chapter' in Australian history. 'For the indignity and degradation thus inflicted on a proud people and a proud culture, we say sorry.' Mr Rudd's gesture had been long resisted by his predecessor John Howard, who served as prime minister for some eleven years. Mr Howard had refused to apologise on the grounds that 'Australians of this generation should not be required to accept guilt and blame for past actions and policies over which they had no control'. ('Rudd's apology', *Sydney Morning Herald*, 12 February 2008.)

8 *Salute* was released in cinemas around Australia in July 2008.

9 Steve Simmons, interview footage, *Salute*, 2008.

10 George Williams, interview footage, *Salute*, 2008.

11 Melbourne 2006 XVIII Commonwealth Games website, <http://qbr.melbourne2006.com.au/?s=baton>.

12 'Gesture spurs sprinter to excel', *Herald Sun*, 20 February 2006.

13 'On the fast track', ABC, 1 September 2004.

14 Peter rated Carl Lewis 'the greatest track-and-field exponent the world has ever produced'.

21

WHERE WERE YOU WHEN I NEEDED YOU?

One day in mid May 2006, Peter Norman felt unwell while at work. His boss Brian Mott agreed it would be best for him to go home. 'He was back the next day looking okay,' recalled Brian.

> But two days later he started to grey a little. He didn't look too good, so we arranged for him to go home. He went straight to the doctor and the doctor said he needed to have some tests. We thought it might be a virus, but I think Peter sensed that it might be something to do with his heart.

Brian was aware that Peter was still a smoker, even though he had attempted to give up smoking several times. 'Peter didn't lie too often, but on a couple of occasions he told me he'd definitely given up smoking. Then I'd go outside at a function and he'd be out there smoking.'

In early June, Peter had a restless night at home. He had trouble breathing. 'I felt pretty ordinary during the night and decided to take myself down to the hospital in the morning. They ran some tests and the doctor said, "You've had more than a little upset. You've had a major incident."'[1] Peter was given an angiogram to check for abnormalities of his heart muscle or valves, and to see if his coronary arteries were narrowed or blocked. Arch Galloway, who was very familiar with the procedure having undergone heart surgery twice, said that the angiogram revealed that Peter had blocked arteries, and 'during the procedure they nicked his artery, but they didn't know that at the time. Peter got dressed and was ready to go home. Then they called him straight back in because they discovered on the screen that his artery was bleeding, so they had to fix the torn artery.'

Jan received a phone call from a doctor at the Western Hospital, Footscray, to say that Peter was sitting up in bed having a cup of tea, and would be ready to pick up in 30 minutes.

> Then I got another call shortly after saying, 'Don't come. He's in surgery. We'll call you.' The next phone call was, 'He's in an ambulance heading into the city to have a quadruple bypass.' That's when it all came out that the doctors clipped an artery.

Peter had the bypass operation at St Vincent's Private Hospital, where his father had also had a quadruple bypass operation in the late 1980s. In hospital Peter was more concerned about others than himself, as Belinda recalled. 'We saw him the day after his operation. He looked terrible and I started to faint and he was fussing over me, asking me if I was all right.' Emma remembered that when her father had his stitches removed, the doctor said it was better for it to have happened that way, rather than Peter sitting around waiting for the bypass to happen. 'Dad agreed. It was done before he even knew what happened to him.'

Max Wells sent Peter flowers from Surfing Victoria and also visited him in hospital the day before Peter went home: 'That was the last time I saw Pete. He was really positive and said he was going to make some changes in his lifestyle, like cutting out smoking.'

Thelma Norman was aware that Jan was flying to New Zealand around the time Peter was going home. 'Her mother had had a heart attack. I knew Jan had to see her mother. I would have gone down to Williamstown, but Belinda and Emma were going home to look after Peter. A few weeks later Jan's mother died.'

At the end of June, Peter's daughter Sandy, her husband Chris and their two daughters were in Melbourne en route to Queensland.

> We visited Dad. This was only a couple of weeks after his heart surgery, which was around his birthday. Maya was asleep in the car and Chris was sick but Laura wanted to see Papa. So Laura and I went in and saw Dad. He wasn't very well. Jan was in

> New Zealand, but Belinda and Emma were hovering over him. Dad tried to play with Laura, but he was pretty tired. She can remember that he poked and prodded her and had a giggle with her during the half hour we were with him.

Peter's friend Robin Kidney had gone through a triple bypass in 1997. In early July, Robin rang Peter when he heard the news of his bypass. 'He answered the phone. I said, "Peter George Norman!" His response was, "Big Rob Kidney, the one bloke I wanna talk to."' Peter told Robin he still wasn't feeling that flash and was having trouble coming to grips with the operation. Peter also said his doctors had given him a timeframe for a typical recovery from such an operation, but he couldn't work out why things weren't going to plan with his recovery. Robin and Peter spoke at length about each other's heart surgery: 'We discussed "war stories" and I feel he benefited from that.'

Ruth's husband Don had also taken sick in late June 2006, and was in a Melbourne hospital on a dialysis machine throughout July. Ruth stayed in Melbourne with a friend. Don died on Wednesday 26 July 2006 and his funeral was held in Echuca on Monday 31 July 2006. The day before the funeral, Peter caught the train from Williamstown into the city centre and then caught another train to Echuca. Peter was totally exhausted by the time he booked into a motel in Echuca after a five-hour journey so soon after major surgery.

Peter made a rare phone call to his daughter Sandy to tell her that he would be at Don's funeral. 'I was surprised because he was still recovering. But I was pretty proud that he felt he needed to come. He was there to thank Don. Dad looked tired and like crap, for want of a better word.' Peter's attendance was a shock to Ruth.

> Even though I'd known Don 30 years and loved him dearly, I still loved Peter because I had his children. I didn't see Peter until we went for a cuppa. He was immaculately dressed in a beautiful suit. I only had a few words with him and that was the last time I saw him. But I didn't think Peter looked well. Coming to the funeral was perhaps Peter's way of saying thank you to Don, because he had opted out of his responsibility. It was probably recognition and respect for what Don had done, looking after his children. I emailed Peter not long after that and thanked him for

> the children. I needed to say that to him. I didn't get a response. I used to send him cards on his birthday. I'd get no response but that was fine.

Peter spent time with Rhonda Kidney at the funeral. Rhonda, who has a nursing background, felt that Peter should have had somebody with him at the funeral. Immediately the service was over, Peter took Rhonda by the arm as they walked up a slight rise to the hall. He leant heavily on Rhonda and it was obvious to her that he wasn't well and should not have been there. 'He told me about having dizzy spells and double vision. I said, "Peter, tomorrow morning you must get back to your specialist. Something is not right."' Rhonda had no doubt that Peter made the trip to Echuca out of great respect to Ruth and Don. 'He probably knew the consequences of going, but was prepared to take the risk. That was Peter! I felt very special because he chose to talk to me, to lean on me at the funeral. It wasn't often that he left my side that day. I just felt that was meant to be.'

Thelma travelled to Echuca by car with her daughter Elaine and son-in-law Michael to attend Don's funeral. 'We offered to bring him home,' said Thelma, 'but he said no because he could get up and walk around on the train.' Peter told his daughter-in-law Lara that his doctor had advised him against making such a long trip, but by catching the train, Peter knew he would be able to get up, walk around and keep his blood flowing correctly. 'He also didn't want people to have to stop all the time,' said Lara, 'so that he could walk around.'

Heather Norman had three weeks' holiday from her teaching position in the Falkland Islands in August 2006, so she went home to Melbourne. She knew Peter had had a bypass and was determined to see him, which she did in mid August.

> We spent the day looking at Peter's videos. He really enjoyed taking movies. Thornbury Salvation Army Corps had recently had a 100-year anniversary. He had taken video of that and he kept pointing out different people we both knew and we reminisced about them.

Heather also saw some of Peter's videos of family holidays in Bali and Thailand.[2] Peter particularly loved Thailand and the Thai people.

Heather and Peter went for a walk with the family's two dogs.

> When we got home, he sat and rested for 45 minutes as he was supposed to do. It was a really lovely day. The girls came over for supper and Peter cooked that. Emma made sure he was looking after himself properly. I stayed overnight, then we walked to the train the next morning and I was off and away.

Based on the way he had spoken, Heather was optimistic about Peter making a full recovery. Peter had initially expected to return to work the following week, but by the time of Heather's visit, his doctor had told him to take another week off. Heather was pleased about this. She knew Peter had had a fright.

> It had shaken him. He'd been taking Belinda and Emma shopping and showing them around. It was as if he was cuddling them back towards him. And he was showing me things. In hindsight it was his last chance. When we talked about Thailand, he brought out a little Thai elephant key chain. When we talked about some of the sporting events he was involved in, he brought out a Rip Curl windcheater.

Peter gave Heather a Commonwealth Games baton and a five-centimetre length of the athletics track that had been laid at the Melbourne Cricket Ground for the Games, to take back to the Falklands.

Belinda and Emma spent their last day with their father at the family home in Williamstown on Saturday 30 September 2006. It was a big day in the Melbourne sporting calendar: the Australian Football League's grand final at the magnificent MCG. 'Belinda, my boyfriend and I were down here,' recalled Emma. 'He must have been quite ill, but he looked after us the entire day. He wouldn't have had it any other way, no matter how bad he was feeling.' Peter cooked four courses during the afternoon and served them to his special guests at the end of each quarter of the grand final, which everyone watched on television. Belinda remembered the four courses: 'At quarter time, we had sausage rolls. At half-time, it was hot pies. At three-quarter time, he served chips. Then we had hot dogs at the end.'

Brian Mott had kept in regular contact with Peter following his surgery. Peter told Brian that he wanted to return to full-time work around the end of August, but his doctor would only allow him to work a maximum of two days a week, beginning in early September. 'He came to work for two days spread across two weeks,' said Brian. 'But shortly after his return, Peter felt a little faint, so he went home and then saw his doctor. He seemed to be on the road to recovery again and then about a week later he died.'

Peter was mowing the front lawn at his home around mid morning on Tuesday 3 October 2006 when he collapsed. An ambulance was immediately called. Ambulance officers tried unsuccessfully to revive Peter on the front lawn. Peter Norman was dead at 64. The official cause was heart failure. Jan said Peter wasn't cutting the lawn on impulse. 'That morning he said to me, "I'm going to give the front lawn a go. If the mower doesn't start the first time, I won't do it." He'd done the back lawn the day before. I think he'd already been for a [bike] ride that day.' Jan knew that Peter 'probably shouldn't have been mowing lawns' but she said he was always pushing boundaries. Emma added that her father wasn't one for lying around doing nothing. Belinda agreed: 'He couldn't sit in bed ringing a bell when he needed something.'

Jan felt there was every expectation that Peter would make a full recovery from the operation, although she conceded that he had been struggling. He had been going to therapy classes, but he wasn't recovering as quickly as he would have liked: 'He was probably a bit impatient.'

Peter's death shocked Brian and other work colleagues. Peter had been a much-loved member of Sport and Recreation. 'Because we had experience of people having bypasses and surviving, we had a false sense of security,' said Brian.

> It's worse with a person like Peter. You think he's immortal. When the phone call came we were obviously devastated, but absolutely surprised. I'd been out to his home to see him during the last recovery period. I thought by the look of him that he was coming good.

Brian had known Peter really well for around ten years and on a casual basis for several years before that. Like Peter, Brian had been a teacher in the technical system. He said Peter was really enjoying his work and 'he was also proud of what his daughters were achieving. He could see great things ahead of them. He was enjoying being on holidays occasionally. Everything was nicely in place. It would have been nice for him to get a few more years of that'.

Couch Production's Bob Stuart had seen Peter at his surprise sixtieth birthday party in September 2006. He hadn't seen Peter for a year before that: 'He was there with Jan and looked remarkably well. Jan told me that he was still pretty crook when he went to the party, but it was something he wanted to do. I thought he was quite happy with the way things were going.' Arch had also thought Peter was progressing well. He had been ringing Peter on a regular basis and saw him two weeks before his death: 'He looked a bit grey but it was soon after the operation. Jan said he had been having problems and he wasn't recovering and that they were doing tests to see what the problem was. I don't drink, but smoke. He did both unfortunately. He was a heavy smoker.'

Jan estimated that Peter would have been smoked at least ten cigarettes a day: 'He tried many times to cut down, but it didn't work. Sometimes he had given it up for months then I guess a bit more stress in his life caused him to go back on it. Peter also suffered badly from asthma and breathing issues.' Belinda knew that her father could have eaten more healthily: 'He liked butter and he'd cut off a lot of cheese.' Peter loved cooking and would pore over recipe books looking for the next culinary challenge. He enjoyed recreating meals that he'd eaten at functions, but his goal would always be to make his meal tastier than the original. He was known to deep-fry quite a lot and particularly loved cooking fresh fried chips, which Jan described as 'exquisite', the best she's ever tasted. But he should not have been cooking them as often as he did.

The news of Peter's death came 'absolutely out of the blue' for Heather. 'It was horrible. I called "Laney" [Elaine] and spoke to her and Mum. I couldn't get through to Jan, so I left a message. I phoned Laurie.' Heather had only a very short time to get her tickets and foreign currency organised before her long flight to Melbourne from the Falkland Islands. Sadly she arrived in Melbourne the day after Peter's funeral: 'We only have one flight each week to get out of the country, so I couldn't get away any sooner.'

Sandy learnt of her father's death when her sister Janita met her outside the hospital where she worked and told her.

> I think Elaine phoned her because Elaine was worried about Mum finding out and being on her own. Gary told Mum while Janita was out collecting me. We all ended up at Janita's office. I was only just starting to level out after Don died, so it was kind of a numb kick. All the outpouring of emotion we had with Don didn't really happen then and there with Dad.

Neville Sillitoe had never contemplated Peter not recovering from his operation. He spoke to Peter by phone about a week before he died and Peter told him that he was coming on fine, adding that he had walked five kilometres that day. Neville asked Peter if he would talk to his Caulfield Grammar athletics team on 15 October. Peter replied in his typical 'no problems!' fashion. Neville and Peter were more than just coach and athlete – they were good mates.

> If I ever asked Peter if he could talk to some kids for me, there was never any hesitation. The answer was always, 'Yes, and when?' The only way I can sum it up is to say that he was an outstanding athlete, but more importantly, an outstanding friend.

Gary Holdsworth had last seen Peter at the Melbourne Commonwealth Games in March 2006. Gary was pleased to see Peter looking well and enjoying his Games role. When Gary heard about Peter's bypass operation, he immediately rang Peter to return the favour of giving support. In 1995 Peter had supported Gary by visiting him in hospital when Gary had an angioplasty following a heart attack. The phone call was to be the last time these two great athletes and friends spoke. Peter's sense of humour came to the fore when he said to Gary, 'Where were you when I needed you?' Gary got the impression Peter was progressing well, particularly when Peter told him he was walking and riding a bike.

> Two weeks later we heard he died. Peter was always very positive. He'd put a good spin on anything, but I didn't think this was a good spin. I accepted what he told me. He didn't sound ill. It was just like he'd had this setback, but he was on his way back. His death was an absolute shock.

Greg Lewis was also shocked: 'He went far too early. He still had a lot of productive contributions to make.'

Peter's death also hit a number of other Australian Olympians hard. Pam Ryan had expected others to die well before Peter: 'He was so young and bouncy. The news of his passing was a shock to everybody.' Bob Lay was absolutely shattered to hear the news: 'I never saw him as one who would leave us so soon.' Perry Crosswhite agreed: 'His passing came as a big surprise to me. Peter was indestructible. He couldn't die!'

NOTES

1 *Sunday Mail*, 7 October 2006.

2 Emma Norman said, 'We have so many videos and Dad is hardly on any of them, because he is behind the camera commentating, but we can hear him.'

22
SPIRIT IN THE SKY

Approximately 1000 people paid their last respects at the Celebration of Life for Peter Norman service at the Williamstown Town Hall at 1 pm on Monday 9 October 2006. Reverend Cheryl Johnson conducted the service. Besides the extended Norman family, attendees included Tommie Smith and John Carlos; Steve Simmons; Judy Patching; Neville Sillitoe; Gary and Glenda Holdsworth; Greg, Carolyn and Tamsyn Lewis; Ray Weinberg; John Landy; Pam Ryan; Ralph Doubell; Bob Lay; Maurie and Daisy Drew; Bob Gardiner; Ray and Denise Boyd; Barry Round; Max Wells; Paul Jenes; Arch Galloway; Danny Corcoran; Brian Mott and other representatives from all levels of government including Justin Madden, then Victorian minister for Sport and Recreation.

The service opened with the reading 'A Time for Everything', after which Emma, accompanied by her sister Belinda, offered a touching and at times amusing reflection on her father.

> He loved the limelight and we loved him for it … We bought him a big thick robe while he was in hospital. The next day we went in to see him for his [last] birthday. He was wearing his robe. It wasn't till later that mum told us he'd sat there overheating for an hour waiting for us. He'd do anything to entertain us. He was so generous and gave us the best advice. He was the first person

we'd call in a crisis. He'd never judge.

Emma related the story her father had once told her of an incident that occurred at a party: 'After a few drinks and no doubt words of encouragement, Dad found himself a lawnmower and mowed the only shag pile carpet in the house.' Emma said her father 'could run the 200 metres in around 20 seconds and if you locked your keys in, he could break into your car in around thirty. Dad inspired a lot of people and most of all us. We will miss his roasts, his chats, his jokes and his stories. We adored you Dad.'[1]

Coach of the Australian 1968 Olympics athletics team Ray Weinberg spoke from the heart of his warm friendship and affection for Peter. He commented on Peter's deep sense of humanity, lack of pretence, charisma, infectious sense of humour and genuine love for sport and life. He spoke of the man who wasn't afraid to display his Christian faith by wearing a tracksuit emblazoned with the words 'Jesus saves'. He recalled, with great pride, Peter's wonderful achievement in Mexico.

Tommie Smith and John Carlos delivered eulogies. Tommie's was brief. He spoke of last seeing his friend Peter, 'the humanitarian who believed that right can never be wrong', at the statue unveiling ceremony in 2005. Tommie related the story of Peter insisting they dance in the hotel's piano bar after the ceremony, despite the late hour: 'So we danced. Now there's a photo folks! Tommie Smith and Peter Norman embracing while dancing.'[2]

John then delivered what sportswriter Ron Reed described as 'a heartfelt tribute … a masterpiece; one of the most stirring funeral orations most had heard'.[3] John stressed that the average young white person at that time would never have had the gumption, nerve and backbone to stand on the dais in Mexico with two young black men who were 'really disenchanted with life' and who had received death threats from around the world. 'Peter said, "I stand with you. I don't stand before you; I don't stand behind you. I stand with you."' John described Peter as a lone soldier who was not only proud to represent Australia but also, even greater than that, was 'proud to represent the human race'. He spoke of Peter running the best race of his life in Mexico: 'When the race was over he felt good. He got second. I got third … I looked at the clock. It said Peter Norman 20 seconds flat. Not 20.06 but 20 flat.' John recalled that he had never seen a photo of Peter where he wasn't smiling.

> He always had a smile. If you were down, Peter would raise you up. He always had a joke for you. He always had a trick to make you want more … He always had that twinkle in his eyes … Peter had pain and hurt but he never ever let you know.

John concluded by saying that Australia had lost a 'great soldier' and that Australians should always remember Peter Norman, the man. 'Make sure you use that phrase, the Man. Because that's exactly what Peter was!'[4]

Steve Simmons then spoke as a representative of the organisation USA Track & Field. He began by reading a eulogy, prepared by Payton Jordan, the head coach of the 1968 US Olympic track-and-field team. Jordan described Peter as being a man for all seasons, a giant of the sport of track and field. 'But more importantly, he was a wonderful human being that always saw the best in others. He was an ambassador for humankind.' Jordan added that Peter's deeds and contributions to make this a better world will never be lost.

> The kind of man he was will be cherished and will always live on in the hearts and memory of those that were enriched and ennobled by the privilege of knowing him. On behalf of the athletes of America and our 1968 US Olympic team in Mexico City, we thank you for sharing Peter with us, and please know the depth we feel in his passing.[5]

Simmons spoke of flying Peter and Jan to Sydney for the 2000 Olympics, and taking them to US Olympian Michael Johnson's birthday party. Simmons read a tribute to Peter from Michael Johnson, who had learned about Peter when he became a huge admirer and fan of Smith and Carlos, 'not only for what these men accomplished athletically, but for the courage and bravery they displayed in standing up for what they believed in on the medal podium at the 1968 Olympic Games'. Johnson, having read much about the story, gained respect for Peter, the Australian athlete far removed from the controversial issues about which Smith and Carlos were protesting but

> who decided to cooperate with the protest and also use the moment to bring awareness to a cause important to him, knowing that this moment and this protest would be controversial and surely not knowing that it would go down as one of the most courageous and

> selfless moments in sports. Peter Norman and Smith and Carlos displayed class and dignity in the way they staged their salute at a moment in which they all could have selfishly celebrated their many years of hard work and the culmination of that hard work leading to success in Mexico City. Instead they decided to use that moment to bring attention to a greater cause. Peter Norman was not only a great athlete but a great individual.[6]

Simmons concluded by reading a 'Proclamation in honor and celebration of Peter Norman' signed by the president and the CEO of USA Track & Field, declaring 9 October 2006 as 'Peter Norman Day' in the USA. Such a proclamation had never been made in the 170-year history of American track-and-field athletics.

Janita and Sandy then shared the reading of 'The Dash'. The poignant poem, which Janita had chosen, was a reminder to all of the importance of how one lives one's life, from the beginning to the end.

Towards the end of the service, Peter's nephew Matt Norman screened excerpts from his upcoming documentary *Salute*, including the complete 200 metres race in Mexico. This drew resounding applause from all assembled as Peter crossed the line in second place. During the service, songs selected by Belinda and Emma were played from Peter's music collection, including Fats Domino's 'Blueberry Hill', Woody Herman's 'Golden Wedding', Joe Cocker's 'Little Help From My Friends', Norman Greenbaum's 'Spirit in the Sky', the Carpenters' 'What The World Needs Now Is Love' and the Proclaimers' 'Sunshine On Leith'.

In a fitting farewell, while Vangelis' 'Chariots of Fire' – another of Peter's favourites – was played, Peter's coffin was carried from the town hall by pallbearers Tommie Smith and John Carlos, Laurie Norman, Gary Norman, Matt Norman, Chris Kadri, Colin Stevens and John Whittington.[7] A private cremation followed the service.

Elaine was overwhelmed by the immensity of the service. She was happy to meet Tommie and John, but she found it

> all a bit surreal with 'the brothers' talking about their 'bro', the guy on the podium. What really touched me and where I found my pleasure was when Ray Weinberg spoke about Peter. That was the brother I remembered. Ray spoke about the guy I had on a pedestal and he spoke about him with such warmth.

Ruth was very pleased that Janita, Sandy, Gary and Chris were involved in the service: 'It was important for my children. It was a good thing they were able to take part.' Jan appreciated the assistance given to her by Ruth and her family following Peter's death: 'Ruth gave me so much support, as did Gary, Sandy and Janita.'

After the service, Ruth and her family went back to Jan's home where they had the opportunity to meet John and Tommie. It was fitting that Ruth finally met the two people who had figured so prominently in Peter's life and indirectly in hers. It gave her a sense of closure.

Over the years, Janita had tended to take for granted the stance her father took on the Olympic dais. 'It had always been there in my life. But meeting Tommie and John bought the significance home and I've thought a lot about it since. Peter was pretty gutsy to do it and I admire him for that.' She too found it 'quite surreal' meeting Tommie and John at the funeral.

> Those guys have always been part of my life too, even if they were just figures. They were wonderful; very warm. In lots of ways, it put the world right for me. I was pleased they came. I went to Melbourne the day before Peter's funeral. I felt compelled to call in on Jan and the girls. John Carlos had just arrived and I got to spend some additional private time with him. That was really nice.

Janita knew that Peter respected her stepfather Don and was grateful to him. She had decided after Don's funeral that 'I wanted to have a good long talk to Peter. The time was right to deal with all that had happened years earlier. I wanted to put things right, where they needed to be, but he died before I had the chance.'

The funeral service had understandably been very emotional for Jan, Belinda and Emma. Jan took great comfort in having her sister Ali by her side throughout the day. The wake held for Peter at their home was wonderful. Everyone enjoyed the opportunity to reflect on the day and have a laugh, which was fitting given Peter's great sense of humour. Jan recalled that she and some friends felt at one stage during the service as if Peter would sit up in his coffin to say that he agreed with all the tributes being bestowed on him. Emma added, 'He would have just been sorry he couldn't get on the stage and talk, especially with everybody there. That would have been his ultimate moment. His ultimate crowd!' Belinda enjoyed hearing all the 'did you know that your father…' stories: 'I'd never heard so many!'

For Jan and her daughters, it was an astonishing experience to meet Tommie and John. 'That was amazing,' said Jan, 'they were the loveliest, loveliest people'. Emma concurred: 'They were so nice. They were telling us stories and I learnt a lot.' She thought she knew the story of the dais protest quite well, but until hearing it from John and Tommie, she hadn't realised that 'they were taking that big a risk'.

Over the last years of her son's life, Thelma hadn't often seen Peter face to face.

> That's why I can't believe he's gone. It hasn't really hit me yet that I'll never see him again. He would call in if he was down this way for a meeting or for a speaking engagement. I'd ring him at home sometimes, but mainly I spoke to him on the phone on his way home from work. The phone was mainly our only form of communication over the last few years.

Glowing tributes were paid to Peter in newspapers throughout Australia, the USA and many other parts of the world. Tributes also appeared on countless internet sites and on television and radio news broadcasts worldwide.

Nicola Roxon, the federal government member for Gellibrand, paid tribute to Peter in a speech to Parliament on 19 October 2006. In part, she said:

> I would like to take this opportunity today to commemorate the life and recent death of a constituent of mine, Olympic medallist and Williamstown resident, Mr Peter Norman … Mr Norman's performance at those Olympics was all the more inspiring for the support that he gave his co-finalists on the podium … Mr Norman's involvement in this protest is something that we should all be proud of … Mr Norman was a role model for all Australians in his stand and support for equal rights. With the American civil rights movement in a way heralded and symbolised by this action, the world began to recognise the right of all people to live free from oppression. Mr Norman's action at the 1968 Olympics, standing in solidarity for the rights of others, is worth reflecting on again today. After all, human rights are all about caring, not

just for yourself but for the plight of others around you.

> Nevertheless, I do not want this moment in history to overshadow his outstanding sporting achievements and lasting contribution to the community … Mr Norman's life shows that our national pastime, sport, can be coupled with a commitment to social justice and equality for all and was perhaps the start of a rich tradition of Australian sportsmen and sportswomen who have used their sporting success to highlight and combat social inequity.

Simon Crean, federal government member for Hotham, also paid tribute in Parliament on 2 November 2006.

> I rise to acknowledge the passing of a great Australian athlete and a great humanitarian … I had the privilege of knowing Peter. Our families went camping together one year … Throughout his life, and in that glorious moment in Mexico City, Peter Norman embodied true moral courage and generosity of spirit. Recently in Australia we have been having a debate about Australian values and what it means to be Australian. Peter Norman embodied what is good about Australia and Australians: good humour, respect, tolerance, humility, honesty, moral principle and great courage. We salute him for his great sporting achievements and his values.

Peter would have enjoyed reading such glowing tributes. After all, had he not revelled in being one of Australia's most famous Olympic medallists? But deep down Peter saw himself as being very much an average Australian, and a very proud Australian at that. Just before his death, he reflected upon his life. Aside from his obvious faults, he believed that he was 'an acceptable character in most situations', although he argued that it would be 'fairer to ask someone else'. He summed up his life by saying that he had 'been lucky enough to be in the right places at the right times on a lot of occasions' and having 'been lucky enough to take advantage of being in the right places at the right times'. Peter decided on an appropriate epitaph for his life:

> Here lies a man, not perfect, not all good, not all bad, liked by some, respected by some, taught some people some things, showed some people some things, did a lot of things.

NOTES

1 Emma Norman, film footage, *Salute*, 2008.

2 Tommie Smith, film footage, *Salute*, 2008.

3 'Track soulmates honour "The Man"', *Herald Sun*, 10 October 2006.

4 John Carlos, film footage, *Salute*, 2008.

5 Payton Jordan, eulogy to Peter Norman, 4 October 2006.

6 Michael Johnson, extract from email to Steve Simmons, 5 October 2006.

7 Colin Stevens was a former teaching colleague and John Whittington, a family friend.

INDEX

Note: PN denotes Peter Norman

ACKNOWLEDGMENTS

The author and publisher wish to thank the following people and organisations for permission to reprint their quotes, text extracts and images. We have made every effort to contact those concerned, and, where this has not been possible, we welcome the opportunity to include acknowledgments in future printing of this publication, should an omission be brought to our attention.

Text

See notes in each chapter for text acknowledgments. All quotes not acknowledged in chapters are courtesy of *Salute* (film) © Matt Norman 2008, or from interviews conducted by Damian Johnstone.

Images

Collection 1

Page 1: all images from Thelma Norman personal collection; page 2: all images from Thelma Norman personal collection; page 3: Thelma Norman personal collection (top), John Francisco (middle), Helen Whelan (bottom); page 4: Thelma Norman personal collection (main and bottom), The Herald and Weekly Time Photographic Collection (top); page 5: all images from Ruth Membrey personal collection; page 6: Peter Norman personal collection (main), Thelma Norman personal collection (right); page 7: Thelma Norman personal collection (top left), Peter Norman personal collection (top right and bottom); page 8: Peter Norman personal collection.

Collection 2

Page 1: all images Peter Norman personal collection; page 2: all images Peter Norman personal collection; page 3: Salute The Movie Pty Ltd; page 4: Bettman/Corbis (top), Peter Norman personal collection (bottom); page 5: Damian Johnstone (top), Peter Norman personal collection (bottom left and right); page 6: Peter Norman personal collection (top and middle), Gary Holdsworth (bottom); page 7: The Herald and Weekly Time Photographic

Collection (top), Peter Norman personal collection (bottom); page 8: Peter Norman personal collection.

Collection 3

Page 1: Peter Norman personal collection (top, bottom left and bottom right), Sandy Kadri (middle); page 2: Peter Norman personal collection (top and bottom right), Sandy Kadri (bottom left); page 3: Thelma Norman personal collection (top), Sandy Kadri (middle and bottom); page 4: Peter Norman personal collection; page 5: Peter Norman personal collection (top and middle), Newspix/Kelly Barnes (bottom); page 6: Heather Norman (top and middle), John Heard personal collection (bottom left), Getty images/Mark Dadswell (bottom right); page 7: Matt Norman; page 8: all images Matt Norman.